Progressive Politics and Conservation

JAMES PENICK, JR.

Progressive Politics and Conservation

THE BALLINGER-PINCHOT AFFAIR

THE UNIVERSITY OF CHICAGO PRESS, CHICAGO & LONDON

Library of Congress Catalog Card Number: 68-15798

THE UNIVERSITY OF CHICAGO PRESS, CHICAGO & LONDON
THE UNIVERSITY OF TORONTO PRESS, TORONTO 5, CANADA

for Barbara

Acknowledgments

I would like to thank Carroll Pursell, Jr., Morgan Sherwood, Donald Swain, Hunter Dupree, Walton Bean, and Albert Lepawsky for their help. My wife Barbara read and criticized the manuscript at every stage of its development. All errors are my own. My parents, James and Annie Penick, generously provided assistance on several occasions. The Committee on Research of the University of California granted funds for research in Seattle. I am grateful to Richard Berner for his many kindnesses. Paul Lietz made help available in the final preparation of the manuscript.

The following individuals and publishers have given their permission to quote certain materials: Mrs. Henry F. Pringle, Mrs. Amos Pinchot, Alpheus T. Mason, Gifford Pinchot, Jr., Princeton University Press, Harcourt, Brace & World, Inc., The Crowell-Collier Publishing Company. Scattered materials in the first three chapters appeared earlier in similar form in *Forest History*, the publication of the Forest History Society, and in volume two of *Technology in Western Civilization* (New York: Oxford University Press, 1967), edited by Melvin Kranzberg and Carroll Pursell, Jr.

Evanston, Illinois

Introduction

In 1909 and 1910 the administration of William Howard Taft was torn by a controversy which left it a shambles. The chief protagonists were Richard Ballinger and Gifford Pinchot. Friction between them began when both were bureau chiefs under President Theodore Roosevelt but erupted into open warfare when Ballinger became Taft's secretary of the interior. When Ballinger began to undo the coordinated policies which collectively comprised the conservation movement, Pinchot moved to stop the attack by any means at hand. He seized it when the opportunity arose to discredit his opponent's integrity. Taft exonerated Ballinger, and in time Pinchot was dismissed. Nevertheless, in a widely publicized congressional hearing Ballinger was branded before the public as anti-Roosevelt, anticonservation, and, in the eyes of many, personally dishonest. Within a year he retired, a sour and defeated man. Meanwhile the controversy added to the mounting bitterness dividing Roosevelt and Taft which eventually split the Republican party in 1912 and made the election of Woodrow Wilson possible.

To contemporaries and to historians ever since it has been known as the Ballinger-Pinchot controversy. As a historical event it has most frequently been treated as an aspect of grander concerns, but two earlier full-length studies exist. The first of these, published by Rose Stahl in 1926, concluded that the major issue was the continuing struggle to bring the power of corporate wealth to heel. This had already become the traditional—one might say the standard—interpretation. The work bristled with the apparatus of scholarship and softly radiated the aura of cool, detached julgment.[1] The calm was deceptive, for many of the later efforts were openly quarrelsome.

Always somewhere near the eye of the turbulence was the ambiguous figure of Ballinger's accuser, Louis Glavis. In 1911, because of his role in the controversy, he was appointed secretary to the two state conservation commissions of California by the progressive governor, Hiram Johnson. Within a matter of months the surveyor general of the state charged that Glavis had used his position to line his pockets, and after a private hearing before the governor in December 1912 he was permitted to resign. Glavis faded from public view, but with remarkable resilience he reemerged in the 1930's as chief of the division of investigation in the Department of the Interior. Although for awhile held in such high favor that he was rumored as a possible successor of J. Edgar Hoover, the old ambiguity continued to cloud his career. Charged with having created a "virtual OGPU" in the Department of the Interior, with running an illegal surveillance system that included the use of wire taps—charges that are confirmed by the recollections of a ranking bureau chief, by the testimony before a Senate investigating committee, and indirectly by the diaries of Harold Ickes—Glavis again resigned under questionable circumstances.[2]

Harold Ickes later claimed to be ignorant of the earlier career of Glavis in California. Although skepticism might be uncharitable, there is little reason to doubt that his sympathies—which as an old follower of the Bull Moose standard, had been with Pinchot in the controversy with Ballinger—accounted for his attraction to Glavis. Certainly when Ickes assumed control of the department there was no figure in American public life for whom he professed more admiration than Pinchot, and it is significant that Glavis fell from favor at a time when Ickes' relations with Pinchot were deteriorating. Ickes dreamed of

[1] "The Ballinger-Pinchot Controversy," in Harold U. Faulkner and Sidney B. Fay (eds.), *Smith College Studies in History*, 11 (1926), pp. 65–126.

[2] For Glavis' career after the controversy, see J. L. Penick, Jr., "Louis Russell Glavis: A Postscript to the Ballinger-Pinchot Controversy," *Pacific Northwest Quarterly*, 55 (April 1964), pp. 67–75.

transforming the Department of the Interior into a home for all the conservation agencies of the government, a place where conservation activity could be centralized and coordinated under one head—namely, himself. Several times he made lightning raids on the Department of Agriculture, where resided the most coveted of prizes, the Forest Service, but always his path was deflected, not only by Wallace but by his old friend Gifford Pinchot. In the mid-thirties, when Glavis passed from the scene, friendship was wearing thin.

At the end of the decade the smouldering feud suddenly burst into open war. Henry F. Pringle gave extensive treatment to the Ballinger-Pinchot controversy in his biography of William Howard Taft, reversing the opinion of thirty years' standing by clearing Ballinger of any taint of corruption, and removing the onus of anticonservation from the Taft administration. Although Charles Beard called it a whitewash, the frustrated Ickes sensed an advantage. Gathering about him the musty archives of an earlier administration, he launched his great effort to discredit the formidable Pinchot. In the *Saturday Evening Post*, and in a longer account published by the government, Ickes corroborated the Pringle thesis, to which he added his own twist: that Ballinger had been the victim of a massive conspiracy engineered by Pinchot, who had used the ambitious Louis Glavis as an instrument. Ballinger, said Ickes, was the American Dreyfus.[3]

Although the assault was less deadly than intended, it did result in a flurry of interest in the Ballinger case. Alpheus Thomas Mason ceased work on his great biography of Brandeis long enough to write a book which vigorously reasserted the traditional view. In 1946 George Mowry defended this interpretation, although with moderation, and with the reservation that Ballinger probably was not guilty of corruption. A year later Pinchot took up his own cause, yielding no ground

[3] Pringle, *The Life and Times of William Howard Taft* (2 vols.; New York and Toronto, 1939); Ickes, "Not Guilty! Richard A. Ballinger," *Saturday Evening Post*, May 25, 1940, p. 9; Ickes, *Not Guilty: An Official Inquiry into the Charges Made by Glavis and Pinchot against Richard A. Ballinger, Secretary of the Interior, 1909–1911* (Washington, D.C., 1940).

to anyone. In this state of disarray the matter stood at the end of the 1940's.[4]

In recent years three books on related subjects have dealt with the controversy. The first of these was the meticulously researched history of the progressive conservation movement by Samuel Hays. He shifted the focus sharply from the old questions of personal morality and the progressive fear of the octopus, and in a sophisticated analysis traced the importance of the controversy for the conservation movement. In a biography of Pinchot, M. Nelson McGeary, although rightly sympathetic to his subject, nevertheless emphasized his rashness and instability as well as his great gifts. In 1962 Elmo Richardson included chapters on the controversy in *The Politics of Conservation*, which effectively called attention to the political turmoil which the conservation movement created in the western public lands states.[5]

Under the circumstances, how still another look at the controversy can be justified is a valid question. Although there has not been a full-length book on the subject since 1940, to point this out is hardly an adequate reply. For myself I am satisfied that it is an interesting story which has never been explored in its full complexity, and although many of its implications have been sufficiently probed, others have been touched on only briefly or ignored altogether. I have tried to restore a basic unity to a historical event long fragmented by several generations of special pleading, considerations of policy, or the brevity imposed by larger purposes.

Although I hope the book will speak for itself, something can be said about my own position in relation to earlier interpreta-

[4] Mason, *Bureaucracy Convicts Itself: The Ballinger-Pinchot Controversy of 1910* (New York, 1941); Mowry, *Theodore Roosevelt and the Progressive Movement* (Madison, 1946); Pinchot, *Breaking New Ground* (New York, 1947).

[5] Hays, *Conservation and the Gospel of Efficiency: The Progressive Conservation Movement, 1890–1920* (Cambridge, Mass., 1959); McGeary, *Gifford Pinchot: Forester-Politician* (Princeton, N.J., 1960); Richardson, *The Politics of Conservation: Crusades and Controversies, 1897–1913*, University of California Publications in History, 70 (Berkeley and Los Angeles, Calif., 1962).

tions. Progressive history, which tended to emphasize the struggle between the "people" and the "vested interests," often has dominated discussions of the controversy. Within this framework it was possible to side with either antagonist. Thus it has been argued that Ballinger was, or was not, the agent of big corporate wealth. This particular argument, whether phrased in the affirmative or the negative, has been extremely difficult for scholars to avoid. It has influenced even the very recent studies—Elmo Richardson's *Politics of Conservation* and M. Nelson McGeary's *Gifford Pinchot*—which contain significant treatments of the affair. In my view, whatever ore this approach can yield has long since been mined. Insofar as the Ballinger-Pinchot controversy was concerned, the question was not whether corporate wealth should be controlled, but what relationship existed between the conservation movement and the trust issue. Pinchot argued that conservation was an instrument of control while Ballinger contended that the movement favored the trust.

I must acknowledge the influence Samuel Hays' *Conservation and the Gospel of Efficiency* has had on my thinking. Yet his treatment of the controversy is also enmeshed in the web of progressive history. Hays seems to suggest that Pinchot was a technical expert concerned primarily with efficiency and Ballinger a conventional politician responsive to traditional political ends—an idea generically related to Pinchot's own view of the affair. At the same time Hays' evidence demonstrates that Pinchot was actually more of a "politician" (in the conventional sense) than his antagonist (who was really out of his element in politics), but a missing ingredient was the extent to which Ballinger's concern for efficiency was an essential part of the story. Indeed, the issue was joined between two different conceptions of efficiency which had rubbed elbows under the mantle of the Roosevelt administrations. Ballinger's controversy with Pinchot was a contest of two competing views of the national interest, both of which claimed to be progressive. To sympathize with one side or the other, at least on matters of policy, has not seemed to me especially fruitful. My intention has been to understand (and I suppose to sympathize with) both sides. To do this and still not suspend judgment is at once the most difficult and the most important task of any historical enterprise. Perhaps in the nature of things the effort can never be entirely successful.

This book is about a clash of personalities over what were considered very high stakes, and as such it contains many of the elements of drama. Paradoxically the roots of the story are buried in a mass of detail in itself of no great intrinsic interest, except possibly to specialists. Faced with the purely mechanical problem of getting at these roots and still preserving the essential drama of the story, I ended with a compromise. I decided on narrative as the best mode of presentation. As I came to understand it, the story could be best revealed only by doggedly peeling it back layer by layer, while at the same time making an effort to keep the personalities involved at the forefront of the unfolding events.

I cannot claim any overriding significance for the controversy, although I certainly think it held various levels of significance. There has been a wide variety of opinion on this subject, ranging from that of Elting Morison who called it "meaningless" to Pinchot's insistence that it was a great crusade to save the land of the people from the spoilers.[6] My own interest kept me from adopting Morison's view, whereas Pinchot's opinion was one of the reasons for my interest. Although there are no doubt genuine spoilers lurking behind the scenery, every generation has a somewhat different version of the villainy they seek to perpetrate, which is usually part fact and part fiction and—in some hands—part policy. I would like to think that I have gone behind the scenery sufficiently to separate illusion from reality without allowing my own devils to intervene; but this is a question on which it is perhaps discreet to suspend judgment.

[6] Morison, *Turmoil and Tradition: A Study of the Life and Times of Henry L. Stimson* (New York: Atheneum, 1964), p. 107.

Contents

CHAPTER ONE

The Conservation Movement 1898–1908

It is symbolic that the bullet of an anarchist raised Theodore Roosevelt to the highest office in the land. No national leader so well embodied the anxieties of the era or so well expressed the need for new controls of the great sprawling pluralism of industrial America. His pronouncements on monopoly, his fear of labor violence, socialism, and class conflict, his concern for the decline of rural life and the problems of rapid urbanization combined to identify him as a spokesman for his generation. Since he had little success in obtaining effective legislation, with important exceptions, it may be that he will be remembered longest for his role as spokesman. But it remained true that no president had ever exercised existing executive powers more forcefully. The "Roosevelt policies" were peculiarly presidential. Except in foreign affairs the powers of the presidency were most discretionary on the federal lands and the public domain. For this reason the conservation movement loomed large in his domestic program.

The conservation movement produced several colorful personalities, but none so dominated the scene as the flamboyant chief forester, Gifford Pinchot. Owen Wister once said, not entirely to flatter, that Pinchot's eyes looked as if they gazed upon a Cause. The setting in which they burned was important to the impression, since a gaze of equal intensity from a fat man might have seemed merely dyspeptic. But the eyes peered out above appropriately hollowed cheeks, over a truculent nose that hovered above ferocious muleskinner mustachios, and the head was attached to as lean and spare a frame as ever suggested austerity and rigor. The total effect was magnificent. If there was little in the impression to suggest the childhood spent rotating between the country estate in Pennsylvania, the town house in New York, and the summers in Europe, there was more than enough to suggest the vigor of the young man who referred to his inherited wealth as unearned increment while declining the leisure it might have afforded.

A romantic streak and a love of the outdoors had combined to arouse his interest in forestry, although the absence of professional forestry schools forced him to seek his training in Europe. At the time there seemed to be little demand for professional foresters, and what there was came from wealthy estate owners like himself. An act of 1891, however, had created the "public" forests by empowering the President to set aside forest reservations, and Pinchot's attention was drawn to them. In mid-decade he served on a study commission of the National Academy of Sciences which reported on the condition of the reserves for the government. In 1898 he was given charge of the Division of Forestry by President McKinley.[1]

Pinchot took command of the forestry bureau at a time when the Department of Agriculture was emerging as the center of science in the government, under the able leadership of its secretary, Tama Jim Wilson. In 1898 the Division of Forestry was an insignificant agency in the departmental research establishment, which comprehended the land grant colleges and the state experiment stations. Yet under the leadership of Pinchot in the progressive era, the bureau became for a time the national focus of scientific and technical public policy, and the tail seemed to wag the dog. Pinchot himself became a Great Captain of federal science in the tradition of Alexander Dallas Bache and John Wesley Powell. Like the Coast Survey of the

---

[1] Pinchot's autobiography, *Breaking New Ground* (New York, 1947), is a good introduction to his career, although it ends in 1910. A full-dress biography is M. Nelson McGeary, *Gifford Pinchot: Forester-Politician* (Princeton, N.J., 1960).

1850's and the early Geological Survey, the Forest Service under Pinchot acquired truly national scope.[2]

In part its influence flowed from an elaborate communications system which hooked up to diverse constituencies outside the government. Pinchot was a great politician of science precisely because his ambitions transcended the technical mission of his agency. Before 1905 those ambitions were centered on acquiring the national forests, which were administered in the Department of the Interior by the General Land Office. This was a situation which dramatized the pluralistic character of federal scientific and technical programs. The forests had originally been created at the urging of urban and irrigation groups concerned with protecting watersheds. Such groups often wanted the reserves entirely removed from commercial use. On the other hand, there were numerous groups interested in the commercial possibilities of the reserves, including lumber and mining interests, cattlemen, sheepmen, and homesteaders. Pinchot bridged the two factions, those for and those against commercial use of the reserves and, for a time at least, successfully welded them into a coalition.

There was no lack of material for bridge building, although it took talent to use it properly. Ready at hand on the bureau level was a body of doctrine concerning the relationship of forest cover to water storage, a legacy of the hydrographic investigations of 1888 which had crowned the efforts of Powell's Geological Survey. This doctrine, which Pinchot adopted, had already become gospel in the irrigation movement in and outside the government. The several phalanxes of that movement joined Pinchot's forces and supported the transfer of the reserves to the forestry bureau. Pinchot, in turn, was an open champion of the Newlands act of 1902, which began the federal reclamation program, and he struck a lasting alliance with Powell-trained chieftains such as Arthur Powell Davis, Frederick Haynes Newell, Marshall O. Leighton, and W J McGee.

[2] A. Hunter Dupree, *Science in the Federal Government* (Cambridge, Mass., 1957), chap. 12, emphasized the scientific character of the conservation movement.

The merger with the irrigation movement won over many groups which might have opposed opening the reserves to commercial use. Meanwhile, Pinchot actively sought the support of the industries most concerned with the forests. The core of "practical" forestry, as preached by Pinchot, was sustained-yield management, a concept designed to maintain a constant supply of timber by insuring that annual cutting did not exceed annual growth. Proponents of the doctrine had captured the American Forestry Association in the 1890's and after 1898 were identifiable as supporters of Pinchot. Their number was increased by representatives of industries dependent upon wood, which after 1900 were experiencing greater difficulty in acquiring satisfactory materials. Hardwood users wanted the Appalachians set aside as a sustained-yield area, and their trade associations lined up behind Pinchot and joined his bloc in the American Forestry Association. That bloc also included the major lumber concerns. The lumber industry faced a critical turn. By the 1890's the pineries of the lake states had been cut over, and the transcontinental railroads had opened the pure stands of Douglas fir in the far Northwest. In 1889 lumber production in Washington was equal to that of Minnesota; by 1909 it led the nation. The lumber industry was mobile and speculative, but with the shift to the Pacific Northwest the last frontier of virgin stands had been reached. Pinchot began preaching management and planning at a time when lumbermen were becoming aware of the need for greater stability in their industry.

Pinchot took a strong stand on grazing in the forests. The Department of the Interior had reluctantly opened them to livestock but continued to view the activity with suspicion. Pinchot shamelessly courted the leading grazing interests. He pointed out the contrast between his views and the past policy of the Department of the Interior, which had always sought to keep commercial use of the forests to a minimum. In convention in 1901 and in succeeding years, the American National Livestock Association passed resolutions favoring Pinchot and recommending transfer of the forest reserves to the Bureau of

Forestry. They were joined by other groups interested in commercial development in the forests, such as the American Mining Congress. At the same time, he built up a highly effective publicity distribution system which kept forestry and his views on forest management before the public eye in newspapers and magazines around the country. When a transfer act was passed in 1905, Pinchot had clearly proved himself one of the great promoters in the history of bureau politics.

Ultimately it was his relationship with the President that transformed him into something more than just an especially vigorous bureau chief. Pinchot had no trouble convincing Roosevelt that he should make a strong conservation statement in his first message to Congress. For many reasons Roosevelt came to look upon conservation as his most important domestic policy. His championing of the bureau doctrines of resource management which had grown up since the time of Powell functioned through a close working relationship with Gifford Pinchot. The latter became a member of the famous "tennis cabinet"—a carrier of presidential influence to the bureau level but also a carrier of bureau doctrine to the presidential level, a conductor cutting across the lines separating the cabinet departments, connecting the working agencies with the highest level of political power. With lines out also to numerous supporting groups in the private community, Pinchot was in a position to dominate federal resource policy in every area of the government.

After 1905 he made good on his promise to open the forests to greater commercial development, and two prominent users, the grazing and waterpower industries, were regulated by the Forest Service. Out of this experience and from the reports of the Public Lands Commission which assembled and restated the bureau doctrines of the preceding twenty years, a new theory of land management evolved. The core of the new program was reform of the land laws, which traditionally revolved around the principle of distributing land and resources to individuals, although by 1900 the most important unit of exploitation was corporate. Roosevelt resource leaders proposed that this system be replaced by public ownership. Resources were to be classified by their actual value and leased, a method of disposal which would permit federal officials to determine priorities and regulate the conditions of use. Part of this program began in 1906, when the remaining coal lands were withdrawn and the Geological Survey began classifying them and opening them for purchase at market value. This was an improvement over the flat statute price which had enabled speculators to acquire the most valuable coal lands and make fantastic capital gains by reselling them at the higher price. As the system was applied to minerals other than coal, it went far to check the practice of acquiring mineral rights under agricultural laws designed to be lenient to the individual farmer. Putting an end to fraud, however, was only the negative side of the new resource policy.

Advocates of the policy hoped to adjust the conditions of resource use to meet the needs of large-scale corporate enterprise and at the same time to arbitrate and control the demands of competing users. The difficulties of implementation were illustrated by the conflict over grazing lands in 1906–7. Stockmen had been advocating the leasing of federal grasslands since the 1890's. In 1906 the Roosevelt administration backed a lease bill which in effect would have applied to the public domain the system developed by Pinchot in the national forests. The stockmen competed with other possible users for federal grass, and the intensity of this competition between sheepman, cattleman, settler, and watershed protection groups produced a deeply partisan arena in which to formulate policy. The controversy revealed the inner tensions of the new policy. The Reclamation Act of 1902 stemmed in part from a desire to prop up artificially a flagging individualist ethic by preserving the family homestead, and irrigators and homesteaders had been part of Pinchot's grand coalition, along with giant corporate interests. Emotional commitment to the small-scale operator and admiration for the efficiency of the large economic unit existed side by side, an anomaly which the lease bill revealed. Most of the urban and irrigation forces left the Pinchot camp at this point

and did not find themselves in line with the administration resource policy again until the fight over multiple-purpose river
development in 1908. Even the cattlemen were split between
the large corporate outfits backing the administration because
they wanted stability for their industry and the small operators
who opposed federal leasing because stability for them could
mean restricted opportunity.[3]

The fate of the lease bill seemed to demonstrate that a well-
developed conservation program for the public domain similar
to that initiated for the forests by Pinchot had to depend primarily on unilateral executive action for its advancement, perhaps in the teeth of congressional hostility, and conditions
proper for this did not come about until 1907. In that year
James R. Garfield replaced the more conservative and legalistic
E. A. Hitchcock as head of the Department of the Interior.
Garfield, the son of the assassinated twentieth president, came
from the Bureau of Corporations, over which he had presided
during the years when the basic elements of the Roosevelt trust
policy were formed, and he tended to look upon the problems
of conservation as germane to the trust problem generally: the
need to control and regulate, rather than destroy, large-scale
enterprise.

The waterpower industry, already regulated on the forests,
presented the most immediate challenge for those interested in
applying the Forest Service system to the public lands. The use
of hydroelectric power was just hitting its stride, and the need
to prevent power sites from going the same way as had the
valuable coal deposits was evident to many. However, the waterpower problem acquired added significance with the appointment of the Inland Waterways Commission in 1908. The
commission was the brainchild of one of Powell's closest associates, W J McGee, who served as its secretary; its membership
included Pinchot, Newell, and the chief of the Army Engineers. The commission report was the culmination of three

[3] E. Louise Peffer, *The Closing of the Public Domain: Disposal and
Reservation Policies, 1900–50* (Stanford, Calif., 1951), is the best account
of the grazing question.

decades of creative thought on the bureau level about natural resources. It proposed the regional development of river systems, but it concerned more than water: flood control, navigation, electric power, irrigation, agriculture, industry, the material development of the nation on every level was involved. It called for the creation of a permanent commission to oversee the regional and national development of the nation's material base. The cost of this vast enterprise was to be defrayed by the production and sale of power by the government.

Although Senator Francis Newlands of Nevada introduced a bill into the Senate embodying the recommendations of the IWC, the Army Engineers had dissented from the report and opposed the creation of a permanent commission; Congress, already disturbed by the effect that new land policies were having on local political arrangements, was in no mood to accept a super planning agency. Thus it appeared, as the Roosevelt years neared their end in 1908, that regional development would be postponed to an undetermined future. It was in this context in December that Garfield began withdrawing power sites from all forms of entry except power development. Doubtless he was concerned with nailing down the lid with the approach of a new and unpredictable administration, by applying the Forest Service system to the public lands. But the recommendations of the IWC were foremost in Garfield's mind, rather than just a desire to regulate power companies. The IWC report had suggested that charges for power would one day defray the costs of multiple-purpose river development, if and when it emerged as a reality, and to safeguard sites for this future purpose, Garfield withdrew the great majority of the waterpower sites under the authority of the Reclamation Act of 1902, which clearly retained ownership in the government.[4]

In the sense that they were a holding action, the late-hour withdrawals were an admission that the conservation program

[4] In this regard see Garfield's testimony in *Investigation of the Department of the Interior and the Bureau of Forestry*, Sen. Doc. 719, 61 Cong., 3 Sess., 4, pp. 1494–1505, *passim.*

had stalled. In 1907 and 1908 the failure of the administration lease bill for range lands was followed by the unwillingness of Congress to pass the Newlands bill and establish the waterways commission. To this had to be added the rise of powerful opposition, of which the Army Engineers were not least. Thus the crusade of 1908–9 was born to some extent of frustration. The governors' conference, the National Conservation Commission, the great inventory, the "international" conservation conference, and the call for the nations of the world to cooperate in the great venture, all were signals that Roosevelt and Pinchot had decided to broaden the movement by appealing directly to the people. Out of this labor emerged the "conservation movement," a product of the publicity talents of Gifford Pinchot, and the willingness of Roosevelt to use the tremendous influence of the presidency to focus attention on the nation's "diminishing resources." What had been the concern of a handful of technical administrators and a restricted number of economic groups, acquired a national audience. The rhetoric of conservation was plugged into the antitrust sentiment of the progressive era. To the public the conservation movement came to mean the movement to keep monopolistic trusts from exhausting the nation's material wealth within a few generations.[5]

The crusade of 1908 was scarcely an unmixed success. In March 1909 Theodore Roosevelt went off to Africa to hunt large vertebrates for the Smithsonian Institution, and William Howard Taft moved into the White House. Pinchot quickly found himself in conflict with the new president and his secretary of the interior, Richard Ballinger. Within a year the forester had been dismissed from the government and had set in motion forces which, all unwittingly, would contribute to the final derailing of the Roosevelt conservation movement. Ballinger began by thoroughly undoing the waterpower policy

[5] The standard scholarly treatment of the progressive conservation movement is Samuel P. Hays, *Conservation and the Gospel of Efficiency: The Progressive Conservation Movement, 1890–1920* (Cambridge, Mass., 1959).

of Garfield. Taft, although Roosevelt's hand-picked successor, had been secretary of war and had taken the side of the Corps of Army Engineers in the fight for the waterways commission. As president, he took the side of Ballinger against Pinchot.

The point has been made that Gifford Pinchot, whatever he may have thought, was not the conservation movement—that it was the product of the talents of many men. Although this was undoubtedly correct, it remained true that Pinchot was utterly committed and identified with the movement, about which he had very definite views and to which he had contributed both direction and purpose. He was not, however, blinded by fanaticism. He was capable of making a realistic appraisal of the character and importance of his personal contribution, and of acting as he thought necessary on the basis of that appraisal. This emerged clearly in his conflict with Taft. Ultimately it was not a question of Taft's opposition to conservation, but rather his unwillingness to allow Pinchot to continue as a virtual member of the cabinet for conservation. At stake were the extraordinary powers wielded by bureau chiefs concerned with conservation during the Roosevelt years, powers which had depended on the peculiar relationship of Pinchot and Roosevelt. After March 1909 Pinchot attempted to perpetuate conditions of the previous administration. His failure, as well as the emotional character of the conflict with Ballinger, obscured the real problem.

The real problem, which persisted and continues to persist, was how to establish a unified system of planning. Departmental autonomy and the jealousies of departments and bureaus each with its own congressional lobby, its own programs, its own jurisdictions, plus the overlapping and duplication, turned dreams of an "administration" program into a nightmare. The Inland Waterways Commission was to have been the central planning agency to carry on the resource programs of the Roosevelt years while launching new ones that had been envisioned. Although Congress had balked at its passage in 1908, some hope for the bill persisted for another decade. It was this hope that gave the conflict with Taft and Ballinger its urgency.

Until the IWC could come into being, the Roosevelt policies based on personal relationships had to be perpetuated.

In February 1909 Roosevelt asked Congress for funds to continue the work of the National Conservation Commission. Not only was the request refused, but Congress passed a measure making it illegal for a federal administrator to aid an executive commission not authorized by Congress. Roosevelt signed the bill shortly before leaving office, although he claimed he would have refused to obey it.[6] Some legislators doubtless voted for the amendment because they opposed the president's resource policies, but many others were reacting less to the substance than to the tone of policy. Increasingly that tone had acquired an antiparliamentary character.

The National Conservation Commission brought to a head certain tensions between the executive and Congress. Many members of the administration, including the president, had adopted a position later to be identified in America with Herbert Croly and *The New Republic*, but increasingly to be recognized as an affliction of many liberals in the western world. It was a position marked by the belief that the liberal bourgeois state was artificial and factional, a mask disguising the real sources of power.[7]

Gifford Pinchot put it bluntly: "the special interests are in politics, [and] . . . in Congress." In the rhetoric of the time the word politics was often used synonomously with special interests, which explained Pinchot's classic description of a pre-Roosevelt government "debased by generations of political control," as well as Roosevelt's own frequently expressed view that the government should be divorced from politics and made to run according to sound business principles.[8]

[6] Theodore Roosevelt, *Autobiography* (New York, 1916).

[7] A good discussion of this subject is John P. Diggins, "Flirtation with Fascism: American Pragmatic Liberals and Mussolini's Italy," *The American Historical Review*, 71 (January 1966), pp. 487–506. Many of its insights are relevant to the era of Theodore Roosevelt.

[8] Hays, *Conservation and the Gospel of Efficiency*, pp. 125, 130, 133; Pinchot, *The Fight for Conservation* (New York, 1910), p. 134; *Breaking New Ground*, p. 296.

When Pinchot's main concern was building the Forest Service into the foremost agency concerned with public lands, he worked smoothly enough with Congress. After 1907 new theories of land management were being applied to the public domain, and the immensely creative movement for regional planning took shape. Policy now concerned many agencies and cut across departmental lines to a greater extent, with more at stake. The need for unity of policy, and the problems of central planning—what agency was to do the planning, who would set priorities and make the necessary allocations—these now came to the fore. Viewing problems from the needs of the center to overcome the pluralism rather than from the position of an agency seeking to survive and compete in the context of pluralism threw a different light on congressional "inefficiency," and gave meaning to Roosevelt's conclusion that "all modern legislative bodies tend to show their incapacity to meet the new and complex needs of the times."[9]

A government organized along business lines was something else. In an era when great moneymen were seeking to stabilize the private sector of the economy by substituting cooperation and control for struggle, men in government talked of adjudicating the conflict of interest groups dividing the community. But the traditional legislative and judicial machinery appeared to be as inadequate to the needs of industrialized America as laissez faire had become. The new policies required bureaucratic and administrative methods, the smooth efficiency of the giant trust then so effectively reordering the American economy.

The broad social concern which contemporaries referred to as the trust problem was at the center of the political rhetoric of the time. Historians are not entirely in agreement on the relationship between the antitrust and conservation movements. Traditionally, conservation has been viewed as a phase in the conflict over the distribution of wealth and therefore closely related to the trust problem. More recently students have sug-

[9] Quoted in Hays, *Conservation and the Gospel of Efficiency*, p. 133.

gested that the real implications of conservation derived from the "political implications of applied science," that is, from the application of scientific rather than political criteria to resource policy, and that administration leaders appealed to public fear of the trust as an expedient for gaining broader support.[10]

The trust question came equipped with a full set of hate symbols which, when evoked, would elicit a public response. Pinchot was delineating the morbid fears of a generation when he described "the separate circles of centralized control" spreading "into the uniform, unbroken, nationwide covering of a single gigantic trust."[11] Just as in a later time a potent political weapon existed in the possibility of connecting an opponent with the internal threat of communism, so in the progressive era a reputation for being soft on corporations was politically fatal.

Opportunism doubtless played its role in such political appeals, but administration leaders were far from unfeeling in their attitudes to the trust. Admiration for efficiency and fear of declining opportunity could and did go hand in hand, along with other feelings that could be quite strong. James R. Garfield, one of the architects of the Roosevelt trust program, experienced actual physical disgust when he first set eyes on John D. Rockefeller.

> Never have I seen a more sinister, avaricious face—repulsive & deceitful. I disliked to shake his hand, but of course could not cause comment by not doing so. . . . I wonder if anyone—outside his family—really cares for him apart from his money. . . .[12]

[10] Rose M. Stahl, "The Ballinger-Pinchot Controversy," *Smith College Studies in History*, 11 (1926), pp. 65–136, states the traditional view; a sophisticated restatement is J. Leonard Bates, "Fulfilling American Democracy; The Conservation Movement, 1907–1921," *Mississippi Valley Historical Review*, 44 (June 1957), pp. 29–57. The Hays study focuses on the political implications of applied science.

[11] *Addresses and Proceedings of the First National Conservation Congress Held at Seattle, Washington, August 26–28, 1909* (Washington, D.C., 1910), p. 100.

[12] Garfield Diary, October 4, 1909, MS in the Library of Congress, James R. Garfield Papers.

On the other hand, W J. McGee, the man credited by Pinchot with pointing out to him the connection between conservation and the trust problem, thought of Rockefeller as a "generous public benefactor" who had "all the opportunity in the world to exact an exorbitant toll and yet . . . charges less for oil than is paid every day for common water." He recommended that the government use similar methods for its own purposes.[13]

Contemporary opinion was sharply divided on the trust. Many people felt the trust was intrinsically evil, and should be destroyed forthwith, and the competitive free and open market resuscitated. This was the view of Robert M. La Follette. Others tolerated the trust as a natural economic development but demanded that it be prevented from engaging in unfair competition. Like the first, this view insisted upon the maintenance of open market conditions, and held that government should intervene only to prevent the trust from blocking the operation of the natural laws of commerce. This was the position of Roosevelt's successor, William H. Taft. A third solution involved the acceptance of the trust as a positive good, when under the proper restraints, and was given its first vigorous expression by Theodore Roosevelt.[14]

Roosevelt's pungent brand of toryism has been disturbing to liberal historians, just as it was to contemporary spokesmen such as Robert La Follette. Yet this was the very quality which made his position distinctive and significant. Roosevelt rejected all forms of radicalism which seemed to indict the character of American society. He argued that good and evil, and not the "system," were the roots of virtue and corruption in society. He hoped to prevent men from turning to "false teachers," the "fifth monarchy" men who denounced the "principalities and powers" and sought to lead an assault on "the system." He

[13] *Omaha Bee*, August 11, 1909.

[14] William E. Smythe, *Constructive Democracy: The Economics of a Square Deal* (New York, 1905), pp. 180–81; Belle Case and Fola La Follette, *Robert M. La Follette, June 14, 1855–June 18, 1925* (2 vols.; New York, 1953), 1, p. 291; Alpheus T. Mason, *Brandeis: A Free Man's Life* (New York, 1946).

attempted to circumvent the Marxian insistence upon impersonal and overwhelming social forces, with its emphasis on group struggle. He faced the increasing organization of society into ethnic, religious, and economic groups by insisting on individual responsibility and, where struggle existed, as between labor and capital, by bringing the "contending forces face to face" and forcing them to resolve their differences in the open.[15] Doubtless there was a touch of reaction in such an approach. The desire to "restore" individual responsibility implied the preservation of the individualist ethic of a pre-industrial, agrarian, and presumably better past. Yet the effort to avoid the implications of group struggle inherent in an urban and plural community was a typically American reaction and one to which the countrymen of Roosevelt readily responded.

The program for the federal control of corporations went to the heart of these concerns. The trust represented all that was wrong with America. Corporate organization was smothering individual enterprise; corporation money corrupted politicians, undermined public morality, and harnessed government to corporate interests; the misuse of power led to the organization of countervailing groups in opposition, encouraged the further breakdown of individualism, and led to class struggle. Roosevelt wanted to use publicity to reveal corporate abuses and to turn the spotlight on malefactors who sought to rely on corporate anonymity to obscure responsibility for their actions. It was on this aspect of the manager as wrongdoer that Garfield focused when he was revolted by Rockefeller. On the other hand, Garfield fully shared the admiration McGee expressed for the methods which Rockefeller had at his disposal. The Sherman Antitrust Act reflected the deep public distrust of great concentrations of power and the ancient common law bias against all combinations in restraint of trade, but its de-

[15] Roosevelt to Lincoln Steffens, June 5, 1908, in E. E. Morison *et al.*, *Letters of Theodore Roosevelt* (Cambridge, Mass., 1952), 6, pp. 1050–53; Roosevelt, "Socialism," *The Outlook*, March 27, 1909, p. 662; Garfield, "Review of President Roosevelt's Administration," *ibid.*, February 20, 1909, p. 393.

mand for the dissolution of the large economic unit aroused scant respect in the Roosevelt administration. The administration saw the trust not only as the symbol of the worst evils in American society but also as a source of solution for the very evils which it represented. In the centralized organization and administrative methods of the modern corporation, many saw a model for carrying on the great enterprise of government itself. Roosevelt hoped to license all corporations in interstate commerce and to use the licensing power to institute "thoroughgoing and effective" regulation. The Sherman act was to be used only on recalcitrant corporations which balked at cooperating with the federal program.

Publicity would restore individual responsibility by submitting the actions of corporate managers to public scrutiny. Regulation would rationalize economic activity by eliminating wasteful competition and enforcing order among conflicting groups. Continuous supervision by a government organized along the same efficient lines as the corporation itself would keep the responsibility for wrongdoing focused on the individuals running the corporations and serve to keep them honest. Thus Roosevelt was calling for a new kind of state, a regulatory state staffed by disinterested administrators. Since it could not exist with "special interests" in the government, part of the Roosevelt trust program called for legislation to keep corporation funds and influence out of politics.[16]

For this ideal of professionalism in government, two guides were at hand. Business seemed to offer the necessary organizational techniques and the businessman, morally reconstituted of course, provided just the right image of the democrat governing himself.[17] Science, sometimes used synonomously with business, also provided a model. It seemed to offer the dash of

[16] *Ibid.*, pp. 389–93; Arthur M. Johnson, "Theodore Roosevelt and the Bureau of Corporations," *Mississippi Valley Historical Review,* 45 (March 1959), p. 573; *Report of the Commissioner of Corporations,* December 21, 1904, H. Doc. 165, 58 Cong., 3 Sess., 51, p. 45.

[17] See Discussion in Barry Karl, *Executive Reorganization and Reform in the New Deal; The Genesis of Administrative Management, 1900–1939* (Cambridge, Mass., 1963), p. 95.

disinterest that the businessman needed to tone up his image. There was a good deal of talk about scientific management. The technical character of conservation may have raised the question whether government administration was best provided by "scientists" whose first loyalty was to the realities of their technical disciplines rather than to any of the warring forces in society. But the ultimate implication lay in the development of a professional class, technical and non-technical, whose first loyalty would be to the state. To Pinchot and Roosevelt scientific management meant unselfish management. They seemed to be moving toward the concept of a professional governing class as a vested interest devoted to its own discrete development. In this way they demonstrated their devotion to the bourgeois ideal of disinterested bureaucracy, with its commitment to a sharp division between the objective and the subjective, the public and the private, the personal and the impersonal.

When Garfield spoke of the "Roosevelt policies" he was referring to a close relationship between federal control of corporations and the conservation of natural resources.[18] It is important to keep this connection in mind. To do so, it is not necessary to accept the progressive theory of history that saw the historical process as a struggle between the "special interests" and the "public interest," with conservation as part of that process. Yet it helps to keep in mind the contemporary belief in such a dichotomy, to ward off the too hasty conclusion that the antitrust rhetoric was a mask for designing politicians bent on manipulating public fears for their own ends. Although doubtless such opportunism was present in some degree, Roosevelt and his captains did not identify conservation with the trust problem in 1908 merely because it seemed the most convenient means of attracting public attention. The identification was made because the two programs were essential features of the same system.

Roosevelt had little hope of getting the legislation needed to launch the program for licensing and regulating corporations.

[18] Garfield Diary, November 29, 1909, Garfield Papers.

On the public lands he could push ahead, often without additional legislation. The Forest Service made creative use of publicity and, with the regulation of the grazers and the water-power industry, pioneered in the methods of permanent and continuous administration, the goal of the regulatory state. Garfield sought to infuse the same spirit into the management of the public lands by the Department of the Interior. The pluralistic structure of the government was a challenge to men who admired corporate efficiency. Roosevelt appointed commissions to study its workings, some of which had to be financed, without the consent of Congress, by wondrous means. Through personal influence, through informal and formal agreements, often department and bureau procedure was short-circuited and working agencies in different departments harnessed in tandem. In short, conservation provided an arena for implementing in some degree the broad solutions for problems believed to be inherent in the complex and plural community of modern America.

The Inland Waterways Commission, with its promise of broad regional and national planning, raised again the question of acquiring legislative support for policy. When it was not forthcoming the Roosevelt men invoked the specter of special interests in politics. But such appeals should not be allowed to obscure the meaning of the conservation program as it emerged in the spring of 1909. Conservation had grown in importance with the recognition that it gave full range to policies with larger significance, and to this extent was part of a system. Yet it was the only part which had been very successful. The IWC, or at least the integrated program which it represented, was by no means a lost cause when the White House changed occupants, and in any case a good deal had already been accomplished. This very accomplishment, in contrast to failure on many other fronts, served to make the conservation movement synonymous with Roosevelt policies rather than just one phase of those policies, as the Roosevelt years came to an end.

CHAPTER TWO

Ballinger in the Land Office, 1907-1908

Steeped in the fulness of unmellowed age, Gifford Pinchot was to remember Richard Ballinger almost affectionately as "a stocky, square-headed little man, of no inconsiderable energy and no little executive punch."[1] Pinchot was tall and Ballinger short, and the geometrical shape of their heads no doubt contrasted sharply, but both men were vigorous and aggressive and both had demonstrated great administrative talents as bureau chiefs under Roosevelt. Yet whatever similar traits they may have shared were more than offset by basic differences stemming from background and temperament. Although Pinchot frequently assumed the rough manner of the outdoorsman and man of action, he was a patrician to his fingertips. He was raised to rule, or to use the euphemism usually employed by Americans when their leaders come from the upper class, he was reared to public service.

Ballinger was cut from the different but equally familiar pattern of the self-made man, that independent, hardy exemplar of middle-class America. In nineteenth-century America the ingredients of the conventional success story required a hero of sound stock, and sufficient hardship and deprivation to test his mettle. Ballinger's career was as well endowed as an Alger melodrama. With little formal education beyond a smattering of Greek and a volume of Burns's poetry committed to memory while herding cattle on the open range, he worked his

---

[1] Pinchot, *Breaking New Ground* (New York, 1947), p. 395.

way through Williams College and went on to become a respected lawyer and a man of substance in the Puget Sound region of the far Northwest. In accepted fashion, he parlayed the sturdy virtues of intelligence, thrift, hard work, and self-reliance into coin of the realm.

In 1907 Ballinger was a partner in an established law firm. He was respected by the bar as the author of an authoritative work on community property as well as of the official code of the state of Washington. His practice had brought him into contact with the influential and powerful of the region, and the possibilities for greater and greater material rewards were only beginning to open for him. Most of his satisfaction was drawn from this practice. Although he was dedicated to getting ahead, and ambitious for the trappings that accompanied the status of "leading citizen," he did not seek political power. Indeed, he had an ingrained suspicion of power. This was perhaps a heritage from his father, who had been an abolitionist editor. Like this parent, Ballinger would not abide with evil in the community, a characteristic which tempered and restrained his material ambitions. He was fiercely upright. His sense of evil was Calvinist rather than Marxist. He sought to fix individual rather than general responsibility. Evil was corruption in public life, or prostitution, or gambling; it was not struggling social classes or decayng societies. The solution was to be found in retribution for all wrongdoers. If he recognized the inexorable working of an overriding historical process, it worked in Calvin's heaven and not in Marx's dialectical materialism. This sense of righteousness had occasionally propelled Ballinger into public life. Such forays were not to his liking and he rarely stayed longer than it took to chastise the rascals.

For a brief period as a fledgling lawyer, Ballinger had been a city attorney in New Decatur, Alabama, and the center of a campaign against dishonesty in local government. In 1890 he moved to Port Townsend on Puget Sound. The following year he became a United States commissioner and tried several Chinese exclusion cases. In 1892 he was chairman of the Port Townsend bar association, which preferred charges against a judge of the Superior Court who, according to Ballinger, was "a faro gambler and corruptionist." When impeachment proceedings failed in the legislature, the unfortunate jurist was turned out of office in the next election and Ballinger succeeded him on the bench. In 1898 he moved to the larger and faster growing community of Seattle. In the same year the city took the full impact of the Klondike gold rush.

Seattle stood at the gateway to Alaska, and the entire gold rush, going and returning, funneled through its portals. As the usual industries appeared to service the transient flood, not all were welcome to the sedate and moral portions of the citizenry. Seattle merchants prospered. Yet civic leaders grew increasingly irate over the enlarged redlight district, the overheated gaming tables, and the alarming growth of the "criminal element." In 1904 Ballinger was elected mayor on a clean government slate. After two years of vigorous effort, organized vice was driven underground, the more obvious bribery and corruption in government were eliminated, and the affairs of the city were organized along "sound business principles." Ballinger retired to private life after one term. But for a brief time in this era of reform mayors, the ripples from the splash in Seattle reached beyond the state of Washington to a national audience intrigued with municipal reform. One consequence of the wider notoriety was a periodic correspondence Ballinger began with a college acquaintance, James R. Garfield, Roosevelt's commissioner of corporations.[2]

This tenuous connection with Garfield ultimately launched Ballinger's national career. When Garfield took up the office of secretary of the interior he brought Ballinger to Washington to reorganize the General Land Office. The broad policies of

---

[2] R.A.B. to E. A. Hanson, January 13, 1910; Albert Searl to R.A.B. March 26, 1909, University of Washington Library, Richard A. Ballinger Papers. There are also numerous biographical sketches in this collection. *Investigation of the Department of the Interior and the Bureau of Forestry,* Sen. Doc. 719, 61 Cong., 3 Sess., 7, pp. 3549–55 (hereinafter cited as *Investigation*). Clarence Bagley, *History of Seattle* (Chicago, 1916), p. 620. Elmo R. Richardson, *The Politics of Conservation: Crusades and Controversies, 1897–1913* (Berkeley and Los Angeles, Calif., 1962), pp. 47–50.

the conservation movement were still in an early planning stage in late 1906 when Garfield was preparing to assume his new position, but his appointment signaled a general departmental reorganization. George Woodruff, a Forest Service legal adviser and major architect of the agency's program on the national forests, became the attorney general assigned to the Department of the Interior. Through him as well as through the close personal relationship of Garfield and Pinchot, the new theories of land management acquired spokesmen at the highest level of authority in the department, and ideas of resource regulation and control were fruitfully combined with a coherent approach to the problem of large corporate enterprise in American economic life.

The General Land Office was an object of their grave concern. Until 1905 it had the responsibility for managing the national forests, which had placed it in the role of adversary to Pinchot in his campaign for their transfer to the Forest Service. The rivalry continued after the transfer. With some justification, Pinchot believed the Land Office to be a haven of inefficiency and archaic procedure. It had a long history as the agency chiefly concerned with the disposition and sale of public lands, and that history had had its notorious and malodorous moments. The land frauds in Oregon, even then being prosecuted, were a glaring contemporary example. In addition, the Land Office was a lawyers' agency and habitually took what Pinchot believed to be a narrowly legalistic approach to resource policy. This attitude created problems for Pinchot even after the transfer, since the success of much of the Forest Service program depended upon the informal cooperation of the Land Office. Furthermore, the Public Lands Commission, of which the commissioner of the Land Office was chairman, had yet to complete its recommendations, and its deliberations emphasized the need for changes in the Land Office. Incumbent commissioner William A. Richards cooperated with Pinchot and Newell on the commission, but perhaps for related reasons, he was not the man to reorganize the Land Office. With his approaching retirement in late 1906, the proponents of the new program were far from indifferent to the question of his replacement.

Pinchot was concerned enough to consider taking the position himself, but political considerations dictated the appointment of a westerner. Pinchot was not slow in providing the president with suitable names, and at least two Pinchot supporters were actually offered the Land Office, but they declined. Finally, in January 1907 the offer went to Richard Ballinger of Seattle on the strength of Garfield's recommendation. Ballinger, too, declined although he changed his mind after personal pleas from both Garfield and Roosevelt. Ballinger was unable to resist Roosevelt's appeal for "support . . . from the men who believe in my way of handling things." Ballinger probably sincerely wanted to avoid the appointment. He had just completed his two years as mayor and he had no taste for public life. He was not a wealthy man and wanted nothing except to return to his practice. Somewhat smugly, he liked to quote Roosevelt as saying that he had "secured a $20,000 man while I was in the commissioner's office, for $5,000." But the sacrifice was real enough. Ballinger's firm specialized in transportation, landownership, the use of natural resources, and other matters requiring close contact with the Land Office. When he became commissioner this business had to be dropped to avoid any question of conflict of interest. The firm was dissolved shortly after Ballinger's appointment as secretary of the interior.[3]

The General Land Office over which Ballinger assumed control was an agency on the verge of transition. Its primary mission of presiding over the disposal of the public domain was not yet completed—between 1900 and 1920 there were twice as many final entries under the homestead laws as in the preceding twenty years. Nevertheless, the great era of settlement was drawing to a close, and the time was not too distant when the Land Office would begin its metamorphosis into the Bureau

[3] *Ibid.*, pp. 47–51. *Investigation*, 2, p. 67; 7, pp. 3551–52. E. E. Morison et al., *The Letters of Theodore Roosevelt* (Cambridge, Mass., 1952), 5, pp. 533, 549, 606.

of Land Management. In 1907 new theories of land management were already setting the tone of federal policy. Land Office procedure may have been working against this current, but something more was responsible for the bureau's unenviable reputation. The Land Office played the role of villain in the general system within which the theories operated.

Middle-class disillusionment with the economic expansion and development of the post–Civil War years was widespread in the first decade of the century. The earlier railroad land grants were only the most notorious demonstration of the way in which it was believed the land and resources of the nation had passed into the hands of corporations, despite a system of land laws designed to foster the interests of the individual. The progressive era was a time of great concern for the "national heritage." The same generation which would soon sanction immigration laws to protect the genetic purity of the American population and would support a National Park Service to protect the heritage of natural beauty awoke somewhat earlier to the revelation that the material wealth had been acquired by a few men who used their great economic power to exploit the farmer and laborer, liquidate the small operator, and corrupt and control the political life of the nation. According to the progressive theory of history, the General Land Office had abetted the great betrayal.

Pinchot was able to take advantage of this disillusionment in his struggle for control of the national forests. But despite the acrimony of the period before the transfer, Pinchot and his colleagues believed that the real trouble with the Land Office was not so much the periodic corruption as the outmoded procedure of a bureau administering outmoded land laws. They were, after all, bureau chiefs with a program to promote, and the progressive theory of the great betrayal was only the context within which the policy was emerging. Elimination of the corruption and inefficiency was important but incidental to the aim of integrating the bureau into the new system.

It was Ballinger's fate to undertake a course of action in the Land Office and later under Taft, as secretary of the interior, which threw the conservation program into confusion and threatened to reverse it altogether. As commissioner of the Land Office this course was only partly intentional. His first offense, by no means the smallest item of an indictment that would grow in length, was his success in achieving what he was appointed to achieve, the thoroughgoing reform of the Land Office. The trouble was, he restored life to the moribund bureau without changing its character. A revived Land Office, honest, efficient, and eager to defend its jurisdictional prerogatives, proved to be more of a threat than the inefficient and corrupt object of scorn and odium of the old days.

The implications of effective reform were not immediately apparent. As Ballinger took hold, he seemed to Garfield to be "doing well." Much of the work of the bureau was done in the field divisions, where special agents investigated and processed claims, where hearings were held before registers and receivers who determined whether the law had been complied with and whether to issue a patent (title). The Washington office, itself divided into special divisions such as that handling mineral lands, coordinated and supervised the work of the field divisions. All but two of the chiefs of field division were removed out of hand; many were retired or demoted and replaced by younger men. For instance, Louis Glavis, a youth of 23 years in 1907, became the chief of the Portland division. Two chiefs of field division, Fred Dennett and H. H. Schwartz, were promoted to the Washington office to be groomed for the leadership of the bureau.

Ballinger estimated that "fifteen percent of the clerical force [in Washington] was totally inefficient because of age and failing powers." Many were elderly women, "pathetic cases" to Garfield, who was called upon to dismiss them. Some were political appointees. Ballinger removed at least one classmate of the president's and one of Taft's, but Roosevelt refused to "try to stop him." The purge of inefficient clerks and agents was supplemented by a shakedown of procedure. Typewriters were introduced in divisions still laboriously copying documents in longhand. The forms for homestead entry were reduced from five to one, and others were similarly shortened and simplified. The general mineral laws were codified and republished. Reforms of this nature hacked at the roots of the old corruption and inefficiency.[4]

Ballinger resigned in March 1908 after twelve months in office. He left, Pinchot later said, because of profound disagreement with the objectives of the Roosevelt administration, but there is little evidence to support the claim. Garfield confided to his diary that Ballinger had "done admirably and leaves with a reputation for ability, industry, and fairness." The former commissioner returned to Seattle with the praises of Roosevelt and Garfield ringing in his ears. He had brought the Land Office to an unparalleled efficiency. Furthermore, to some observers, he appeared to have rendered valuable yeoman service to the conservation movement. For instance, with Pinchot, Newell, and Garfield, Ballinger defended the Roosevelt resource policies in June 1907 at the Denver public lands convention, the first organized expression of western anticonservation sentiment. Ballinger seemed to be one of the leaders within the Department of the Interior carrying out Roosevelt resource policies.[5]

At the bureau level it was a different story. Ballinger had struck sparks against Pinchot and Newell on several occasions. It is easy to overemphasize the extent of this friction because of later events. Nevertheless, it seems unlikely that either Pinchot or Newell found much to regret in Ballinger's de-

---

[4] U.S. Department of Commerce, *Historical Statistics of the United States, Colonial Times to 1957* (Washington, D.C., 1961), p. 237. *Investigation*, 7, p. 3556. R.A.B. to Frederick H. Gillette, March 25, 1908, Ballinger Papers. Garfield Diary, entries for March 5, 1907, March 7, 1907, May 16, 1907, October 5, 1907, Garfield Papers.

[5] *Ibid.*, entries for June 6, 1907, November 2, 1907, March 2, 1908. Garfield to R.A.B., June 4, 1907; R.A.B. to T.R., January 4, 1908; T.R. to R.A.B., January 6, 1908; Glavis to R.A.B., January 31, 1908; F. D. Smith to R.A.B., December 19, 1907, Ballinger Papers. For background on the Public Lands Commission, see Peffer, *The Closing of the Public Domain: Disposal and Reservation Policies, 1900–50* (Stanford, Calif., 1951), pp. 45–53; Hays, *Conservation and the Gospel of Efficiency: The Progressive Conservation Movement, 1890–1920* (Cambridge, Mass., 1959), pp. 61–90, *passim*; Pinchot, *Breaking New Ground*, pp. 243–50, 395.

parture. The commissioner had been openly critical of the Reclamation Service and its director Newell. Partly this was a question of personalities, but the conflict over policy was uppermost. For instance, as commissioner of the Land Office Ballinger was also chairman of the Public Lands Commission, which had yet to report on mineral and coal lands when he took office. The forester and Newell had prepared a report recommending leasing. Ballinger threatened to make a separate report supporting sale, although at an appraised market value. After "a good deal of bitter discussion," the Pinchot-Newell report was shelved; the two men felt that a divided report was worse than no report at all.[6]

The relations of Pinchot and Ballinger were, at the very least, abrasive. The commissioner resented the influence of George Woodruff, the department attorney general, whom he correctly identified with Pinchot. On at least one occasion Ballinger questioned the legality of Pinchot's use of the Forest Management Act of 1898, which, liberally construed, had become the instrument for regulating waterpower and grazing on the forest reserves. In his annual report Ballinger recommended that the remaining timber in the public domain, exclusive of the national forests, be knocked down to the highest bidder, with the condition that the timber be removed from the land by the buyer within a fixed period of years so that the land could be disposed of under the homestead laws, a suggestion which did not conform to Pinchot's idea of scientific forestry. Ballinger further infuriated Pinchot by recommending against the creation of the Chugach National Forest in Alaska on the grounds that such reserves were unnecessary in the northern territory.[7]

There is an obvious point concerning the relations of these two men, so obvious that it might easily be overlooked. Unless a man acts according to the requirements of the position he occupies, he will cease to occupy the position, or he will

---

[6] *Investigation*, 4, p. 1146. Pinchot, *Breaking New Ground*, p. 395.

[7] *Investigation*, 4, pp. 1147–49; 7, p. 3613. R.A.B. to Garfield, August 5, 1907, Ballinger Papers. U.S. Congress, Sen. Doc. 283, 61 Cong., 2 Sess., p. 36.

continue to occupy it, but weakly. Ballinger and Pinchot faced
one another as chiefs of rival bureaus with overlapping jurisdictions, and both jealously protected their own programs and
prerogatives. Even had they begun as the best of friends it is
difficult to imagine them remaining so, assuming that both
vigorously championed their own interests.

Most galling of all to Forest Service administrators, who
had complained long and loudly about Land Office inefficiency,
was the fact that Ballinger brought his agency to a peak of
efficiency; moreover, he left it a new leadership with the will
to resist Forest Service "encroachments" on Land Office jurisdiction. This new spirit upset the administrative arrangements
which allowed the Forest Service to settle land claims in the
national forests legally the concern of the Land Office.

The act of February 1905 transferring the national forests
to Pinchot from the control of the Land Office was the main
source of friction. It gave the secretary of agriculture—that is,
Pinchot—full authority to administer the reserves, but it left
determination of all questions affecting title to land to the
Department of the Interior. This meant, in effect, that the
Land Office would pass on mineral claims in the national
forests.

The gap was intolerable to Pinchot and was quickly closed. In
May 1905 Roosevelt directed Secretary of the Interior Hitchcock to refer "to the Secretary of Agriculture all questions of
fact [concerning land claims in the forest reserves] and accept
his findings with regard to facts." Commissioner Ballinger was
never happy with this arrangement, already in operation when
he arrived. Undoubtedly it brought more order to Forest
Service administration, but one man's order was another's
confusion. The Land Office was required by law to pass on
title to land in the national forests, but it was stripped of the
power to issue any patents without the virtual consent of
Pinchot, a chief in another department. The situation became
worse in June 1906 when Congress passed a law permitting
agricultural entry in the forest reserves. The secretary of agriculture was to determine the extent of agricultural lands in the

forests so that the secretary of the interior could dispose of them under the homestead laws. The act was nullified from the beginning by the agreement of May 1905 as far as the jurisdiction of the Land Office was concerned. Garfield cooperated by withdrawing mineral and agricultural sites in the forests, under the guise of ranger stations as an added insurance. Land Office objections were given short shrift by the Forest Service. The result was deep, slow-burning resentment. "The constant reiteration," Ballinger's successor Fred Dennett asserted peevishly, "on the part of the Forestry of antagonism and of dissension with them on the part of the Land Office was . . . done with a purpose. They were anxious to discredit this office in order that they might build themselves."[8]

"Voluntary cooperation" between two dynamic bureaus often meant that one side had succeeded in mustering sufficient influence and power to gain its ends at the expense of the other. Most of the "cooperation" between the Land Office and the Forest Service was of this character. Nevertheless, there were many ways in which the Land Office could frustrate the daily operation of the Forest Service program, and Pinchot was equally unhappy with the need to rely on cooperation between the two bureaus. Shortly after Ballinger resigned, the forester moved to consolidate all facets of reserve administration under the control of the Forest Service. He prepared a letter for Garfield's signature asking the secretary of agriculture to assume the functions which the Department of the Interior still performed under the Transfer Act of 1905. Pinchot was particularly anxious that the Forest Service be empowered to prosecute offenders of the power development policy in the national forests, rather than forwarding the evidence to the Department of the Interior for prosecution. The Land Office resisted. Commissioner Fred Dennett and his assistant, Harry H. Schwartz, wired each of the chiefs of field division for an opinion; the replies were antagonistic to this interpretation of

[8] *Investigation*, 2, pp. 138, 723–24. M. D. McEniry to R.A.B., December 11, 1909, Ballinger Papers.

"cooperation" by the Forest Service. Schwartz forwarded the replies to Garfield, and Pinchot's letter went unsigned.[9]

The forester did not drop the subject. At his urging, Garfield took up the question once again the day before he left office and forwarded the letter, signed, to the secretary of agriculture. Three days later, Richard A. Ballinger—"the first Commissioner to assert the independence and to require recognition of the jurisdiction of [the Land Office]"—now secretary of the interior, asked Secretary James Wilson to suspend action on the Garfield request. It remained in suspension. Ballinger meant to exercise whatever jurisdiction in the forest reserves remained to the Department of the Interior. Given his experience in the Land Office, any other position would have been illogical and out of character.[10]

It seems clear that Ballinger's ideas on conservation during his commissionership were readily discernible in the stands he took on specific policy. These ideas were critical and a threat to the entire program if they should acquire a platform, as happened when he became secretary of the interior. Because Ballinger as secretary did come up with a conservation program, it has sometimes been assumed that the primary differences with the Roosevelt men were over the question of the scope of executive powers, i.e., whether the excutive already possessed sufficient powers for a broad program or whether it was necessary to seek broader powers and more specific legislation from the Congress.[11] Ballinger and Taft did insist on the need for more congressional approval, but the legislation they sought was very often antithetical to the program of the Roosevelt men. This has been the source of some confusion.

9 *Investigation*, 2, pp. 260–61, 264.

10 A conference on cooperation between the departments and bureaus was held in November 1908. A questionnaire prepared in the Forest Service was sent to specific bureaus; a copy is in the Ballinger Papers; also H. H. Schwartz to R.A.B., November 1, 1909. See also *Investigation*, 2, p. 263.

11 This interpretation is argued in Henry F. Pringle, *The Life and Times of William Howard Taft* (2 vols.; New York and Toronto, 1939). A recent restatement is in Richardson, *The Politics of Conservation*.

Was Ballinger a conservationist who differed from his antagonists chiefly in regard to method? Or did he make noises like a conservationist to disguise a concerted assault on the entire program? Unfortunately, either question has operated to cloud an understanding of the nature of Ballinger's attack on the conservation movement; and although the controversy itself is a subject for later chapters, this seems an appropriate place, against the backdrop of his career as a bureau chief in the Roosevelt administration, to examine the roots of Ballinger's ideas on conservation.

Some of Ballinger's attitudes became more understandable when placed in the context of the city of Seattle, from roughly 1890 to 1910. Seattle was young, of course. In 1875 it had been little more than a village. In its early years its businessmen and civic leaders were engaged in a desperate struggle with Portland, which controlled the mouth of the Columbia River, for the trade of the ranches, farms, mines, and lumber of the great inland empire of Washington east of the Cascades. In the 1890's the balance rapidly favored Seattle once James J. Hill had decided to make it the terminus of the Great Northern Railroad. Seattle prospered in the shade of Hill's benevolence. But many who had hoped to benefit from the transcontinental railroads had nurtured a more daring dream.

The Orient beckoned from Seattle's privileged position on the Pacific Coast. Commanding the finest harbor north of San Francisco, with Snoqualmie pass at its back opening on the vast hinterland of the Columbia basin, linked by the railroad with the settled metropolitan centers of the eastern United States and through them with Europe, Seattle boosters dreamed of dominating the trade of the Pacific, the United States, and Europe. The problem as they saw it was to progress from the exploitative economic phase featuring the dominance of extractive industries such as lumbering, mining, and agriculture, to the more advanced manufacturing stage with iron and steel reduction industries as its base. The raw materials, the iron and coal, they insisted, were there in sufficient quantity. It was capital that was needed, capital to finance the mining of the coal and iron of the region and make possible the building of the heavy industry that was the necessary foundation of the economic dominance they envisaged.

In the first decade of the century it was clear that the dream had not materialized. Seattle was prosperous. It commanded its own inland empire. But the Orient if anything became more elusive with the rise of Japan; the old dream of rivaling and eventually surpassing the settled metropolitan centers of the East and Midwest seemed farther away than ever. The periodic coal and iron bubbles had invariably collapsed. The dream was founded on a pre-Mesabi pattern of economic de-velopment and doubtless was impractical. There was no lack of capital imported into the region, but it was seldom attracted to new industries when enormous profits beckoned in timber, utilities, and rising urban land values. Although the railroad had opened local markets to the eastern manufacturer, it had not opened eastern markets for the far Northwest, except for extractive industries such as timber or agricultural products. At the same time, Hill had done nothing to promote the iron industry; he saw lumber as the logical year-round traffic. Thus it happened that by 1905 the Seattle booster was already ac-quiring something of the "plundered province" psychology which is so much a part of the intellectual history of the Amer-ican West.[12]

The "plundered province" is a myth often perpetuated in American scholarship. In some ways the picture it has painted is an objective representation of reality according to the lights of the people it once served. It portrays the region west of the 100th meridian as being different from earlier frontiers in that it could not be developed in what reminiscence called the old individualistic way, with an ax and a strong back. Whether in agriculture, mining, or lumbering, special equipment was needed. Essentially it was a region where big capital had to precede settlement; that is, the railroads opened up the area

[12] This view of Seattle's economic development is argued in great detail in Robert C. Nesbit, *"He Built Seattle": A Biography of Judge Thomas Burke* (Seattle, 1961).

and then the machinery of credit made settlement possible. In this view the West was a region from which wealth was drained from the beginning, and westerners often saw themselves as colonials who did not own their own country.[13]

Unfortunately this portrait of the westerner as a man bereft of his heritage overlooked the extent to which the westerner himself was often a promoter. It was in the nature of its early economic development that the West was highly speculative and fluid. Migrating capital was essential to maintain the proper rate of escalation. The West as a region, and the businessmen of Seattle were no exception, ardently courted and solicited the aid of outside capital. The capital, however, flowed from settled metropolitan and manufacturing centers and it flowed primarily into the extractive industries, preventing development of the mixed industrial economy that truly ambitious promoters wanted. Great fortune and prosperity often attended the development of these industries, as in Seattle, but real economic and political power continued to reside east of the Mississippi and showed no signs of moving west.

The struggle between East and West dramatized in the myth of the "plundered province" was over the question of how the West should be developed, with those who controlled the machinery of credit having the final say. The pattern gave rise to a curious ambivalence. Mining promoters came up against the names of Guggenheim and Rockefeller, and those seeking their fortune in timber had to contend with Weyerhaeuser, and so it went in agriculture, in the cattle industry, in utilities, and in real estate. Such men loudly denounced the tyranny of the absentee landlord even as they frantically sought the aid of outside capital to finance their own enterprises. They contended, however, not with Wall Street but with the agents and spokesmen of the absentee landlords, who were westerners themselves. Beneath the rhetoric, the conflict raged as much between west-

---

[13] The classic statement of this view of western development is Bernard De Voto, "The West: A Plundered Province," *Harpers*, August 1934, pp. 355–64.

erner and westerner as between westerner and easterner. The West, struggling as a unified section to throw off its chains, simply did not exist.

Ballinger confronted Pinchot with views that were highly colored by his long residence in Seattle and the far Northwest, which included sympathy for the problems of the "independent" entrepreneur and a pronounced dislike of monopoly and absentee landlords. The Forest Service program touched on all of these questions and raised the additional one sometimes called federal landlordism. But although opposition was strong and feelings ran deep, it went without saying that Pinchot's program would have been unworkable unless it could count on considerable support among westerners. The new policies had to find adherents among two factions at war over how the economic development of the West should be shaped.

Pinchot has said, with a sincerity that it is unnecessary to doubt, that the slogan of the Forest Service was "better help a poor man make a living for his family than help a rich man get richer still." It was a noble gospel, but its very nobility probably helped to elevate it to the level of a Platonic ideal. Pinchot, however, was head of an institution that functioned in an earthbound historical setting, and he found accommodation as useful a force for building as it was a safe guide for survival. Very often support for the Forest Service program and other land management theories promoted by the conservation movement was generated in the camp of the "predatory big man" that the rhetoric of the movement was quickest to condemn, whereas the "democracy" frequently emerged as the potent opposition.[14]

14 Pinchot, *Breaking New Ground*, p. 259. The question of who in the West supported conservation has still not been adequately examined as a separate subject, but a mine of information is in Hays, *Conservation and the Gospel of Efficiency*, and Richardson's *Politics of Conservation* is a major recent contribution. It is apparent that support was diverse and complex and not simplistic. For instance, at times Pinchot could rely on considerable urban backing in the West where the water problem and protection of watersheds were crucial. As in the Hetch Hetchy controversy Pinchot could be relied upon to take the practical view and sympathize with the urban problem. See Richardson, "The Struggle for the Valley:

That the large enterprises dependent upon the public domain and the national forests often supported the early conservation policy was hardly surprising. The bureau chiefs who led the movement were not slow to see the greater efficiency of larger corporate units, and established interests were quick to recognize the benefits of parts of the new program. For instance, the highly competitive livestock industry had long been plagued by overgrazing and vicious range wars. In the national forests grazing was regulated by permit, and range wars were eliminated by federal supervision. Stockmen demanded more of the same on the public domain at large. The great sheepherders were an exception, but their enmity was compensated for by support from the great cattle barons.[15]

Opposition to the grazing policy in the national forests often focused on the charge that Pinchot was retarding western development. J. Arthur Eddy of Denver, who spoke for a large bloc of grazers opposing the forestry program, charged that the grazing policy on reserves was favored by the large stockmen who felt imperiled by the homesteader and small stock-

California's Hetch Hetchy Controversy, 1905–1913," *California Historical Society Quarterly*, 38 (1959), pp. 249–56. My intention here is not to insist upon a simplistic division over conservation between the big and the small man as the sole line of division but rather to call attention to an aspect of the western dialogue which affected Ballinger's position. In any case, my interest is not in whether such a view was in fact correct, but only that it was widely held, and operated on the men who held it.

15 See J. H. Jastro, "Grazing and Stock Raising," paper read at the Conference on the Conservation of Natural Resources, White House, Washington, D.C., May 13–15, 1908, Library of Congress, MS in the Amos Pinchot Papers. Jastro, a Kern County (California) stockman, contended that the "manner in which these forest lands have been handled [by the Forest Service] points out in a most convincing and almost unanswerable way the course [on which] to proceed if the balance of these lands are to be saved. . . .

"Under some plan of government these lands can be managed so as to secure to the users, the stockmen and settlers, a permanency in their business which they do not now . . . enjoy. . . . The range wars that have been so bitter [and] have . . . seriously retarded . . . development . . . will cease, as they have upon the National Forests. These lands should be segregated, and the different areas devoted to the kinds of stock for which they are best adapted according to the feed produced and the local conditions."

men and who, through their control of the stockmen's associations, also controlled the cooperative agreements with the
Forest Service.[16] Men like Eddy maintained that the permit
system favored the well-established stockman but, in a highly
competitive industry, was detrimental to the enterprising but
unestablished contender. Advocates of the program replied
that the small operator was protected against monopolization
in the livestock industry; but it nevertheless remained true that
large operators supported licensed cooperative grazing, while
small operators resisted the new system.[17] It was not protection
the small operator wanted, but wealth as substantial as that already cornered by more fortunate competitors. The new system probably stopped the big fish from swallowing his smaller
fellow, but it had to face the charge of freezing the status quo.

Much the same pattern developed in the lumber industry.
Stumping the state of Indiana during his campaign for reelec-
tion to the Senate in the fall of 1910, Albert J. Beveridge condemned the "Weyerhaeuser lumber and timber trust" as the
"greatest foe of" the Forest Service. Leonard Bronson, manager of the National Lumber Manufacturers Association, was
aggrieved. "Perhaps it does not occur to you," he wrote to
Beveridge, "that from a selfish standpoint alone the heavy timber owners of the West are heartily in favor of the reserves;
for the mere establishment of these reserves has increased the
value of their holdings very heavily by withdrawing from the
market timber which otherwise would be competitive. . . .

> There is intense competition in the West. There are a few
> very large holdings of timber, but many smaller ones; and
> many millions of capital are waiting to develop timber if it can
> be secured. The only real hostility to the forest reserves on
> the part of lumbermen comes from some young men in the

16 *Rocky Mountain News*, July 25, 1910.

17 In regard to this, see W. J. Cross, "Ideas in Politics: Conservation Policies of the Two Roosevelts," *Journal of the History of Ideas*, 14 (1953),
pp. 421–38.

business who objected to the opportunities which were open to the present larger holders being closed to them.[18]

The Forest Service argued that it was precisely such "intense competition" which posed a serious threat to the introduction of intelligent forest management practices. The Weyerhaeusers of the industry had their differences with the Forest Service on the question of intelligent management, but they understood the advantages of less competition, or greater stability as they would probably have preferred to call it.

Stability and instability became definable terms when viewed from the standpoint of related interests. Obviously, Pinchot's opponents among resource users thought the Forest Service program bred considerable confusion in their affairs. And many were men of affairs. The most burning conflict in the West was not between the poor and the rich of Pinchot's slogan. As Leonard Bronson pointed out, there was a good deal of capital looking for a home, and its owners were often aware of the degree to which the lessening of risk could also curtail return. They could afford the legal assistance of firms such as Ballinger's which dealt extensively in matters concerning landownership and the use of natural resources, and which served a variety of clients rather than a few giant corporations paying large fees.[19]

Ballinger joined the Roosevelt administration with a general attitude toward the ideas of land management promoted by Pinchot and his colleagues which hardened into specific and concrete opinions during his career in the Land Office. He opposed the inclusion of grazing lands and unforested lands within the national forests and objected to the grazing lease plan for the public domain. He argued that too much land was

[18] November 9, 1910, Library of Congress, Gifford Pinchot Papers. See also J. B. White to G.P., September 30, 1910, *ibid. Bellingham Herald* (Washington), September 11, 1910.

[19] Some of the records of Ballinger, Ronald, Battle, and Tennant, 1898–1908, are in the Ballinger papers. See Richardson, *Politics of Conservation,* p. 49.

withdrawn under the Reclamation Act. He was opposed to the coal leasing bill and to the plan for leasing waterpower sites on the public lands, preferring outright sale. And he was against administrative arrangements which allowed the Forest Service to settle land claims in the national forests.[20] His own recommendations for conservation called for classification of natural resources to eliminate fraud in their acquisition, legislation to speed up the determination of claims for legitimate claimants, and protection against monopoly. In essence his was a position which favored retaining the broadest possible opportunities for economic development by private capital, with provision for certain reforms to remove unnecessary administrative obstacles to investment, and with some protection for the investor from the large pools of established capital against which he would have to compete.[21]

When the controversy broke into the open during the Taft administration, Pinchot's supporters actively promoted an image of Ballinger as champion of the "special interests," meaning the giant corporations, and by and large the label has stuck. Contemporary supporters of Ballinger in the West had a somewhat different view. They saw him as champion of the small man and labeled Pinchot as favoring the "interests." At times, among such supporters, there was even the hint of belief in a conspiracy. The East, with its control of the machinery of credit, was seen to have retarded western development, while eastern capital cornered and exploited western resources. Pushed by men whose social standing and associations identified them with the oppressive "masters of capital," conservation appeared to be an eastern plot to protect the holdings of

[20] Hays, *Conservation and the Gospel of Efficiency*, p. 151. Richardson, *Politics of Conservation*, p. 52 and *passim*. R.A.B. to Taft, July 24, 1911, Ballinger Papers.

[21] The complete collection of Ballinger's speeches in the Ballinger Papers, if used with care, provides a broad profile of his views on conservation. For specific recommendations consult the annual reports of the Department of the Interior during the years Ballinger was commissioner and secretary of the interior.

easterners, who first acquired the riches of western resources and then used their power and influence to support a government program which eliminated competition. In this view, Ballinger had behind him "the ever hopeful prospector" and the "small rancher," and against him "the monopoly and aristocracy of wealth."[22]

Strangely enough, Ballinger would never be able to accept the view that he was a threat to Roosevelt policies. He considered himself a "follower of Theodore Roosevelt." When he was commissioner of the Land Office in the Roosevelt administration, he clashed with Pinchot and he would clash with Pinchot as a member of the Taft administration, but he never seemed to understand the difference—that it was one thing to contribute to the dialogue within the Roosevelt administration and quite another to attack established policy from a position within the Taft administration.

Ballinger never lost his desire to be a "follower" of Roosevelt, nor did he cease to think of himself as a "progressive." The man who became Taft's secretary of the interior was the same man who had served under Roosevelt. He favored civil service reform, city planning, introducing business methods into government; he was against "invisible government." He supported tariff reform, a corporation tax, the income-tax amendment, a federal incorporation law for Alaska—with stringent antimonopoly provisions—and the accelerated antitrust activity of the Taft administration. But a secretary of the interior could overturn policy where a commissioner of the Land Office could only question its wisdom. In the end, it was Ballinger as a progressive who came into conflict with Roosevelt policies. But his progressivism was shaped by his experiences as a Seattle lawyer. He was an antimonopolist in the classic sense. Like Grover Cleveland, he saw the tariff as the mother of trusts, and his solution was tariff reform and stepped-up activity under the

[22] *Inter-Mountain Globe* (Hulett, Wyo.), December [?], 1909, clipping in Ballinger Papers. Editorial sentiment such as that quoted is plentiful in this fine clipping collection covering the years Ballinger was secretary of the interior.

Sherman act. He rejected the Roosevelt-Pinchot-Garfield admiration for the efficiency of sheer bigness as long as it behaved, and he rejected the Roosevelt conservation movement because he believed it was geared to promote the interests of sheer bigness.[23]

[23] R.A.B. to Taft, July 5, 1909, and July 16, 1909; R.A.B. to Richard W. Parker, December 3, 1910; R.A.B. to F. H. Gillette, March 25, 1908, Ballinger Papers. *Investigation,* 5, p. 2085.

CHAPTER THREE

Ballinger and the Roosevelt Policies

Richard Ballinger's influence in Washington state politics, which began with his term as mayor, had been enhanced by his career in the Land Office. He returned to Seattle as an important force in local politics. Even before he left the capital he was being canvassed as a possible gubernatorial candidate, although he wanted no part of it. Nevertheless, he was unable to turn his attention entirely to his own private law practice. Almost immediately he was immersed in efforts to secure his state's early endorsement of Taft. Ballinger made himself useful to the Republican party as fund raiser, organizer, and speaker in the Northwest and was appointed to the party's national committee. At the national convention he was chairman of his state's delegation and sat on the resolutions committee. Throughout the campaign he worked closely with Garfield and other party leaders on matters of party strategy. The day following the election he wired Taft, "I congratulate you and the country. The Lord of Hosts was with us." Yet Ballinger knew that the Lord helped those who helped themselves, and he knew he could expect to be rewarded.[1]

Ballinger was not actually offered the Department of the Interior until the latter part of January; nevertheless he was aware for some time before the offer that his name was being considered. To the flood of well-wishers he responded with a

[1] R.A.B. to F. W. Baker, February 29, 1908; Miles Moore to R.A.B., February 7, 1908; Dennett to R.A.B., May 21, 1908; R.A.B. to Taft, November 4, 1908, Ballinger Papers. R.A.B. to Garfield, September 27, 1908; Garfield to R.A.B., October 11, 1908; R.A.B. to Garfield, March 18, 1908, J. R. Garfield Papers.

stock answer: he did not want the position and he hoped Garfield would be reappointed. This familiar refrain recurred at every point where Ballinger assumed public office, and as always the matter did not drop with the refusal. His name continued to circulate as a probable appointee. The Pacific Coast was to have membership in the cabinet, and Ballinger, a western man associated with Roosevelt policies, was the likely candidate. Despite professed reluctance, Ballinger had his chance to turn down the appointment without embarrassment. Yet just as clearly, he avoided accepting as long as the possibility of Garfield's reappointment existed.[2]

The reappointment was considered crucial to the perpetuation of the conservation policies. Although Taft was the hand-picked successor of Theodore Roosevelt, Pinchot like many of the Roosevelt men was uneasy. The president-elect had been Roosevelt's secretary of war and, on the level of department and bureau, had been something less than an enthusiastic supporter of the new conservation machinery, especially that which posed a jurisdictional threat to his own department. Much later Pinchot claimed that the president had wrung from Taft a promise of loyalty to conservation and the resource policies developed by Pinchot and Garfield. It was a pledge which Pinchot thought was quickly violated when the new president refused to continue the National Conservation Commission in the face of congressional injunction, and torpedoed the international conservation conference which Roosevelt had hoped to see convene in the Hague Peace Palace. Selection of the new cabinet had provided even earlier evidence of bad faith.

Cabinet appointments were awaited anxiously, all the more since Taft kept his own counsel. Five of the nine men eventually appointed were corporation lawyers, as the outstanding men under Roosevelt had been. The attorney general, George Wickersham, was known to conservationists for his lack of sympathy with important aspects of the new water policy. But

2 Frank Pierce to R.A.B., January 8, 1909; Jonathan Bourne to R.A.B., January 28, 1909, Ballinger Papers; Garfield Diary, February 1, 1909, Garfield Papers.

the replacement of James Garfield by Richard Ballinger aroused the greatest concern.

Ballinger was careful to seek out his former chief before accepting. That Garfield had ardently hoped to be reappointed was no secret. But shortly before Ballinger's visit Garfield had learned from Taft that he was not on the cabinet list. He thought Taft "weak and not sincere," but he was kind to Ballinger: "I told him I definitely am out & if he is offered it & wants it to certainly accept." About the same time, late in January, Frank Baldwin of *The Outlook* apprised Taft of a "comment made by Gifford Pinchot . . . concerning Dick Ballinger: 'I couldn't work with him as I have with Jim [Garfield]. Jim and I think alike. . . . Ballinger and I might clash.' "[3]

Although greatly disappointed, there was no evidence that Garfield was as concerned about his successor as many of the bureau chiefs were. Concern was not long in developing, however. Within a few short months most of what Garfield considered accomplishment had been overthrown by Ballinger. Although Taft and Ballinger would continue to insist that they approved of the broad program of the former administration and that such differences as existed were over details and methods, it was plain from the beginning that a concerted attack was being made on the fundamental character of the conservation movement.

When Ballinger said he was against certain methods, he meant the machinery of conservation. But very often it was the machinery which made the policy possible. Significantly, the cooperative agreements between departments, particularly those between the Forest Service and General Land Office, drew the new secretary's fire. He honored the 1905 agreement giving the Forest Service control over mineral entries in the forest reserves although he disapproved, but he moved forcefully against the Garfield innovations. Pinchot was foiled in his last-ditch effort to sweep into the Forest Service all remaining

[3] January 23, 1909, February 1, 1909, *ibid*. Pinchot quoted in Henry F. Pringle, *The Life and Times of William Howard Taft* (2 vols.; New York and Toronto, 1939), 1, p. 479.

aspects of reserve administration still controlled by the Land Office. Agreements were canceled which had permitted the Forest Service to initiate legal proceedings under the land laws rather than turn the evidence over to the Land Office for prosecution.[4] Ballinger called a halt to the withdrawal of several hundred acres near national forests for use as ranger stations, authorized by Garfield at the midnight hour. Ballinger had seen the ruse employed of withdrawing power sites in and around national forests under the guise of ranger stations. Although it passed from the scene with the late-hour withdrawals of waterpower sites, whether under the Reclamation Act or under the concept of the supervisory power of the executive, the practice had left in its wake a wary suspicion of ranger station withdrawals.[5]

Of the same character as the agreements between the Land Office and the Forest Service was a natural cooperation which grew up between Pinchot's service and the Office of Indian Affairs in the Department of the Interior. Although charged with the management of fifteen million acres of forest lands on the Indian reservations, the Indian office had no trained foresters and became accustomed to calling upon the Forest Service for assistance. In January 1908 Pinchot and Francis Leupp, the Indian commissioner, formalized this arrangement. An agreement approved by Garfield provided that foresters would undertake the management of the Indian forest lands, that their salaries would be paid by the Indian office, but that the men would remain on the rolls of the Forest Service, "responsible directly and only thereto." This work began immediately, but with what Pinchot described as "inevitable friction . . . during the early stages of its application." Part of the problem, he thought, was the extent to which routine work was still handled by the Indian office. Yet in September 1908 when the comptroller-general ruled illegal a Forest Service attempt to

[4] See pp. 29–30.

[5] McEniry to R.A.B., December 11, 1909; R.A.B. to Frank Baldwin, May 10, 1909, Ballinger Papers. *Chicago Record Herald,* July 21, 1909.

transfer a clerk to the Indian office, Pinchot dropped the matter rather than call the whole arrangement into question.[6]

The cooperation was even less smooth after the change in administration. As the fire season approached in 1909 a reluctance to assign the Forest Service the funds to pay for the cost of fire wardens became apparent. At first the delay was caused by the opinions of Oscar Lawler, who had replaced George Woodruff as department attorney general, and of Edward Finney, a former Land Office official promoted by Ballinger to his own office. Both men declared informally to inquiring foresters that the agreement was illegal unless the Forest Service experts were transferred to the rolls of the Indian office. The secretary of the interior, they argued, could not abdicate his responsibility to care for the timber on the Indian reservations to another department. In early June Ballinger left on an extended western tour which would keep him away from Washington for the entire summer. At the end of the month an impatient Pinchot, over the heads of Lawler and Finney, called on Acting Secretary Frank Pierce personally to take action on the Indian forest question, thus setting in motion the chain of events which led to the abrogation of the cooperative agreement. As it happened, Pierce, learning from the new commissioner of Indian affairs, R. G. Valentine, that the Indian office lacked trained men to do the work, recommended to his chief that the agreement be extended. Ballinger, however, agreed with Lawler and Finney. On July 20 Pierce notified Secretary Wilson that the relationship was formally dissolved.[7]

Pinchot was furious. Ballinger had already thwarted a last-minute attempt by Garfield and the forester to transform the Indian reservation forests into national forests to bring them entirely under Forest Service jurisdiction. After the abrogation of the cooperative agreement Pinchot argued that no question

[6] *Investigation of the Department of the Interior and the Bureau of Forestry*, Sen. Doc. 719, 61 Cong., 3 Sess., 2, pp. 90–91, 95; 4, pp. 1186–1260.

[7] "Memo on abrogation of agreement," October 9, 1909; Pierce to James Wilson, July 20, 1909, Gifford Pinchot Papers. *Investigation*, 2, pp. 89, 93, 95, 96.

had ever been raised by the auditor of the Department of the Interior about the transfer of funds. Two months later in September, Ballinger revealed that the basis of the department's decision was the earlier ruling of the comptroller-general in September 1908 that the transfer of a clerk from the Forest Service to the Indian office was illegal. Pinchot insisted that the ruling applied only to the question of the clerk and not to the entire agreement. From Valentine's office he learned that a copy of the agreement had not even been sent to the comptroller at the time Garfield requested a decision. Nevertheless, neither Pinchot nor Garfield had evinced any desire to discover the comptroller's opinion on the agreement. At the time the question over the clerk arose, Garfield had described the cooperative agreement to the comptroller. His reply had not encouraged further inquiry. Indeed, it explicitly declared the agreement to be illegal.[8]

Pinchot believed that Ballinger's course represented a major assault on the Forest Service, a view which was the basis for his later claim that he was always on the defensive in his struggle with Ballinger.[9] The growing conflict was greatly exacerbated at the time of the decision on the ranger stations. Ballinger refused to discuss the question with Pinchot. In the Land Office he had resented the freedom of movement accorded Pinchot in the Department of the Interior, which he interpreted as interference from the chief of a rival bureau in the business of another department. Ballinger insisted on dealing with Secretary of Agriculture Wilson. At the same time Pinchot's old freewheeling practice of dealing directly with subordinates in the Department of the Interior was, at least formally, brought to an end. This stand was as serious to Pinchot as anything the secretary did. It greatly curtailed Pinchot in his coordinating

[8] Hays, *Conservation and the Gospel of Efficiency: The Progressive Conservation Movement, 1890–1920* (Cambridge, Mass., 1959), p. 158. G.P. to Wilson, July 23, 1909; "Memorandum for Mr. Wells," October 21, 1909; G.P. to Valentine, October 7, 1909, Gifford Pinchot Papers. *Investigation,* 4, p. 1260.

[9] McGeary, *Gifford Pinchot: Forester-Politician* (Princeton, N.J., 1960), p. 158.

role as promoter of a broad program. Unless this function was exercised the whole question of an "administration" program was endangered.

By jamming the machinery of interdepartmental cooperation and denying Pinchot his role as coordinating agent, Ballinger threatened the ad hoc system of unified planning which made the conservation movement a "movement." At the same time, he lashed out at the policy decisions of his predecessor which had been designed to integrate the Department of the Interior, and therefore the public domain, into the system.

Garfield scratched earnestly in his diary on April 3: "The burden of the fight for the Roosevelt policies under this administration will fall on Gifford's shoulders."[10] Even as he wrote, the weight of the burden was growing. Two weeks earlier Ballinger met for the first time with Arthur Powell Davis, chief engineer of the Reclamation Service, whose career, like Newell's stretched back to the time of John Wesley Powell. They talked about the waterpower sites withdrawn by Garfield in the closing months of the previous administration. Ballinger insisted they were illegal. That he chose Davis to broach this to rather than Newell was significant. Ballinger and Newell had clashed when they were both bureau chiefs under Roosevelt, and probably Ballinger had already decided to remove Newell as soon as it was expedient to do so. But ignoring the personal animosity which each felt for the other, Newell was deeply involved in the withdrawals and defended them with vigor. Davis, on the other hand, had argued against the use of the Reclamation Act to make the withdrawals. He felt that they had involved committing the service to a policy beyond reclamation work, which, because of its unpopularity in the West, would unnecessarily attract criticism of the service. Ballinger could expect, with some justification as it turned out, that Davis would not actively oppose a decision to restore to entry the land withdrawn under the Reclamation Act. Newell fought every step of the way, thereby completing his fall from

[10] Garfield Diary, Garfield Papers.

grace; but Davis maintained a working relationship with Ballinger, whom he felt it idle to antagonize unnecessarily.[11]

The waterpower question was really a complicated skein involving most of the components of the conservation movement. The model for the system which Garfield sought to impose on the public domain with the "midnight" reserves was, of course, the regulation of hydroelectric power in the forest reserves. Pinchot, with the legal assistance of George Woodruff, had used the Right-of-Way Act of 1901 to impose this regulation, but because the act was supposed to be administered by the secretary of the interior, a formal agreement between the Departments of the Interior and of Agriculture had to be sealed to enable the Forest Service to administer it in the reserves. Hence, the cooperation of the Department of the Interior was essential to the effective continuation of the Forest Service program.[12]

The decision to extend the Forest Service system to the public domain was sparked by the deliberations of the Inland Waterways Commission. However, the legality of what was essentially a new area for the government had to be hammered out at every step along the way. From the standpoint of the Roosevelt leaders the problem was to determine the extent of federal jurisdiction over hydroelectric power development on navigable streams, as well as on the headwaters of navigable streams on the public domain. The IWC provided a philosophy for broadly integrated policy. The permit system developed by Pinchot for the national forests provided a practical pattern for federal regulation and control. Roosevelt's efforts to use the General Dam Act of 1906 to regulate hydroelectric power on navigable streams, much as Pinchot had used the Right-of-Way Act in the forest reserves for nonnavigable headwaters, were hampered by the attitude of the Corps of Army Engineers and his secretary of war, William Howard Taft, who insisted that the Constitution allowed Congress to regu-

[11] *Investigation*, 5, pp. 1696–97, 1707; 7, p. 4198.

[12] *Ibid.*, 5, pp. 1641–42. Philip P. Wells, "Personal History," Gifford Pinchot Papers. R. W. Williams to G. P. McCabe, February 18, 1910, Ballinger Papers. Hays, *Conservation and the Gospel of Efficiency*, p. 74.

late dams for navigation only. But federal regulation of hydro-electric power on the public domain advanced rapidly.[13]

Although the majority of the sites were withdrawn under the Reclamation Act, many were located far from reclamation projects. For these Garfield used the "supervisory power of the executive," a concept of broad executive discretion conceived by the ingenuity of George Woodruff, who had moved to the Department of the Interior after Garfield became its head. Full powers, Woodruff reasoned, were vested in the executive to protect the interests of all the people of the United States. Though the extent to which these powers were exercised was governed entirely by the discretion of the president, the "stewardship duty" was clear. The duty of the executive to conserve natural resources was inherent in his historic role as custodian of public property.[14]

The policy of the Forest Service of granting permits which were subject to government regulations was adopted by Garfield for the entire public domain. There were already permits in existence, as well as the "ranger station" sites in and around the national forests. The secretary revoked the older permits and reissued them under the new regulations. Finally on March 2, 1909, the day before he left office, Garfield joined with the secretary of agriculture, James Wilson, to restore ranger stations that had been withdrawn the previous summer to protect power sites and then promptly withdrew them from all forms of entry except those made under the act of 1901, using the supervisory power of the executive. The views of engineers of the great waterpower companies were solicited and considered in setting the scale of fees to be charged under the new permits.[15]

---

[13] *Preliminary Report of the Inland Waterways Commission*, Sen. Doc. 325, 60 Cong., 1 Sess., pp. 15–32. Hays, *Conservation and the Gospel of Efficiency*, pp. 115–21.

[14] *Investigation*, 4, pp. 1156, 1158, 1496. A summary of a brief prepared in the Department of the Interior in the summer and fall of 1908 to give a legal base for the supervisory power of the president to withdraw land is on page 1499.

[15] *Ibid.*, 4, pp. 1504–5; 5, pp. 1642–44.

Ballinger later testified that he felt there was no supervisory power vested in the secretary of the interior to make withdrawals or to suspend the public land laws. Yet it was the withdrawals made under the Reclamation Act, not those made under the supervisory power, which first commanded his attention. Although the supervisory power, too, "in the wider sense" was considered illegal in the early discussions when restoration of the sites was first considered, there was at least some question whether or not to draw the line at reclamation withdrawals. There was no dispute about the secretary's authority to withdraw land under the Reclamation Act; the question was whether the sites had been withdrawn for reclamation purposes or whether the withdrawal power in the Reclamation Act had been used as a ruse to segregate waterpower sites.[16]

Two men figured prominently in early considerations. Edward C. Finney prepared a list of the existing withdrawals for the secretary early in March, and had his own opinion about their legality—no doubt influenced by the view of the Land Office, which turned a jaundiced eye on land removed from settlement and brought under the control of another agency. Next to those of Ballinger himself ranked the opinions of Oscar Lawler. A Los Angeles lawyer brought in to replace George Woodruff as chief law officer of the department, Lawler was described cheerily to Ballinger by an old friend as "one of the squarest toed, and most substantial chaps I have ever known"; but square toes and all, Lawler was commended to Pinchot as a machine politician whose law firm represented power interests inimicable to conservation. He had replaced the man considered only less indispensable than Garfield. The concern his appointment aroused was justified by subsequent events, in the view of the Roosevelt men to whom he quickly became a bugbear. An eccentric, outspoken character, he returned in kind the repugnance in which he was held by Pinchot and his friends. So suspicious that he wrote many of his letters to Ballinger in longhand rather than trust a stenographer, Lawler was intensely loyal to his chief, whose burdens he tried

16 *Ibid.*, 5, p. 1925; 7, p. 4187, pp. 4193–94.

to shift to his own shoulders. "I realize that my own opinions," he would later write in his tight, crabbed hand, "have to some extent been responsible for the present conditions. . . . For my error . . . if there be any, you will, of course, most freely hold me accountable."[17]

Ballinger, Finney, and Lawler held a number of conferences with the officers of the Reclamation Service about the Garfield withdrawals. Newell in particular resisted their restoration. But finally on April 1 a letter went out to Newell from the secretary's office directing Newell to explain why the withdrawals should not be restored to entry. This was done mainly at the insistence of Newell, who wanted something in writing. The question was already settled orally and the restorations were well underway before Newell replied on April 10. Actually, Newell never replied directly. Just before leaving on a scheduled western trip he had drafted a letter containing an urgent plea to keep the sites withdrawn and had left it in the care of Davis. Newell's evident intention was to make a record of his objections. However, Davis disapproved. The letter was long and argumentative, two traits which, as the chief engineer knew by this time, Ballinger objected to in Newell's communications. The chief engineer wrote a second letter over Newell's facsimile signature which stated simply that the withdrawals had been made because it was believed that a danger of power monopoly existed, but whether the withdrawals were legal involved "points of law and of administrative policy upon which this office is not competent to judge."[18]

When the chief engineer walked into Ballinger's office on April 23, most of the Garfield withdrawals had been restored. Davis was dismayed to hear the secretary inform him that the restorations had to be rewithdrawn. As acting director with

[17] *Ibid.*, 6, p. 3035. Albert Searl to R.A.B., March 26, 1909; Lawler to R.A.B., July 21, 1909; Lawler to R.A.B., August, 1909. Ballinger Papers. J. B. Lippincott to G.P., March 27, 1909, Gifford Pinchot Papers. Lawler did not take office until April 6, but he was about the department through most of March becoming familiar with his new job.

[18] *Investigation*, 4, p. 1168; 5, p. 1717. Davis to R.A.B., April 10, 1909, Ballinger Papers.

Newell still in the West, Ballinger's order to rewithdraw the sites presented Davis with a delicate problem. He solved it by arguing that the service lacked the funds to carry out the rewithdrawals and by suggesting that the Geological Survey had appropriations for hydrography and topography which could be used for such a purpose. Ballinger's letter to George Otis Smith, director of the survey, instructing him to investigate and determine power sites to be withdrawn, was evidence of Davis' success in preventing the Reclamation Service from moving back into an area of which he disapproved; but clearly Garfield had preferred to use the Reclamation Act wherever possible in order to retain ownership of the sites in the government. Moreover, the new withdrawals were from all forms of entry, including those under the Right-of-Way Act of 1901, so that all development was suspended. A Lawler legal opinion early in May explained that temporary withdrawals in anticipation of congressional action were legitimate.[19]

Pinchot's intervention was behind Ballinger's decision to reverse himself and rewithdraw the sites. At some time in mid-April he may have approached Ballinger to protest the restoration of the Garfield withdrawals. If so, the forester got little satisfaction. He then complained to Taft himself in two interviews on April 19 and 20. On April 23 the rewithdrawals began. Davis later testified that Ballinger said he was acting under orders from the president, and not only the forester but Garfield believed that "through G's intervention Taft has stopped Ballinger." Though Pinchot was accustomed to the door of the White House being open to him in conservation matters, and indeed had assurances that it would remain open under the new president, Taft had his own opinions about the propriety of such interventions. As secretary of war under Roosevelt, Taft had disagreed with the new hydroelectric policy which evolved from Pinchot's permit system in the forests. Yet Roosevelt had informed Taft bluntly that the opinion of the forester should become the opinion of the war department.

[19] *Investigation*, 5, pp. 1738–39; 7, p. 4205. R.A.B. to G. O. Smith, April 23, 1909; R.A.B. to R. M. La Follette, May 25, 1909, Ballinger Papers.

Beyond doubt Taft resented his forced reliance on a subordinate in another department for his official attitude in war department affairs. "The truth is," he later wrote, "the whole administration under Roosevelt was demoralized by his system of dealing directly with subordinates. It was obviated [a small conceit on Taft's part] . . . under Root and me, because we simply ignored the interference and went on as we chose. . . . The subordinate gained nothing by his assumption of authority, but it was not so in other departments."[20]

Garfield, from his vantage point in West Mentor, hoped that the forester would be able to show "Taft the follies his subordinates are ready to commit." In April it appeared that Pinchot had successfully defended his special access to the president, which had become doubly important when Ballinger curtailed his influence in the Department of the Interior. But a difference of opinion eventually developed among those directly involved. Taft was to insist later that he had defended Ballinger's course of action and that Ballinger had always intended to rewithdraw all of the sites under the aegis of the Geological Survey. Ballinger, too, long maintained that he had meant to have the survey rewithdraw the sites, and that his only mistake was "in not having the restorations and rewithdrawals made concurrently." He retracted the claim before the congressional committee investigating the conflict in the spring of 1910. On balance, therefore, the rewithdrawals were probably made because of Pinchot's intervention with Taft, the statements of Taft and Ballinger to the contrary notwithstanding; but Ballinger never accepted this. To the end he insisted that the decision to rewithdraw the sites was made independently of Pinchot, indeed before the forester's visits to Taft.[21]

[20] G.P. to Newell, April 9, 1909; "Memo prepared by Arthur P. Davis . . . ," Gifford Pinchot Papers. G.P. to Taft, November 4, 1909, Ballinger Papers. Garfield Diary, May 8, 1909, Garfield Papers. Hays, *Conservation and the Gospel of Efficiency*, pp. 116–19. Pringle, *The Life and Times of William Howard Taft*, 1, p. 492. Note that Taft's reaction in the Department of War is similar to Ballinger's when as commissioner of the Land Office he was forced to "cooperate" with the Forest Service.

[21] Garfield Diary, April 23, 1909, Garfield Papers. R.A.B. to Taft, November 15, 1909, Ballinger Papers. G.P. to Taft, November 4, 1909;

The evidence clearly indicates that Ballinger had been caught with his withdrawals showing. So complete was the exposure, Garfield thought it might "mean B's leaving the cabinet—at least his usefulness is seriously impaired." Yet one curious aspect of the whole affair remained unresolved. The secretary maintained to the end that the restorations were made "upon the report of the Acting Director of the Reclamation Service," Arthur Powell Davis. In the spring of 1910 before the congressional committee, Davis testified that the service did not recommend the restoration of any power sites except when they were directed to do so by the secretary. Nevertheless, the impression remained in Ballinger's mind that the chief engineer had lent him something more even than tacit support, and the secretary felt betrayed after Davis' testimony. Clearly Davis had not recommended the restorations openly, at least not in writing. Something approaching the truth was expressed by Ballinger in a letter to Frank Baldwin of the *Outlook* staff: By "recommendation" Ballinger meant that the "Reclamation Service [i.e., Davis] was unable to inform him that any of [those] withdrawals contained feasible irrigation projects."[22] He might have added that Davis had gone to great pains not to.

Pinchot derived some satisfaction from the thought that he had checked Ballinger's attack on conservation. "I think we

---

Taft to G.P., November 24, 1909, Gifford Pinchot Papers—copies also in Ballinger Papers. *Investigation*, 7, pp. 4201, 4207.

[22] Garfield Diary, May 8, 1909, Garfield Papers. R.A.B. to Frank Baldwin, May 10, 1909, and R.A.B. to R. M. La Follette, May 13, 1909, Ballinger Papers. *Investigation*, 4, p. 1171; 5, pp. 1900, 1901. On the subject of Davis, Ballinger's own testimony was pained: "As to Mr. Davis, I reposed a great deal of confidence in him throughout, which I now see was misplaced." *Ibid.*, 7, p. 4164; see also p. 4196 and *passim*. Prior to Davis' testimony Ballinger's correspondence is riddled with animus toward Newell, but Davis is either commended or not mentioned. See Ballinger Papers.

Section 3 of the Reclamation Act of 1902 provided, in part, that the secretary of the interior could "withdraw from public entry the lands required for any irrigation works . . . and . . . restore . . . any of the lands so withdrawn when, in his judgment, such lands are not required for the purposes of this act." *The Statutes at Large of the United States of America*, 32, p. 388.

are going to come out where we ought to have begun," he wrote Newell exultantly. "The reversal of policy in the case of power withdrawals is so striking . . . that I think we have reason to be hopeful." Except for the blood in his eye he might have found the rewithdrawals more ominous than the restorations which made them necessary. When the secretary withdrew land he withdrew it from all forms of entry, including those under the act of 1901, thereby bringing "odium upon the whole conservation movement, because it was done in the name of Conservation," as Pinchot remarked when his eye had cleared. At stake, of course, was the entire permit system which Pinchot had developed on the national forests and which Garfield had applied to the public domain as a whole. Despite the embarrassment of Ballinger, the system was effectively destroyed except in the national forests.[23]

President Taft disagreed with the heart of the Roosevelt power policy. Yet he operated in the shadow of the former president, to whom a number of his subordinates continued to grant their first loyalty. The forester, particularly, kept pushing for greater commitment to policies which the president could neither accept entirely nor repudiate openly. Yet Taft's insistence upon going his own way became increasingly apparent. In October he attempted to explain his views on hydroelectric power to Pinchot. He felt that the federal government could legally utilize and control waterpower on navigable streams as long as the primary purpose of the work was the improvement of navigation. The government had a right to a fair return from such works, said the former department head of the Corps of Army Engineers, and a right to control the rates charged the public; but it was powerless to control conditions on nonnavigable streams where the work was not a government project. The mere duty, he said, to apply to the government meant only a declaration by the government that power works would not interfere with the navigability of a stream, and this did not give the government the right to im-

[23] G.P. to Newell, May 22, 1909; G.P. to S. A. Kean, August, 1910, Gifford Pinchot Papers.

pose conditions for its use. The subordinate who had once told the secretary of war how to think on this very issue in his own department was unable to continue in the same role when the secretary became president. Both men were aware of this issue between them.

> I do not know whether I make my distinction clear to you [Taft closed with heavy irony], but if you will examine some other of my correspondence in the War Department, you will see how often I have made the distinction.[24]

Despite this enunciation of administration policy, Pinchot refused to get in line. Indeed, he continued privately to assert, and publicly to imply, that it was Taft who was out of line. In December in an article published in the *Outlook*, Pinchot defiantly insisted that the government had a duty to regulate waterpower on nonnavigable streams—although he conceded in passing that constitutionally the United States exercised direct control only over navigation.[25]

In his first annual report Ballinger observed that "the best thought of the day is not that development shall be by national agencies, but that wise utilization shall be secured through private enterprise under national supervision and control." In thus registering his opinion of the assumptions underlying the use by Garfield of the Reclamation Act to withdraw power sites, the secretary felt he was sharply delineating the differences between himself and his predecessor. Garfield and Newell clearly used the Reclamation Act to insure that title to the sites remained in the government, although short-term leases they hoped would provide for continuous development. Ballinger feared such a program would attract short-term investors while discouraging investment by businessmen who sought permanent ownership. He effectively blocked the plan by using the Geological Survey to rewithdraw the sites from all forms of entry.

Ballinger used the survey for this purpose, he insisted, because it was better prepared to identify accurately the land

[24] Taft to G.P., October 12, 1909, *ibid.*

[25] *The Outlook*, December 1909, pp. 770–72.

most valuable for power development. Undoubtedly, the sweeping nature of the blanket withdrawals was offensive to him. Garfield and Newell, in haste and anxious to insure that every possible power site was included, had swept in a great deal of extraneous land which they intended later to segregate and restore to entry. Ballinger's rewithdrawals reduced the acreage and included besides a number of sites which his predecessor had missed.[26]

Although Ballinger withdrew power sites from all forms of entry, he was not a reluctant reservationist who locked resources away in a deep-freeze of nondevelopment in lieu of an active policy. To conceive of him as such would be an essential oversimplification. Waterpower recommendations in Ballinger's annual report might have been written by Pinchot—in essence: reserve, classify, and lease for maximum thirty-year periods with provisions for a fee and a maximum rate in the lease. "Ballinger's annual report out yesterday," Garfield recorded, "he *now* is in favor of all the things we fought for. I do not understand what he really would have done if Gifford had not brought the water power question etc. to Taft's attention." Ballinger was quite obviously not in favor of his predecessor's water policy. For one thing, he did not envision a fu-

[26] For annual report, see U.S. Congress, Sen. Doc. 283, 61 Cong., 2 Sess., p. 25. Figures have a way of varying, depending upon the source. Possibly those of the Geological Survey are the most dependable. The total withdrawals originally made under the supervisory power totaled 1,615,940 acres; later rewithdrawn by the survey under Ballinger's direction to the number of 235,850. A total of 2,510,303 acres were originally withdrawn under the Reclamation Act; later rewithdrawn by the survey, the figure was reduced to 373,164 acres. In addition, Ballinger withdrew 844,628 acres which had not been included in the original Garfield withdrawals. *Investigation*, 7, pp. 3442–45. See also U.S. Congress, Sen. Doc. 283, 61 Cong., 2 Sess., p. 30, for extracts from Ballinger's annual reports. Note that the ratio of lands withdrawn by Garfield under the supervisory power to those withdrawn under the Reclamation Act was nearly one to two. As for the discrepancy between the Garfield and the Ballinger withdrawals, it should be pointed out that Garfield and Newell had nominally swept in large areas of privately owned lands which were, of course, excluded from the provisions of the withdrawals, although they increased the total figure on paper. Nevertheless, the haste in which the Garfield withdrawals were made had obviously resulted in many sites being overlooked, as the Ballinger withdrawals, exclusive of those made by Garfield, indicate.

ture role for the government as a producer of power to sell to meet the costs of regional development; nor did he plan to use the Reclamation Service as a haven for power sites which the government might one day want to develop itself. Furthermore, his annual report was in no way inconsistent. Like Taft, Ballinger maintained that nonnavigable streams belonged to the states. This left two alternatives. Either national water conservation could deal only with the public domain, or Congress could legislate to make continued regulation possible after land had passed from federal hands. In his annual report the secretary recommended that since the waters in the streams remained in the domain of the states, Congress should pass laws making possible the classification of lands along streams valuable for power, which could then be disposed of by granting easement but preserving title to the government. The weakness of his case in the eyes of the anguished Roosevelt administrators was the reliance upon congressional action; whereas, the spokesman for western anticonservation in the House, Frank Mondell, thought the secretary of the interior was leading the country down the primrose path to socialism.[27]

Ballinger was not a reservationist by intent; nevertheless, the Taft administration failed to develop an active water policy while Ballinger was secretary of the interior. Ballinger infuriated western anticonservationists in the spring of 1910 by supporting a withdrawal act, but Roosevelt administrators were little happier with a request that the legality of the withdrawals of the previous administration be ratified. Conservationists succeeded in substituting in committee a bill more to their liking. For a time Pinchot, no longer the forester but head of a powerful conservation lobby, supported it as "the one conservation bill most needed." Yet the final act conformed mainly to Ballinger's recommendations, although the opposition succeded in changing the wording in an important way. The

[27] Garfield Diary, November 30, 1909, Garfield Papers. Speech before State Conservation Convention, St. Paul, March 16, 1910; Albert Shaw to R.A.B., December 13, 1909, enclosure; Mondell to R.A.B., November 15, 1909, Ballinger Papers. U.S. Congress, Sen. Doc. 283, 61 Cong., 2 Sess., p. 25.

original bill authorized the secretary of the interior to withdraw land from entry until Congress acted, but in the absence of congressional action the land would be restored to entry. As finally passed, the bill provided that the land would remain withdrawn until revoked by the president or Congress. Ballinger described this act as "the greatest step in Conservation that has ever been attempted." It withdrew coal lands for classification and appraisement and waterpower sites and oil lands until Congress provided for their disposal. The secretary insisted that the lands were not withdrawn "for future generations," because they would be opened up as soon "as the best possible method of disposing" of the land was found. "This," he said, "is what I call progressive conservation."[28] The different uses to which they put the same terminology defined the distance between Ballinger and Pinchot.

Ballinger's feud with the Forest Service had grown to dangerous proportions by midsummer of 1909. Many of the administrative arrangements so carefully devised by Pinchot with other resource bureaus went by the board. The power policy which he had nursed in the forests and proudly watched as it expanded over all the public lands had been pushed back again within forest boundaries. The forester began to search frantically for any means at hand to stop Ballinger. The secretary, on his part, refused to look upon developments of the spring and summer as a personal struggle between himself and the Roosevelt administrators. Undoubtedly this was somewhat unrealistic.

Nevertheless, Ballinger continued to take a high plane; his role, he insisted, was to clean up the mess he found and in the pursuit of this duty he was willing to anger Pinchot or risk the friendship of Garfield. The Roosevelt men were devoted to the aim of making government run like a sound business, and it was therefore infuriating to them to discover that Ballinger

[28] Philip P. Wells to G.P., March 1910; G.P. to C. W. Eliot, March 9, 1910; G.P. to Elting A. Fowler, June 7, 1910, Gifford Pinchot Papers, *The Outlook*, February 12, 1910, pp. 320–21. Clipping from *Leslie's Weekly*, September 1, 1910, Ballinger Papers.

believed that many of their methods were in opposition to good business principles. But they must have recognized that he was at least consistent. A similar approach lay behind his reforms in the city of Seattle and the General Land Office. The tactics of the Forest Service, he maintained, bred confusion and, worse, resentment, which hampered good administration. Far from producing greater efficiency, a worthy aim in itself, their efforts, he felt, often muddied the lines of jurisdiction and thus of responsibility. It was a desire to restore the lines of responsibility which led to the abrogation of the cooperative agreement between the Forest Service and the Indian office. A similar desire lay ultimately behind his attempted reform of the Reclamation Service.

The Reclamation Service was a union of both political and engineering elements, out of which most of the problems of government reclamation arose. The secretary attributed the difficulties of the service to the political and administrative ineptitude of engineers. To a man of his pronounced views, "inefficiency" was a spur not to be ignored and, when combined with his animus against Director Newell, inevitably reflected upon the abilities of reclamation personnel. Ballinger's were the first of a great number of changes inflicted upon the service between its creation out of a division in the Geological Survey in 1907 and the end of the decade of the 1920's. His actions were part of the history of the Reclamation Service, described by Robert Yard in 1928 as being one "of constant investigation and change significant of efforts to develop efficiency out of conditions and complications not clearly understood during years of experiment." The secretary worked from a viewpoint of marked distrust for the autonomous expert and sought to bring the service under greater political control.[29]

Yet something more than concern for efficiency, or hostility toward Newell, was behind Ballinger's policy changes in rec-

[29] R.A.B. to R. H. Thomson, April 19, 1909, *Investigation*, 8, p. 4464. Yard, *Our Federal Lands* (New York, 1928), pp. 169–70. For Ballinger's weakening of the service, see John T. Ganoe, "Some Constitutional and Political Aspects of the Ballinger-Pinchot Controversy," *Pacific Historical Review*, 3 (1934), pp. 323–33.

lamation. A decade earlier, in 1900, irrigation work in the West had been at a standstill. So many private companies had failed that irrigation securities were unmarketable; this had led to the original demand for government intervention. By 1909 investment of federal funds had resulted in a resurgence of interest by promoters of private irrigation. Ballinger, who owned irrigation stock at the time he became secretary of the interior, was aware of this development.

> While the government has invested over fifty million dollars in irrigation works, many times that amount has been invested since the passage of the Reclamation act by private enterprise. ... [A] large portion of these private investments have resulted from government example and encouragement. . . . [I]t has not been and is not the policy of the national government . . . to hinder . . . the investment of private capital. . . . I am not a believer in the government entering into competition with legitimate private enterprise. Its functions . . . are not of this character, and I am sure that when private enterprise had done what it can there will still be thousands of acres of public lands reclaimable only by government aid. . . .

Technically, Newell and Pinchot could have quarreled with few of these sentiments. The need for government reclamation arose because of the unwillingness, or inability, of private capital to build large storage dams and expensive engineering works which required long-term investment without holding out the promise of quick return. Yet the two bureau chiefs unquestionably thought Ballinger's emphasis was weighted in the wrong direction.[30]

Ballinger's persistent efforts to bring the Reclamation Service more under his control were of a different character than his skirmishes with the Forest Service. The Reclamation Service was by law directly under his control. Yet his control was nominal. The service was a conservation model in some respects. Its enabling act of 1902 provided it with a fund derived from the sale of public lands, thus freeing it from dependence upon annual appropriations. Cost of construction

[30] Quoted in *Official Proceedings of the Seventeenth National Irrigation Congress Held at Spokane, Washington, August 9–14, 1909* (Spokane, 1909), pp. 222–28.

was to be charged to landholders served by each project, the assessment against each land allotment to be paid in ten annual installments by the settler. The issue of patents to final title of the land was made contingent upon payment of the last installment within the ten-year period. In this way it was hoped a revolving and perpetual fund would be created. The secretary of the interior was empowered to withdraw from entry, except under the homestead act, all lands which might possibly be deemed useful for irrigation. The service was organized after the pattern of a self-sufficient pyramid with an engineering, a disbursing, and a legal section at the base, all directly responsible to the director at the apex. The secretary of the interior retained ultimate review of reclamation decisions, but operational problems involved in making a final decision were ironed out at the director's level.[31]

Federal reclamation had social implications making it an extremely sensitive area with which to tamper. The movement which had culminated in the Newlands Reclamation Act of 1902 was a combination of adjustments between modern technical requirements and agrarian assumptions of American development. It had support in government and out, from Powell-trained hydrographers like Newell to promoters and publicists like George Maxwell, a California water-law expert who hoped to cure social problems by draining city populations back onto the land; one and all they paid homage to the images of agrarian America. "The nomadic herdsman, the restless miner and the wandering laborer add little to the strength or safety of the community," Newell said, explaining the importance of reclamation, "but let one of these men become attached to the soil; let him own a small farm which is sufficiently productive to furnish his family with needed subsistence and comforts, and he becomes a citizen who can be depended upon."[32]

The movement came to fruition during the 1890's, a time of great crisis in rural America. The People's party and populism

---

[31] *Investigation*, 5, p. 2023.

[32] *Official Proceedings of the Seventeenth National Irrigation Congress*, p. 53.

were symptoms of a more deep-seated disturbance; the nation was changing rapidly from a small-town, rural, federal, decentralized, and nontechnical civilization to a predominantly urban, national society rooted in rapid technical change. Support for federal reclamation was an outlet for concern. "No country can continue to thrive and prosper unless its rural population continues greatly to outnumber its city dwellers," said California's Governor George Pardee, a reclamation enthusiast.

> England, when she came to fight the Boer War, found that, because of the undue increase of her urban population, it was impossible for her to recruit her armies with men up to the military requirements. London and the great English cities had swallowed up too great a proportion of the sturdy yeomen who had made her armies once invincible, and had, within a few generations, transformed them into physical and mental degenerates and weaklings.[33]

These attitudes, combining veneration for old ideals with faith in the unlimited horizons of science and technology, were most dramatically expressed by Theodore Roosevelt. Deeply concerned with social and economic divisions in American life, he was also an enthusiastic supporter of federal reclamation, which he hoped would buttress a declining rural life. "I warn my countrymen," he said, "that the great recent progress made in city life is not a full measure of our civilization; for our civilization rests at bottom on the wholesomeness, the attractiveness, and the completeness, as well as the prosperity of life in the country."[34]

The obvious intent of the Newlands Reclamation Act was to make the service as autonomous as possible, free from political considerations not only from Congress and local politicians but from the executive establishment itself. Applied science and advanced technology were to be enlisted in the service of cherished but threatened beliefs. With their help, it would be possible not only to overcome the physical obstacles imposed

[33] *Ibid.*, p. 231.
[34] *The Outlook,* April 10, 1909, quoted on the cover.

by environment but also to preserve frontier ideals by artificial means, to revitalize rural life, to protect the idealized yeoman farmer, whose virtues—vigor, manliness, independence, individualism, and democracy—were romanticized as the blood and bone of national life. "The nation is concerned in this work [of reclamation]," Newell said, "not only because of the resulting internal development, but also because of the improvement in citizenship and in stability of American institutions."[35] Federal reclamation therefore involved one of the fundamental assumptions underlying the conservation movement, that the specialist was best suited to deal with sensitive social problems. The Reclamation Service built dams, canals, tunnels, and power plants, each a highly technical business which it was thought should be managed on engineering principles and the facts of the environment as determined by science; no politician should be allowed to make decisions which could only be made realistically by experts. Yet the service never enjoyed the freedom from political considerations envisaged in this romantic dream.

The Newlands act obviously applied primarily to the public lands, but as the search for construction sites began it became clear that much of the irrigable land in the West had already passed into private ownership, either incidentally or in anticipation of the passage of the act. As sites were chosen, private lands were often involved, and competition developed rapidly between sections in the arid West hoping for attention from the federal reclamation program, generating problems which defied the precision of the drawing board.[36]

A provision that a major portion of the money coming from sale of lands within a given state be spent by the Reclamation Service within that state was another dangerous flaw in the act. Money came in from Oklahoma and North Dakota where feasible sites were scarce, whereas Nevada had many feasible sites but poured little money into the fund. An effort was made to begin a project in every public-land state within the

[35] *Official Proceedings of the Seventeenth National Irrigation Congress,* p. 53.

[36] Peffer, *Closing of the Public Domain,* pp. 58–62.

first ten years after the passage of the act. By 1909 California and Oregon, where opportunities were plentiful, had several projects each, but a possible site had still not been discovered in Oklahoma. Thus the choosing of construction sites was something short of purely scientific.[37]

On the projects under construction science failed to dominate politics. The land hunger of the settlers caused trouble at once. Construction could not be completed for years, yet even where the land was not privately owned already, the Reclamation Service was unable to prevent it from being taken up as soon as preliminary surveys began. Secretary Hitchcock ruled that the Reclamation Act did not authorize him to withdraw land from all entry until the project could be watered; Garfield ruled otherwise, but most of the harm was done. Settlers roosted on waterless land which could bring no return for many years. Fairly or unfairly, the impasse reflected on the Reclamation Service. Critics were strengthened by the overextension of the reclamation fund—too many projects begun too soon. As Newell himself admitted, the works then in progress would require all of the reclamation fund for several years.[38]

Continuity in construction was hampered by problems endemic in government service. Engineers and other employees obtained through competitive civil service examinations could be removed only by filing specific charges. Government salaries were woefully inadequate. Furthermore, as Newell was well aware, a government engineer had to be something more than just an engineer. Skill in the less scientific but more ancient and subtle art of political maneuvering was necessary. With settlers on the projects long before they were completed, technicians were confronted immediately with the democratic process in the form of water users associations. It could not be said that Newell and his fellow engineers always enjoyed

[37] A. P. Davis to C. W. Baker, October 3, 1909, Gifford Pinchot Papers. *Engineering News,* March 10, 1910, p. 284.

[38] Davis to Baker, October 3, 1909, Gifford Pinchot Papers. *Official Proceedings of the Seventeenth National Irrigation Congress,* p. 54.

the relationship. The need to "do business with a large body of men" too often produced only "unceasing talk," Newell felt. He suspected that associations were concerned primarily with the " 'recognition of the union' rather than the physical needs of the Valley." Yet this combination of characteristics of layman and expert was a necessary adjunct to reclamation affairs, which, no less than the quality of the works constructed, commanded the future of federal reclamation.[39]

Ballinger attributed most of the difficulties of the Reclamation Service to sloppy administration, and his first efforts at reform were directed toward gaining more control of reclamation matters. Almost literally refusing to work with Newell because of old animosities, Ballinger first tried to cultivate the chief engineer. Yet Davis resisted these efforts for the same reason which had caused him to frown on the use of the Reclamation Act by Garfield and Newell to withdraw power sites—his first concern was for the Reclamation Service. The secretary brought in a young engineer as a "special inspector" in mid-April and sent him into the field to inspect reclamation projects on the ground and, incidentally, to wreak havoc in field morale. Accompanied by Davis, Ballinger began a summer-long tour in the West in June to see for himself what the service was producing. The inspection coincided partly with a junket of the Senate committee on irrigation and reclamation.[40]

After two months in the West Ballinger reported to the president. The service, he said, had too many projects outstanding, more than it could "complete with reasonable businesslike dispatch with the funds at its disposal. . . ." Not only the number of the sites came under his criticism. "I am impressed

---

[39] Newell to L. W. Hill, October 8, 1909, *Investigation*, 5, p. 1819. See series of letters bearing date September 29, 1912, from Newell to Samuel Adams, in the Library of Congress, Walter L. Fisher Papers.

[40] *Washington Herald*, August 17, 1909. *Investigation*, 5, pp. 1874–75. R.A.B. to R. H. Thomson, April 19, 1909, *ibid.*, 8, p. 4464. Thomas H. Carter to R.A.B., July 21, 1909; R.A.B. to Ormsby McHarg, August 7, 1909, Ballinger Papers. *Chicago Examiner*, June 26, 1909.

with the belief that some of the projects have been entered into without due consideration as to their feasibility, taking into consideration climatic conditions, soil, the cost of construction, maintenance, and operation. I have no doubt that political pressure has had something to do with these conditions." The irony of the agency created to be autonomous of politics being accused of succumbing to political influence was no less striking than the sight of engineers on the run before a politician determined to introduce them to efficiency and "businesslike" methods. The irony was sharpened further by the secretary's obvious belief that the cure for reclamation ills lay in making the service more responsive not only to himself but to Congress. In order to insure the completion of existing projects with "reasonable businesslike dispatch" he recommended that authority be secured from Congress "to issue bonds against the reclamation fund."[41]

"I am not very much surprised," the president replied. Supporters of Newell insisted that the difficulties of government reclamation were attributable to flaws in the enabling act, not to the reclamation engineers, but Taft had his own opinions. In April he had offered the secretary of the interior the services "of any of the army engineers whom I may desire in connection with this service," but Ballinger had declined. "I am not satisfied that they are specially equipped to handle a service of this kind, which comes in contact with water users and settlers on the public domain, where a vast amount of diplomacy and business judgment is necessary." Nevertheless, the president continued to press the offer of his old bureau upon the secretary of the interior, and within a year the Corps did assume a role in reclamation affairs. Taft was convinced that the "enthusiasm with which this Reclamation Service was entered upon was almost certain to lead to enterprises which were

[41] R.A.B. to Taft, August 2, 1909, *Investigation*, 5, p. 1908. See also R.A.B. speech before Spokane Irrigation Congress, August 12, 1909, and speech before North Yakima Commercial Club, August 24, 1909, both in Ballinger Papers.

in advance of the possibility of profitable return," and that a great deal of money had been spent unwisely.[42]

In the spring of 1909 Ballinger altered several of the administrative arrangements which under his predecessor had become reclamation policy, on the ground that they were practices not authorized by the Reclamation Act. In June he turned on a policy which had come to be viewed as essential to the federal program, the use of "Garfield currency."

Often located on barren, sun-baked soil, with mounting payment for water rights looming in the future, the settlers on incompleted reclamation projects had been a major problem from the beginning. Moreover, the reclamation fund was quickly tied up in many of the states where the money could be spent legally, and a shortage of funds developed. To solve these problems, a scheme was devised whereby the government employed the farmers in construction of the works. They were paid in script—certificates that so much work had been done—which the "company" stores accepted as currency and

[42] Taft to R.A.B., August 10, 1909; *Investigation*, 5, p. 1909; R.A.B. to R. H. Thomson, April 19, 1909; *ibid.*, 8, p. 4464; H. S. Whigham to D. M. Carr, August 16, 1910, Ballinger Papers. Francis Newlands of Nevada, author of the Reclamation Act of 1902, admitted that less feasible projects had sometimes been given preference over more suitable sites but insisted that this was the fault of the act with its mandatory provision of geographic distribution of sites. *Engineering News*, March 10, 1910, p. 284. Shortly after the inauguration, Senator Guggenheim of Colorado approached the president in March with a request that a position be found for his secretary, a Denver man named John Vivian. In due course Taft ordered his secretary of the interior to find the protégé a place in the department. Ballinger decided upon the Reclamation Service, and only Vivian's commendable desire to further the education of his offspring led him to decline the position as too niggardly to support two boys in college. Although Ballinger, who disliked this sort of thing, may have deliberately maneuvered Vivian into the position of declining, the episode left Newell thoroughly shaken and aroused the friends of the Reclamation Service as did no other act of Ballinger. The original Newlands act had been partly designed to protect the service against the evil of political appointments. Francis E. Warren to Taft, March 19, 1909, and D. Guggenheim to Taft, May 4, 1909, Library of Congress, William Howard Taft Papers, Presidential series 1; Vivian to R.A.B., May 18, 1909, R.A.B. to Vivian, May 19, 1909, Vivian to R.A.B., May 24, 1909, *Investigation*, 7, p. 3853. See *Engineering News*, 63, *passim*, for reaction of friends of federal reclamation. For Newell's reaction see his letter to C. J. Blanchard, June 17, 1909, *Investigation*, 8, p. 4649.

which the government stood ready to redeem at face value when the project was completed.[43] Approved by Garfield in 1908, the system was ingenious. The reclamation fund was augmented because labor was used for no actual cash cost, and the farmer received a script which he could later present to the government against his ten-year debt.

Responsible for issuing final title to land, the General Land Office was disturbed by the arrangement from the beginning. Since cash payments had to show on their books they took a dim view of certificates for work. Dennett and Schwartz protested to Garfield, and eventually a ruse was devised by which, Dennett hoped, "the skirts of the Land Office" would remain clean. Under the modification, the Reclamation Service deducted the value of certificates from the total amount of the debt and notified the Land Office of the amount due on a particular entry.[44]

Ballinger was apprised of the difficulties his old bureau had experienced with the certificates, but their legality might never have been questioned by him officially had not the reclamation officers overplayed their hand. The service was anxious to begin a new project in Grand Valley, Colorado, and although, as Davis explained, the "number and magnitude of the projects already taken up will absorb the available funds for some time to come," a solution had been devised for this "one tangible objection." Simply put, the scheme was for the water users' association to supply both cash and labor up to a certain amount, which the government would match by an allotment of its own. The government, in other words, would bear only half of the actual cost. Certificates would be issued by the association to cover the subscription of work, which would be accepted by the government, as under the ordinary script sys-

[43] Hays, *Conservation and the Gospel of Efficiency*, p. 154. McGeary, *Gifford Pinchot*, p. 124. For descriptions of the system, see Garfield's testimony, *Investigation*, 5, pp. 1548–55; see also newspaper sources, for instance, *Portland Oregonian*, June 27, 1909.

[44] See Fred Dennett to R.A.B., April 6, 1908, and April 18, 1908, *Investigation*, 5, pp. 1602–3. Dennett said any "other practice would be one of deceit," but he was still unhappy with the arrangement.

tem, as payment for water rights. In reply to this contrivance, Ballinger dashed off a letter to Attorney General Wickersham asking for an opinion on the legality of all cooperative certificates. Wickersham replied in effect that the system of cooperative certificates was a virtual amendment of the Reclamation Act, since it augmented the reclamation fund from sources other than those authorized under the act.[45]

To Newell the issue was the survival of federal reclamation. He contended that the decision would have been different had the Reclamation Service had an opportunity to phrase the request for a legal opinion. The attorney general, Newell said, had been under the impression that the use of script was devised because the Reclamation Service was short of funds.[46]

In mid-July Senator Francis Newlands of Nevada gave a dinner in his home. The guests were the president of the United States, a number of senators and congressmen including the entire irrigation committee of the Senate, and Frederick Haynes Newell. After the meal the guests filed out on the senator's spacious lawn and smoked their cigars comfortably under a large oak tree while Newell entertained them with stereopticon slides thrown on a square of canvas stretched against the house. The president said nothing, one of the guests later remarked, but "he understood the general purposes of the meeting." The general purposes became even clearer a few days later when the attorney general, who had been visited by several senators, asked Oscar Lawler to have the Reclamation Service submit a statement on the cooperative certificates so that he "might re-examine the question and review his former opinion."[47]

An exasperated Lawler proved to be at least as cantankerous as the engineers were determined. Twice a statement came

[45] See testimony of Finney, *ibid.*, 6, pp. 3062–69, with relevant correspondence included. R.A.B. to Wickersham, May 18, 1909, *ibid.*, 5, pp. 1566–70. Entire decision is in *ibid.*, pp. 1570–76. See also R.A.B. speech at Mitchell, Nebraska, June 28, 1909, Ballinger Papers.

[46] *Investigation*, 6, p. 3066.

[47] Thomas H. Carter to R.A.B., July 21, 1909; Lawler to R.A.B., July 30, 1909, Ballinger Papers.

out of the Reclamation Service destined for the attorney general's office, only to be returned with dispatch accompanied by a cranky note from Lawler. "I received this morning," he reported to Ballinger in Seattle, "a statement . . . which . . . was some sixty pages in length, what, to my mind, was an argument, the facts in which could only be obtained by a very careful examination." After the second try a story appeared in the *Washington Herald* which brought Lawler to the end of his none too lengthy patience. Under congressional pressure, the paper reported, Taft "made the move that is construed as a reflection upon his Secretary, for he asked the Attorney General if he would consent to give consideration to another reclamation case, and he insisted that the case be prepared by officers of the Service rather than by the legal force in the Secretary's office." The *Herald* account then closed with a fact of which only these few men were aware: Lawler, Finney, and the officers of the Reclamation Service; Lawler was reasonably certain of Finney's silence, and sure of his own. The new case had yet to be presented to Wickersham, the newspaper story disclosed, because "it had been held in the Secretary's office for three weeks, a law officer there protesting against the form in which it had been prepared, and urging that it be amended to suit his ideas rather than the ideas of Director Newell."[48]

Lawler's response was prompt. The law officer of the Reclamation Service, Morris Bien, experienced an uncomfortable hour during which Lawler apprised him of his "crass inability." After which

> I then prepared a statement myself, and sent it to him [Bien] . . . with a request that he make any suggestions which he thought proper . . . [and] to prepare a letter for transmission thru the Dept to the Atty Gen'l.

Although no one since has conceded him the war, Oscar Lawler won the battle. In due time a second opinion emerged from the inner confines of the Department of Justice. Gently

[48] Lawler to R.A.B., July 30, 1909, *ibid.*

Wickersham denied that he had misunderstood the script system in his first opinion. The objection, he said, "was not that the moneys subscribed by the water users' association was not in the reclamation fund," but that there was no provision in the Reclamation Act for "augmenting" the reclamation fund "by private enterprise." On September 9, the day following the final blow, the secretary instructed Newell to discontinue the use of reclamation certificates.[49]

"At the very outset" of his administration, Ballinger recalled, "I encountered Newell's resistance." Although he sounded puzzled, there was little to evoke surprise. The two men had clashed often when both served under Roosevelt. The burden of enmity was too heavy for either to bear graciously under Taft. In a letter written to Gifford Pinchot while travelling through the West in mid-April, Newell remarked, "I am embarrassed by leading questions as to why Garfield is out and I am at a loss usually as to what to say. His successor will have a hard time getting any general satisfaction."[50] And, indeed, Ballinger did meet with difficulties. A lack of frankness, sometimes downright untruth, characterized some of his efforts, particularly the early moves against the Reclamation Service, which contrasted oddly with his earlier reform of the Land Office. Yet his goals in each case were identical: to bring the agency in line with what he thought of as the best principles of modern business methods, and above all to insure that within his own jurisdiction the lines of responsibility were clear. But as secretary of the interior he discovered that reform of the Reclamation Service and his earlier reform of the General Land Office were two different things. As in the case of the power sites episode he was alternately furtive and direct, forceful and weak, aggressive and defensive. Such vacillation on the part of a man who took pride in his forthrightness at-

---

[49] Lawler to R.A.B., August 18, 1909; Lawler to R.A.B., August 19, 1909; Lawler to R.A.B., August 1909, *ibid.* Entire decision is in *Investigation*, 5, pp. 1583–85. R.A.B. to Newell, September 9, 1909, Gifford Pinchot Papers.

[50] See memo "In Re Reclamation Service," in Ballinger Papers.

tested to the tensions which developed in an admirer of Roosevelt who was at odds with close Roosevelt advisers, an official of an administration dedicated to preserving Roosevelt policies but temperamentally incapable of utilizing Roosevelt means.

Clearly Ballinger intended from the very beginning to jettison Newell. Perhaps before coming to Washington to assume his new duties Ballinger had decided upon Reginald Thomson, the city engineer of Seattle, as his choice for director. The decision was an open secret in the Reclamation Service, and indeed Chief Engineer Davis, as adept at survival as he was adroit in covering his tracks, began privately corresponding with Thomson in April. Though not averse personally to the change, Taft urged caution. Hence the rumor circulated *in vacuo* all through the spring, and at a very early date Newell was aware that efforts to "save" the service from the secretary entwined inextricably with the problem of saving his own scalp. On June 11 Newell's morning coffee was spoiled by the sudden emergence of the rumor in more concrete form, a *Washington Post* story that he would soon be removed by the secretary. Privately later in the day Ballinger admitted the accuracy of the account to Davis, but publicly he disavowed the news story. In the meantime papers throughout the country picked it up. Pinchot once again visited Taft, but little doubt existed in government circles that Newell's position was shaky. The "slip" to the newspaper was a tactical error. Ballinger knew that the president would not permit Newell's dismissal before September 1. Perhaps the secretary hoped Newell would take the hint and resign. He thought Newell weak and vacillating, but he mistook the mettle of his man.[51]

"A serious attack is being made upon Newell & the Reclamation Service," Garfield remarked the day the *Post* story appeared. That same day Pinchot arrived in West Mentor for a protracted stay. The two friends intended to collaborate upon a history of the Roosevelt policies; but history was

[51] R.A.B. to Frank Baldwin, August 25, 1909; R.A.B. to Thomson, May 22, 1909, Ballinger Papers; Thomson to R.A.B., April 13, 1909; R.A.B. to Thomson, May 11, 1909; *Investigation*, 8, pp. 4462, 4464; 5, p. 1766. McGeary, *Gifford Pinchot*, p. 124.

shunted aside by current events, and Ballinger dominated their talk. On June 15 they decided to "see that he is not permitted to overturn all we did." Ballinger later complained that he was the victim of a malignant conspiracy. If by conspiracy he meant the acting together of a closely knit group of men dedicated to his undoing, then his assessment was accurate. Garfield and Pinchot vehemently denied the charge, however. Always, they insisted, their actions were defensive. "We were engaged upon our book," Garfield later explained, "but after Ballinger's attack upon Newell, the Reclamation Service, and the Water Works withdrawals, we took the actions with which you are familiar."

At first an effort was made to bring Newell actively into the circle. His role was viewed as key. "Newell, Davis & Bien must not resign," Garfield wrote, "if they go Ballinger must dismiss them and assume the full responsibility for his act." Newell, of course, had no intention of resigning, but although he kept in close contact with the forester throughout the summer, he coyly sidestepped the schemes of the West Mentor cabal. Especially after the Newlands dinner and the subsequent request of the attorney general that the question of cooperative certificates be resubmitted, Newell felt that the situation was under control, for a short time at least.[52]

Garfield and Pinchot had no overriding scheme to entrap the secretary of the interior. What "Ballinger has been doing & how we are to meet his attacks," was their main concern during that summer, and by and large they responded to situations as they arose, searching always for the leverage they needed. Thus, when the opportunity arose at the end of the season to ensnare Ballinger, they were more than ready to snatch at it. In the meantime their efforts were expended in several di-

[52] Garfield Diary, June 11, 1909, June 15, 1909, Garfield Papers. Garfield to G. W. Pepper, May 10, 1910, Amos Pinchot Papers. See the following correspondence in *Investigation*, 8, pp. 4649–56; Newell to C. J. Blanchard, June 17, 1909; Blanchard to E. T. Perkins, June 23, 1909; Perkins to Blanchard, June 28, 1909; Perkins to G.P., June 29, 1909; G.P. to Perkins, July 15, 1909; Perkins to Newell, July 19, 1909; Newell to Perkins, July 21, 1909; Thomas R. Shipp to Perkins, July 23, 1909.

rections. Both men felt deeply that "Taft [was] a sore disappointment." "The whole tone of the administration" was "adverse" to that of Roosevelt's. Yet Taft had "stood by Gifford" in the power sites episode "against Ballinger's attack," Garfield believed. The slender hope remained that the president would come around. At the same time the forester was certain that the fidelity of the president would scarcely suffer from a little bolstering, and an "active campaign" began in early summer to bring to bear as much influence as possible upon Taft. In line with these efforts Pinchot and Garfield met at the Colonial Club in Cambridge, Massachusetts, at the end of July in company with an imposing array of conservationists, including two future cabinet members under Taft: Ballinger's successor Walter L. Fisher and Henry L. Stimson. On the spot they organized the National Conservation Association, a conservation lobby. The organization was not officially announced until early November and so played only a small part in the activities of the summer, of whose anxieties it was a product.[53] In the meantime unofficial pressure was of growing importance as the summer waned and with it faith in the efficacy of Pinchot's "visits" to the president.

During the summer a newspaper campaign of mounting intensity was directed at the secretary of the interior. With almost ostentatious propriety the Roosevelt men refused to comment to an inquiring press. It was "yet too early to judge Taft," Garfield told reporters, and "of course" he "could not criticize Ballinger." The secretary, who had his own newspaper contacts (for instance, Walter Eli Clarke of the *New York Sun*), was aware that the source of much of this information was the press bureaus of the Forest and Reclamation Services. Commenting on this development to his chief in Seattle, Oscar Lawler wrote, testily:

> I think the whole problem in the present situation is the apparent inability of Messrs. Pinchot and Newell to realize

[53] Garfield Diary, June 11, 1909, July 18, 1909, July 29, 1909, August 5, 1909, Garfield Papers. Newell to C. J. Blanchard, June 17, 1909, *Investigation*, 8, p. 4649. *The Outlook*, November 6, 1909, p. 522.

that an opinion that certain action is not legally justifiable does not of necessity involve the conclusion that the persons so opining are enemies of their plans; and this in turn, comes perhaps, from a habit derived from former practice of forcing opinions, not in accordance with legal conceptions, but to suit individual desires and purposes.[54]

Yet in July this analysis was somewhat off target. The conclusion mentioned by Lawler might not have been the necessary one from the standpoint of pure logic, but it was hard to avoid nonetheless. Newell was on the verge of being discharged from the government, and the Reclamation Service was in a chaotic state of demoralization. Pinchot had watched the destruction of many cherished policies that had been carefully designed to fortify the Forest Service, and had seen his own influence in the administration decline. Garfield rankled under the charge that as secretary of the interior he had been outside the law as often as within. Ballinger was a stubborn man, but the cornered rat usually walks off with the laurels for ferocity. The newspaper campaign of July indicated the existence of an opposition willing to take the offensive if the occasion should arise. The theme of the campaign was the growing antagonism in the president's official family, with Taft siding with Pinchot against the enemy of righteousness, Ballinger, whose retirement was viewed as imminent. The hope of Ballinger's dismissal was a continuing thread through Garfield's diary in the summer of 1909, upon occasion becoming delusionary. "If only Gifford were made Secy of Int.," he remarked on August 5, "a great victory would be won."[55] Gifford never achieved this goal but great victories lay ahead nonetheless.

[54] See *Washington Herald* for July and August; also extensive clipping collections in the Ballinger Papers and the Newell Papers. Garfield Diary, July 21, 1909, Garfield Papers. Clarke to R.A.B., August 1, 1909; R.A.B. to Clarke, August 7, 1909; R.A.B. to Frank Baldwin, August 25, 1909; R.A.B. to Ormsby McHarg, August 7, 1909; R.A.B. to Thomas H. Carter, July 30, 1909; Lawler to R.A.B., July 21, 1909, Ballinger Papers.

[55] Garfield Papers.

CHAPTER FOUR

The Alaska Coal Imbroglio, 1902–1909

Through the spring and summer of 1909 the conflict between Ballinger and Pinchot gathered momentum. Yet great as the issues were, they revolved around considerations of policy open to more than one interpretation which could lay claim to legitimacy in the political arena. Furthermore, the controversy raged between federal officials and administrators divided into two camps, their congressional allies, and the limited number of interest groups in the general community supporting one side or the other. Pinchot could insist that Ballinger was unfit for his position, but his reasons were necessarily grounded in the difference over policy. At the same time it became increasingly apparent that Ballinger now seemed to have the support of the president that Pinchot had enjoyed earlier. The forester fell back more and more on his allies outside the government; but without the ear of the president the specific interest groups were too narrow a base. The opportunity to widen the struggle unexpectedly fell to Pinchot. Like an apple long in ripening, the Alaska coal imbroglio dropped into willing hands.

Although immediately at odds with most aspects of the Roosevelt conservation movement, Ballinger was reasonably comfortable with the coal land policy of his predecessor. Earlier, as commissioner of the Land Office, he had helped Garfield draw up the new regulations for sale at the classified price, and as secretary he tripled the maximum valuation. He had opposed Garfield's leasing measure, but not inflexibly. In his first annual report in 1909 he qualifiedly supported leasing as an alternative to sale, although he continued to prefer the latter. As commissioner, and as secretary of the interior, Ballinger recommended that coal deposits be separated from title to the surface of the land, as an added insurance against fraudulent entry under the agricultural laws in order to acquire mineral rights. In the summer of 1910, this proposal became law.[1] The new coal land policy not only escaped Ballinger's censure; it received his active support. Yet, ironically, it was a conflict over coal land which eventually destroyed his effectiveness in the Taft administration.

The coal question antedated Ballinger by many years. At the turn of the century the law governing the disposal of federal coal lands provided that an individual could obtain title to 160 acres upon payment of ten dollars an acre for land located fifteen miles or more from a railroad or twenty dollars for land within that distance. An association of four or more persons could enter as much as 640 acres. Only surveyed lands could be entered. The government, which surrendered all title to the land in the sale, was left with no means of regulating development. The private owner was free to exhaust his deposit, take out only the heart of the vein, or hold it undeveloped for speculation. The law was a failure. As late as 1909, less than 500,000 acres of public land had been disposed of as coal land since the passage of the law in 1873, a small figure compared with the disposal of other mineral lands. Areas of 160 acres were considered too small for economical mining. Furthermore, the agricultural land laws provided a more convenient and profitable, though fraudulent, access to coal land.[2]

Concern about the fraudulent acquisition of coal lands

[1] *Investigation of the Department of the Interior and the Bureau of Forestry*, Sen. Doc. 719, 61 Cong., 3 Sess., 7, pp. 3556–57; 6, p. 3349. R.A.B. speech before Conservative Club of Rhode Island, January 29, 1910; and R.A.B. to Breckons, October 15, 1910, Ballinger Papers.

[2] *Report of the National Conservation Commission*, 3, U.S. Congress, Sen. Doc. 676, 60 Cong., 2 Sess., pp. 417, 420. B. H. Hibbard, *A History of the Public Land Policies* (New York, 1924), pp. 518–19; Roy M. Robbins, *Our Landed Heritage* (Princeton, N.J., 1942), p. 359.

prompted action under Theodore Roosevelt. Beginning in 1906, the remaining coal-bearing land in the public domain was withdrawn from all forms of entry.[3] The goal of the Roosevelt administration was classification and disposal of the coal land at market value. Garfield and Gifford Pinchot preferred lease at a per-ton royalty, but after failure of the administration lease bill in Congress, they began to search for a way to raise the price of coal land by administrative means. The Geological Survey was given the opportunity to apply the fund of information it had been gathering since 1879 to the systematic classification of the withdrawn lands. Once classified, by the simple expedient of interpreting the statute price as the minimum, the land was opened to sale at prices not less than the minimum prescribed, but corresponding more to its true economic value; in other words, the statute was interpreted as meaning that no less than ten dollars could be charged by the government but a maximum price approximating market value could be set.[4] The same system was extended to the federal territory of Alaska, but there the conservation goal of maximum economic resource use was distorted by circumstances.

Between 1906 and 1909 nearly nine million acres of land believed to contain coal-bearing rocks were withdrawn from all forms of entry in Alaska. There was little question of classification, since most of the surface of the territory had yet to be geologically surveyed. In any case, only along the south and southeasterly coasts was the coal of sufficient quality to be potentially marketable. The flurry of railroad building in Alaska during the first decade of the century aroused some interest in the coal. Indeed, by 1909 the railroad boom had begun to slacken chiefly for lack of a domestic fuel supply. By then it was increasingly doubtful that coal could be exploited in Alaska in the immediate future because the new policy of classification and sale at market value seemed inapplicable to local conditions. Classification worked in the

[3] By November 1909, 79,650,002 acres had been withdrawn, exclusive of Alaska.

[4] U.S. Geological Survey Bulletin, 537, pp. 35–37.

United States, where most of the public domain had been surveyed, and where the most valuable coal was already in private
hands and being successfully exploited; but very little of Alaska
had been surveyed, the coal industry was nonexistent, and the
normal criteria for determining economic value—accessibility,
transportation, and nearness of markets—were absent.[5]

As the editor of the *Outlook* once remarked, Americans
were "prone to think only of gold" when they considered
Alaska.[6] Yet the first flush of gold fever had scarcely subsided
as the century turned, when men began to look elsewhere for
profitable ventures in the territory. Southeast of Prince William Sound and east of the Copper River delta, the Bering
River flowed from the mountains southwest into Bering Lake
and wound south into Controller Bay. Above the lake and
between two large glaciers lay the Bering River (sometimes
called the Katalla) coal fields, comprising some 30,000 acres
of workable coal of varying quality. To this area in the summer
of 1902, attracted by the reports of coal, came Clarence Cunningham, a promoter and businessman of a type not unknown
in the history of the American West. He found a few prospec-
tors on the scene already. The coal samples which he picked
up for analysis were promising, and after returning to the
United States to interest friends of a similar venturesome bent
with capital to invest, Cunningham arranged with the prospec-
tors to purchase their discovery rights. Only after this initial
outlay did he learn that the general coal law was inoperative
in Alaska. Congress had extended the law to the territory in
1900, but it applied only to surveyed lands. The year before,
the system of public-land surveys had been extended to Alaska;
but unfortunately, since no money had been appropriated,
the coal land law was a dead letter. Undaunted, Cunningham
returned to Alaska in February 1903, ran lines, staked out
twenty-two claims and had them recorded in Juneau under

[5] Joshua Bernhardt, *Alaska Engineering Commission* (New York, 1922),
pp. 1–17. *Report of the Railway Commission*, U.S. Congress, H. Doc. 1346,
62 Cong., 3 Sess., p. 131.

[6] *The Outlook*, 1909, p. 384.

the general mineral laws. Recording his coal locations under the mineral laws was the first of a long line of bumbling mistakes. Pirate or merely typical American businessman, and he has been pictured as both, Cunningham showed at times an appalling lack of talent for either role.[7]

Clarence Cunningham was back in the coal field in May 1903 with men and provisions. During the year he made over three hundred openings and expended something more than $20,000, but his plans went awry again in April 1904. Congress passed a law providing for private survey and entry of unsurveyed coal lands in Alaska. This was the first of two laws, the second coming in 1908, passed by Congress to ameliorate the coal land situation in Alaska. Both brought chaos to Cunningham's affairs. He had to relocate immediately under the coal land law. The new survey, which had to be run on different lines, ended by embracing thirty-five claims. In the final recording Cunningham located thirty-three.[8]

Despite his setbacks, Cunningham had the least suspect of all the Alaska coal claims. There were nine hundred altogether by 1907. All claimants except Cunningham and his group were known to be strawmen, or dummy entrymen—men who for a fee located claims for individuals or corporations ineligible to make the locations for themselves. Even without this common knowledge of fraud, Alaska claimants were suspect because of the feeling that the ordinary businessman would hesitate to locate in a region where the risks were so great. Cunningham's progress was slowed again in 1905. A special agent of the General Land Office, Harry K. Love, was assigned to investigate the Alaska coal claims.[9]

In 1905 the Cunningham group appeared to be an exception to the general run of Alaska claimants. They were businessmen

[7] U.S. Geological Survey Bulletin, 442, pp. 56–57. Background on Cunningham is to be found here and there throughout the *Investigation*. See, for instance, his affidavit, drafted by Ballinger, of September 4, 1908, in 2, pp. 498–99.

[8] *Ibid.*, p. 499.

[9] *Ibid.*, p. 107. Schwartz to R.A.B., November 1, 1909, Ballinger Papers.

of moderate means, widely known in the northwestern states of Washington, Oregon, and Idaho for their venturesome forays in such enterprises as sawmills and mines. Throughout their erratic career these claimants were never charged with being dummies. Furthermore, there was no evidence of other fraudulent violations. There were several stages through which one went to acquire title to land—location, entry, and final entry with the issue of the patent—and each had its formal stipulations. It was illegal, before locating, to plan to combine several claims, but such plans were not illegal once the claims had moved to entry. In 1905 there was no indication that before location the Cunningham claimants had illegally agreed to combine their interests once title had passed from the government. They were allowed by Love to move to entry, the final stage before issue of patents, in which land claimants pay the statute price for the land. The thirty-three Cunningham claims comprised 5,280 acres. Between February and October 1907, the Cunningham group paid the ten dollars an acre price, a total of $52,800. The claims had been properly advertised, no protests had been filed, and seemingly only the slow, inexorable grind of government machinery stood between the group and final title to their claims. Of the nine hundred Alaska claimants, only the Cunningham group ever came so close to success.[10]

With the issue of patents approaching, the Cunningham claimants moved to cement a relationship with the Morgan-Guggenheim syndicate, the single most powerful economic interest (excluding the federal government) in the territory. The syndicate was a combination of the wide-ranging financial empire of J. P. Morgan and the Guggenheim fortune, which had integrated the copper mining, smelting, and refining of the Far West on a grand scale in the American Smelting and Refining Company. In Alaska the principal mining venture of the syndicate was the Kennecott-Bonanza copper mine, and to tap this they began construction of the Copper River and Northwestern Railroad. With an apparently inexhaustible fund of capital, the syndicate seemed to many Alaskans to be a grow-

10 *Investigation*, 2, pp. 175, 222; 3, p. 432.

ing threat to their economic independence. The "Guggies" ruthlessly suppressed competition wherever they could muster the power and carried on constant warfare against other railroad companies struggling to survive. No champions of the entrepreneurial urge, they squelched all enterprise dangerous to themselves.[11]

The syndicate railroad was a going concern. Its line to the copper mine was the only operating road in the territory in 1907; but its goal of bridging the interior and the southeastern coast had been thwarted by the absence of a domestic supply of coal. In 1908 the average price of run-of-mine coal mined in Alaska at the pit's mouth was $4.83 per short ton, whereas the cost under similar conditions was $2.74 in Oregon, $2.93 in California, and $2.21 in Washington. Yet with transportation added, imported coal was the more costly. Actually, in these years the coal most consumed by Alaskans was imported from a foreign source, usually British Columbia. The price finally paid by the consumer varied according to conditions. When Juneau and other towns on the Pacific slope built a public wharf and spent public funds in bringing up coal from British Columbia to sell at cost on the wharf, the price averaged $10. But when the courts restrained the towns from dealing in coal, the price averaged $18–$20 a ton.[12] Struggling already under hazardous climatic conditions, without the emoluments granted by the national government to earlier promoters in the United States, the Alaskan railroaders regarded a cheap domestic supply of coal as essential to continued railroad development.[13]

The Alaska syndicate moved a step ahead of its competitors toward the goal of an assured coal supply in July 1907 when its representatives sat down at a table in Salt Lake City with members of the Cunningham group, the only coal claimants who seemed likely in the near future to be producing coal in

[11] Dennett to R.A.B., July 13, 1907, Ballinger Papers. *Investigation*, 2, p. 36.

[12] U.S. Geological Survey Bulletin, 442, pp. 66, 83, 87; *Congressional Record*, 63 Cong., 2 Sess., 51, p. 14496.

[13] Bernhardt, *Alaska Engineering Commission*, pp. 1–17.

Alaska. The result of the meeting was an option agreement to create a corporation under the equal control of both groups. The syndicate agreed to provide the money to improve and develop the coal fields and in return was guaranteed an unlimited supply of coal for a twenty-five-year period. It was illegal for claimants to combine their resources before location of the claims, but the option agreement was made after entry when they were free to make any agreement with regard to their claims that they chose.[14] Had the option ever taken concrete form, the Copper River and Northwestern Railroad would have attained undisputed dominance over its competitors.

The year of the option agreement witnessed a further setback to the Cunningham fortunes. The Alaska coal investigations were taken away from Love in June and given to a special agent in the Portland office, Horace T. Jones. The change was intended to signify a more severe investigation of the Alaska claims. The year 1907 was the period of Ballinger's shakedown of the Land Office, and Love belonged to a category marked for pruning. Love was a political appointee, a former Rough Rider, and a protégé of Theodore Roosevelt.[15] He was removed from the Alaska investigation by Dennett and Schwartz because his investigation had not progressed beyond the limits of Alaska, whereas the majority of the nine hundred claimants, as was typical of land speculators in American history, were scattered from Washington state to West Virginia.

Although Jones was appointed to complete the cases, he was prevented from making a rigorous investigation. When he returned to Seattle from Juneau where he had copied the locations and entries recorded there, he was ordered by Commissioner Ballinger, who was visiting his home city, to make only a partial investigation for the time being. Four coal land bills, two of them dealing specifically with Alaska, were pending the coming session of Congress, and Ballinger wanted prelimi-

14 The agreement is in *Investigation*, 5, pp. 2131–33.
15 *Ibid.*, 6, p. 2470.

nary reports on Alaska to enable him to testify knowledgeably before the congressional committees. Then because the reports were needed quickly and because he was in Seattle and unoccupied, Love, who had just had the cases taken from him, was assigned by Ballinger to help Jones. Because of the shortness of time they took affidavits only in the Puget Sound and Spokane areas, where the majority of the claimants lived. In August Jones made two reports to Ballinger, which normally would also have been signed by Love, who had assisted in the investigation. But the two men detested one another, and Love refused to sign the Jones reports. Instead, on August 2 Love reported independently.[16]

Very shortly thereafter the Portland office acquired a new chief of field division. Louis Russell Glavis had worked under Fred Dennett and was a close friend of Schwartz. He was an intelligent and tireless investigator, and although quite young (under 25) in 1907, he was given charge of the Portland office as part of Ballinger's program of promoting youth and talent over age and seniority.[17] He was not long in taking an interest in the unfinished coal land investigations of his subordinate, Horace Jones.

After an exchange of correspondence with his superiors on the subject, Glavis was invited to Washington for a conference with the commissioner. When he returned to Portland he had been given charge of the Alaska coal investigations. Just a week before Glavis arrived in the capital, on December 7, the Morgan-Guggenheim syndicate formally accepted the option proposed by the Cunningham group the previous July. Thus it transpired that within a few days of the agent's departure for Portland, Miles Moore, a former governor of the state of Washington, an acquaintance of Ballinger, and one of the Cunningham claimants, called at the commissioner's office. Queried

---

[16] *Ibid.*, 2, pp. 5, 75; Schwartz to R.A.B., November 1, 1909, Ballinger Papers.

[17] Dennett to Commissioner of GLO, October 24, 1905, Records of the Department of the Interior, Correspondence of the Office of the Secretary, National Archives.

about the status of the Cunningham claims, Ballinger sent for Schwartz. The two men went over the records of the case in the Land Office file and concluded that the claims could be clearlisted, that is, transferred to the division in the Land Office responsible for issuing final patents. Prodded by Moore's complaints of the long delay, Ballinger ordered the Juneau office to forward the plats which were necessary before patents could be granted.[18]

On January 7, 1908, Glavis was informed in Portland that the claims were being clearlisted. Fifteen days later he protested, although if the plats had not been delayed at Juneau his action would have come too late. The Love reports, Glavis explained, were unreliable. Love was an active candidate for federal marshal in Alaska, and "while not questioning his integrity, still his judgment is likely to be a little warped." Glavis' action halted the clearlisting. A month later Ballinger wired an inquiring Moore: "Temporary delay caused by report of field agent."[19]

Glavis' motive for halting the clearlisting is not entirely clear. The bad blood between Jones and Love over the reassignment of the cases raises the question whether Glavis' attack on Love was prompted by Jones. Certainly the Cunningham claims were different from other claims in the Alaska cases; they were not dummies, and they had been permitted to proceed to entry, the final stage after which the issue of patents was normally a formality. Glavis later claimed his suspicions were aroused because the clearlisting had been ordered despite the contents of the Jones and Love reports, available to Ballinger and Schwartz when they considered the Cunningham file. Strangely enough, it is quite unlikely that these reports aroused any suspicions in Glavis in January 1908 any more than they had in Ballinger or Schwartz, because they tended to enhance the validity of the Cunningham claims.

Jones's first report, on August 10, closed by suggesting that

18 *Investigation*, 2, pp. 6–8, 67; 3, p. 42; 5, p. 2146. R.A.B. to Moore, January 13, 1908, Ballinger Papers.

19 *Investigation*, 2, p. 8; 7, p. 3965.

"the majority of the statements taken in this matter seem to indicate that the lands which are subject to this investigation appear to have been taken under, to say the least, a misapprehension of the rights of the parties to combine and locate together under one financial arrangement." Jones suggested a number of groups where close investigation was "particularly necessary," among which the absence of the Cunningham claimants was remarkable if he believed their actions to be fraudulent since they of all claimants were the closest to receipt of final title. In his second report, on August 13, Jones expressed a feeling that "the disposal of the lands all tends toward one direction, and that is the Guggenheim companies," which was amazing in light of the existing evidence. The loathing for the syndicate and the Cunningham group on the part of independent operators was common knowledge throughout Alaska and the Northwest.[20] As a matter of fact the Cunningham group was mentioned only once in the reports of Jones. He attached without comment to his report of August 10 two affidavits by Cunningham claimants which, if accurate, corroborated the earlier favorable reports of agent Love in that they did not indicate that intent to combine efforts existed among the claimants prior to location.[21] Moreover, a report by Love dated August 2, 1907, was in the file of the Land Office at the time of the clearlisting. Cunningham, Love said, had informed him of an intention among the group to combine after the issue of patents. He ended his report by remarking: "I believe the action of entrymen toward the formation of a company pending patent . . . to be allowable under the law" since the action was taken after the claims were located.[22] Thus there existed in the Land Office file at the time Moore approached Ballinger no adverse report against a set of claims which had by all appearances fulfilled the requirements of the law and moved to all but the final stage but yet had been delayed and

[20] *Ibid.*, 2, pp. 25–26, 114.

[21] Affidavits can be found *ibid.*, p. 28. See also Schwartz to R.A.B., November 1, 1909, Ballinger Papers.

[22] *Investigation*, 2, pp. 35, 98–99.

kept pending for over three years. The issue of good faith was another question (even Love refused to believe in "the perfect nonexistence of any intent or hope" to combine among the claimants), but one which at this point had not arisen in the absence of adverse evidence.[23]

Glavis contributed something to the issue of good faith on April 20, 1908, when he transmitted to the Land Office a copy of the journal of Clarence Cunningham, which seemed to prove conclusively that the Cunningham claims were indeed fraudulent. Both Secretary Garfield and Gifford Pinchot were shown the damning entry, which was looked upon at the time as a remarkable piece of evidence. Glavis had secured it in curious fashion; Cunningham gave the journal to him voluntarily. On March 6 the Portland chief and agent Jones had visited Seattle. They found Cunningham at his headquarters in the Rainier Grand Hotel. Both Jones and Glavis were concerned with the rumors of Guggenheim control. Because the option agreement was now common knowledge Cunningham was anxious to prove that the syndicate had exercised no previous control over the claimants. With touching sincerity he turned over his books to the inspection of the agents. Unfortunately the journal contained an entry for February 1, 1903 (prior to the date of location under the coal land law), which described an agreement subscribed to by each claimant "to deed his interest to a company to be formed for the purpose of developing and marketing said coal" once final title had been secured from the government. The journal disproved the charge of control by the Guggenheims but, as Glavis reported, "conclusively proved collusion and fraud on the part of the claimants themselves." The two agents disguised their elation and, incredibly enough, secured the journal from the unsuspecting Cunningham long enough to make a copy.[24] Few guilty men have shown such childlike innocence.

On May 2, 1908, within a matter of days of the receipt of the Cunningham journal at the Land Office, Louis Glavis was ordered to discontinue his investigation of Alaska coal claims.

[23] *Ibid.*, pp. 9–10.   [24] *Ibid.*, pp. 10, 99, 469, 474, 495–96.

The Land Office was concerned about a large backlog of cases, the prosecution of which would soon pass from the government under the statute of limitations. Many of the Oregon land-fraud cases were especially pressing. Glavis, who later came to view this as another attempt to thwart his Alaska investigation, was ordered to turn his entire force of agents to the Oregon cases endangered by the statute of limitations.[25]

In the chain of suspicions which forged the Ballinger-Pinchot controversy, no link was more important than the dreary story of the Oregon and California timber frauds. They came to light in 1903 during Roosevelt's first administration. By 1908 twenty-six convictions had been won by the government, and more were to come. Three men were responsible for this success. The special prosecutor, Francis Heney, had worked smoothly with the most famous detective of the day, William J. Burns, borrowed temporarily from the Department of the Treasury. One of the least appetizing of the suspects, Stephen A. Douglas Puter, produced most of the evidence for the convictions including the most notable, that of Senator John H. Mitchell, Oregon's long-time political boss and a respected national figure.[26] Very early in the prosecutions a commissioner of the General Land Office, Binger Hermann, resigned under a cloud and in the spring of 1910 would eventually be brought to trial (though not convicted) by Heney.

The chief of field division in Portland who preceded Glavis was Thomas Neuhausen, who had also acted as a special inspector for the Department of the Interior, assisting Heney and Burns. For reasons not entirely clear Ballinger as commissioner sought to force Neuhausen to resign and apparently only Neuhausen's relationship to Secretary Garfield as a special inspector for the department saved him.[27]

[25] *Ibid.*, pp. 10–11, 114, 228. Ballinger retired from the GLO in March 1908.

[26] Puter, *Looters of the Public Domain* (Portland, 1908), pp. 452–54.

[27] Thomas Ryan to Thomas B. Neuhausen, August 14, 1906, Records of Department of the Interior, Correspondence of the Office of the Secretary, National Archives. Ballinger to Frank Pierce, June 30, 1908, Ballinger Papers.

Garfield had asked his old school friend Ballinger to surrender a lucrative law practice and accept the position as commissioner partly because of the corruption and inefficiency in Land Office procedure earlier revealed by the Oregon frauds. Ironically, it was his effort to reform procedure in Oregon which caused Ballinger to be tarred with suspicion in the land frauds. Shortly after Ballinger retired as commissioner, S. A. D. Puter wrote a book with the help of Horace Stevens, a clerk who worked for Neuhausen. Though primarily a history of the California and Oregon frauds, it made charges against Ballinger as commissioner. According to Puter and Stevens, Mount Rainier was made a forest reserve in 1897, and two years later a national park, because most of the land involved belonged to the Northern Pacific Railroad, which desired to take advantage of the lieu land law. Using the park as a basis of exchange the railroad set out to get good timber in return for an "unprepossessing" mountain composed mainly of glacier and rock. Despite the protests of Neuhausen, the account continued, Ballinger permitted the railroad to exhaust its base (i.e., the park) for good marketable timber—that is, exchange the mountain, considered valueless to the railroad, for timber lands. This exchange took place under the cover of a "humane spirit" which professed to be concerned that the "poor, honest, homesteader" should "get his patent in a hurry." Ballinger had ordered the chiefs of field division to pass to patent all entries about which there was no evidence of fraud and against which no protest had been filed for at least two years.[28]

The action of Commissioner Ballinger had been an administrative measure to clean up the perpetual backlog of cases which always dragged behind Land Office business. In the hands of Puter and Stevens it came very near to being a charge that

[28] Puter, *Looters of the Public Domain*, pp. 368, 377. Early forest reserves had encompassed private lands, and in 1897 an act of Congress provided that the landowner in such a situation could exchange his holding for public land elsewhere. The land selected did not have to be equal in value with that relinquished. The railroads, as the largest landowners in the West, profited most from the law. See E. Louise Peffer, *The Closing of the Public Domain*, pp. 43, 46–48.

Ballinger had granted patents to entries which he knew to be fraudulent, although, as it turned out, only a few of the questionable claims were ever actually filed and most of those were still being investigated when Puter's book appeared. Ballinger was enraged, and although a private citizen in June 1908 he sought again to have both Neuhausen and Stevens removed from office for the "libelous statements" in Puter's book, for which Ballinger held the two Portland men responsible.[29]

The entire incident was prophetic. For five years Oregon had been a breeding ground of suspicion. The trail had led to the doors of the great and the powerful, some of whom had been seen to tumble with astonishing ease. The making of reputations had been uncomfortably connected with the breaking of reputations. Several strands led from Ballinger's small feud with Neuhausen. Glavis, who had worked on the land frauds as an agent in Seattle in 1905, had taken over much of Neuhausen's work in Portland including the assistance to Heney. Glavis' assistant, Horace Jones, who more than anyone else interested the Portland chief in the Alaska coal land cases, was a brother-in-law of Thomas Neuhausen.[30] The information about Ballinger with which Horace Stevens had supplied Puter came from files for which Glavis and Jones were responsible. Probably neither of the Portland agents was directly involved in the episode; neither could have been unaware of its significance. It was the background against which they interpreted Ballinger's role in the Cunningham imbroglio, from his action in curtailing Jones's investigation in the summer of 1907 through the clearlisting episode.

Action on the Cunningham claims hung in abeyance in the summer of 1908. However, Dennett and Schwartz were convinced after the transmittal of the Cunningham journal that the group had filed fraudulently. In October Schwartz ordered

[29] Puter, *Looters of the Public Domain*, pp. 368–77. R.A.B. to Frank Pierce, June 30, 1908, Ballinger Papers.

[30] Fred Dennett to Commissioner of GLO, October 24, 1905, Records of Department of the Interior, Correspondence of the Office of the Secretary, National Archives. A. W. Lafferty to R.A.B., June 29, 1908, Ballinger Papers.

Glavis to proceed once again with his investigation. A new Alaska coal land law had been passed in May under which the claimants might have refiled. Schwartz continued:

> This office has been informally advised that the various entrymen . . . have concluded to stand upon the old law and ask for a patent upon the now pending applications. The reports as made by you to this office show that these applications were fraudulent and should be canceled. Proceedings will be deferred, however, until such time as you advise this office that you have completed your investigations and are ready to sustain the Government's case in the hearing.[31]

Glavis believed that field investigations in Alaska, which weather conditions precluded in the fall, would yield additional evidence of fraud, but his investigation was not resumed until April 1909.

The new coal land law which the claimants had decided to ignore had been passed on May 28, 1908. Applicable only to Alaska, it had struck at the embargo on coal development in the territory by providing that all persons who had made locations prior to 1906, that is, those whose claims were pending at the time the new policy of classification began to go into effect, could consolidate their claims or locations into a single entry of as much as 2,560 acres. This figure, though haphazardly arrived at as a "fair and reasonable limitation," eliminated one of the principal faults of previous coal land legislation, the unrealistic 160-acre limitation.[32] Of all the Alaska claimants only the Cunningham group was in a position to take advantage of the new law. Yet they declined out of distaste for the rigid antimonopoly clause.

The act of May 28 was the only coal land bill to pass Congress of four which had been pending during the winter of 1907 and the spring of 1908. The most important of those to fail was the administration's lease bill, sponsored by Knute Nelson of Minnesota. Another measure, applicable only to

[31] Schwartz to Glavis, October 7, 1908, and Schwartz to Dennett, September 23, 1908, *Investigation*, 2, pp. 35, 36, 501.

[32] Quoted from *Congressional Record*, 60 Cong., 1 Sess., 42, p. 6924. *Investigation*, 2, p. 174.

Alaska and drafted in the General Land Office, had also failed to pass. Known as the Cale bill, it had been the reason for Ballinger's shortening of the Alaska investigation by Horace Jones in the summer of 1907.[33]

In the hearings held on the various bills Ballinger and Garfield had differed over the question of lease, though not radically. Garfield went so far as to tell the Senate committee on public lands that "I am by no means so clear in my own mind as to which of those systems [sale or lease] is correct as to say that I would not be perfectly willing to accept either one." Ballinger opposed the leasing of coal lands, Garfield remarked, "on account of the difficulty of enforcing the regulations."[34] Both Ballinger and Garfield approved of reform of the acreage limitation; both desired that any bill applicable only to Alaska should make some provision for implementing the new policy of classification in the territory. Finally, they both hoped that Congress would provide relief for the Alaska coal claimants who had been forced to file under poor laws.[35]

It was partly the pending coal land legislation which was responsible for the Land Office order to Glavis in the spring of 1908 to discontinue temporarily the Alaska coal investigations. Ballinger had resigned before the new legislation was passed and the task of formulating regulations for its administration passed to his successors, Schwartz and Dennett. The main problem, raised long before the act's passage, was a disagreement over the fate of the nine hundred claimants who had previously filed on coal land locations in Alaska. Garfield, Pinchot, and George Woodruff maintained that the old law had been responsible for most of the fraud. Although admitting the "culpability of such evasion," they were willing to interpret the new legislation liberally to erase the last traces of a bad law.[36] A circular of regulations drafted by Woodruff for the

[33] *Ibid.*, 4, pp. 1507, 1508, 1511.   [34] See testimony, *ibid.*, 2, p. 162.

[35] *Ibid.*, p. 635; 5, p. 1517. Garfield to the Committee on Public Lands, Senate, April 15, 1908, Ballinger Papers.

[36] Garfield to Committee on Public Lands, House, April 20, 1908, and G. W. Woodruff to Charles F. Manderson, November 23, 1907, *ibid.*

administration of the act of May 28 interpreted the existing coal locations benignly. Dennett, and especially Schwartz, objected strenuously that the circular would validate the claims of dummies and of entrymen who had illegally agreed to combine their efforts under the old law. The Land Office lawyers were unwilling to allow the new legislation to erase the earlier fraud. Garfield and Woodruff were less concerned with legality than they were with efficiently promoting coal development in Alaska under a system which permitted a degree of federal control. In the end the protest of Schwartz and Dennett resulted in a compromise. A new circular was issued in which dummy entrymen were still to be viewed as illegal, but those whose offense was intent to combine before entry were to be treated liberally.[37] Of the nine hundred Alaska claimants, this new circular opened the door only to the thirty-three Cunningham claimants. Had the Cunningham claimants not shied away from the new law because of the regulatory features they could have gained title to their claims under the Woodruff circular, provided the patents had been issued before the attorney general under Taft had declared the Garfield and Woodruff interpretation to be unwarranted.

Busy as he was with the election year, the erstwhile commissioner of the Land Office did not escape involvement in the affairs of the Alaska claimants. A member of a firm which specialized in land matters and a former chief of the Land Office, Ballinger was immediately sought out by men with business interests snagged by Alaskan conditions. In late March he was visited by one of the Cunningham claimants. "I think," he wrote his successor, Fred Dennett, "that it will be a mistake to continue to hold up the entries in this field against which no reasonable protest exists, and that it would be good policy to speedily clear up the situation."[38] Glavis had not yet forwarded the Cunningham journal to the Land Office.

In June 1908 Clarence Cunningham called on Ballinger. In

[37] *Investigation*, 2, pp. 108, 157, 169–70, 219–21; 5, p. 1601.

[38] *Ibid.*, pp. 1600, 1602; R.A.B. to Frank Mondell, March 30, 1908, Ballinger Papers.

injured tones the coal claimant described the manner in which his journal had been secured by Glavis. Ballinger was not always frank about what happened next. Over a year later he said: "I never appeared in the Cunningham coal land cases. I gave them some casual advice in my office."[39] More accurate was his report to President Taft in September 1909:

> I made, during the summer, a special trip to West Mentor, Ohio, to see Mr. Garfield in respect to this matter, and also spoke to Mr. Dennett about it, my principal contention being that the book that was in dispute was not proper evidence to show conspiracy against the individual entrymen who had no knowledge of the matters noted therein, and for the further reason that the memoranda were made prior to the locations upon which they were seeking patents and upon locations which were attempted to be made under the placer mining laws, which were claimed to have been subsequently abandoned and reentered under the law of April 28, 1904.[40]

None of this was very strong reasoning. Cunningham was quite obviously speaking for the other claimants in his journal. As for the second point that the agreement was made while the claims were located under the mineral laws, Schwartz said when he saw the affidavit, "It is ingenious, but not convincing, although the showing is ex-parte and made after several weeks of very careful consideration by Cunningham and his attorneys. No law warranted the location" of coal land under the general mineral laws. The affidavit drafted by Ballinger attempted to explain away evidence which under the old coal land law was injurious to the group. The lawyer knew the weakness of the argument which he formulated, and his strongest advice to the claimants was to refile under the new law of May 28.[41] This was precisely the course which the Woodruff circular on the new law aimed to promote. Had the claimants followed this course Ballinger's intercession with Garfield would have been more effective.

Shortly after Ballinger's visit Garfield forwarded the affida-

---

[39] R.A.B. to F. F. Randolph, August 26, 1909, *ibid.*

[40] *Investigation*, 2, p. 69. Entire affidavit: *ibid.*, pp. 498–99.

[41] *Ibid.*, p. 70; 3, p. 147.

vit to the Land Office with instructions to Dennett "to go over it carefully and bring to my attention on my return. No action to be taken till I come."[42] An important question which the affidavit raised was ethical. An 1872 statute prohibited a former government officer from "prosecuting any claim against the United States" which had been pending during his employment for at least a period of two years after his employment had ceased. In 1885 Secretary of the Interior L. Q. C. Lamar interpreted the rule as applying to both money claims and land claims. In 1893 Secretary Hoke Smith interpreted it as applying only to money claims and as not extending to "a former employee of the General Land Office who appears before the Land Department on behalf of an applicant for a tract of public land." Garfield was dubious about the Smith ruling and late in 1908 directed Woodruff to determine broadly what departmental policy should be in such cases. Eventually the department attorney general advised that the question "be left as it stands. . . . A new promulgation would hurt only the honest attorneys." In early November Ballinger appeared before the department representing someone in a claim. Assistant Secretary Frank Pierce suggested tactfully that he "have some other counsel sign the brief." Ballinger immediately withdrew from the case.[43]

After March 1909, his assistance to Cunningham the previous summer became a problem for Ballinger. The new secretary of the interior was visited almost immediately by Falcon Joslin of Alaska, representing the American Mining Congress, who argued for quick action on the coal cases. Shortly thereafter former governor Miles Moore announced that he expected consideration now that Ballinger had had "time to become established" in his new position. The secretary's solution was to disqualify himself from acting directly in the Alaska cases because he had been consulted professionally by the Cunningham claimants. Assistant Secretary Frank Pierce assumed responsibility for the coal cases. On March 3 the General Land Office was given an

[42] Garfield Diary, September 15, 1908, Garfield Papers; *Investigation*, 3, p. 145.

[43] *Ibid.*, pp. 307, 311, 312; 7, pp. 3632–34.

appropriation of $1,000,000 for "bringing up to date old work in the field."[44]

The pleas of Joslin and Moore, which had been shunted to Pierce, and the additional funds increased the pressure exerted on Glavis. On March 10 he was ordered by Dennett to submit full reports on the status of the coal land investigations. A week later Glavis was transferred to the Seattle division, which had been closed for lack of funds, in order to bring him closer to the scene of his investigations. Within a month of Dennett's order Glavis forwarded seventy-three reports to the Land Office. As a whole they indicated that few of the cases were completed.

The report on the Cunningham claims in particular raised hackles in the Land Office. That "I am surprised at its general tenor," Schwartz remarked, "is putting it mild." The investigation had originally been delayed, the agent hinted darkly, because of the "political ambitions" of Harry Love. Glavis might have completed the investigation in the spring of 1908, the report continued, "but before sufficient time was allowed to complete this work I was directed to postpone taking further action." Though maintaining that the Cunningham journal "conclusively" proved the claims to be fraudulent, the agent insisted upon a field investigation in Alaska. He closed with an accusation against unnamed officials in the Land Office.

> In the course of investigation heretofore made I was greatly embarrassed in my work . . . [because] many of the claimants appeared to be fully informed as to recommendations previously made by me and concerning the work which I had been directed to perform. It will readily suggest itself no doubt that one is greatly handicapped by being confronted with such a condition, and I respectfully recommend that hereafter due care be taken to prevent the claimants or any one interested from knowing what has been done or is contemplated.[45]

On April 20 an irritated Schwartz ordered Glavis to complete the Alaska coal investigations within sixty days. The protests of Glavis were unavailing. Although beginning to doubt

[44] *Ibid.*, 2, pp. 70, 120, 231, 284, 513.

[45] *Ibid.*, pp. 11, 115, 233, 235, 505–8, 510.

his "ability of ever getting a final report out" of the young agent, Schwartz held firmly to the deadline.[46]

In mid-May Glavis arrived in the capital. Among other things, he was concerned with the loophole the act of May 28, 1908 offered the Cunningham claimants under the Woodruff circular. Without too much difficulty he convinced Schwartz of the need for a clarifying decision, and together they constructed a letter to the attorney general. Edward Finney, who approved of the original decision and looked on the letter as an attempt by Schwartz to reopen a settled question, rerouted the letter to a lawyer in the Department of the Interior, and on May 19 a new decision was signed by Pierce reinforcing the earlier interpretation of Garfield and Woodruff. The act was "curative," said the Pierce decision, "and should be liberally construed." It should not "refuse the privilege of perfecting . . . claims under its liberal provisions solely because of . . . previous arrangement or agreement."[47]

The Pierce decision reiterating the position of the previous administration was not allowed to stand. Beginning on May 20 Miles Moore launched a drive to attain special consideration for the claimants from department officials. Both Pierce and Ballinger repeated what had been said on other occasions: If the charges against the claims were sustained titles could not be granted under the old legislation. Moore refused to consider refiling under the new act. Instead he announced his intention to bring his case before the president. The threat sent Ballinger himself hurrying to Taft. The meeting halted Moore's offensive but reopened the question settled by the Pierce decision.[48] At the end of May Ballinger approached Wickersham with a request that the issue be taken up, when he learned incidentally, that Glavis had already on his own initiative complained of the Pierce decision to the attorney general. Two weeks later in a decision dated June 12 Wickersham overturned the

[46] *Ibid.*, pp. 15, 37, 511–12.

[47] *Ibid.*, pp. 16, 17, 176–77, 180–81, 207–8; 6, pp. 3020, 3032–33.

[48] *Ibid.*, 2, pp. 71–73, 176–77, 181.

Pierce decision and, for that matter, the earlier Woodruff circular. Claimants, Wickersham said, who had not filed in good faith under the old coal land statute could not receive patents under the new law.[49]

The decision of the attorney general on the act of May 28, 1908, bolted fast the last door open to the Cunningham claimants. They had stubbornly resisted the advice of department officials to refile under the new law. After the Wickersham decision, refiling could no longer improve the legality of their claims.

In any case the claimants remained inflexible in their determination to seek title under the old law. Miles Moore and Pierce had fought over this question in mid-May. Moore had found this meeting a "disappointment" because of the procedure outlined by Pierce should the claimants persist in seeking patents under a situation in which the evidence indicated fraud. Moore was told that charges would be served against him. Pierce promised a prompt hearing, but if the claimants decided to forgo a hearing, the claims would be canceled without further ado.[50] Moore's abortive appeal to the president had been a last-ditch effort to avoid this procedure. When the effort was thwarted by Ballinger the claimants anxiously awaited the Wickersham opinion on the act of May 1908. Finally on June 24, they glumly informed Pierce that they wanted a speedy trial, as he had promised in May.[51]

True to his word, Pierce notified the Land Office that the "department" desired early action on the Cunningham group. Ironically, it was understood the claimants had undertaken to stand without hope. Yet every step taken toward an early hearing convinced Glavis that they were receiving favorable treatment. Ordinarily when the government's case was completed, Land Office procedure required that the evidence be sent to the register and receiver in the district where the locations had been filed originally, for a decision "in the first instance," be-

[49] *Ibid.*, pp. 39–40, 244. G. Wickersham to R.A.B., September 3, 1909, Ballinger Papers.

[50] *Investigation*, 2, pp. 176–77.   [51] *Ibid.*, pp. 182–83.

fore being sent to Washington, whence patents were issued. Pierce asked that evidence in the Cunningham case be forwarded to Washington for decision in the first instance, thus bypassing the local land officers in Juneau. Glavis interpreted this as an attempt to skirt the normal procedure in favor of the claimants. In reality Pierce was attempting to protect the case of the government: The register at Juneau had financed his son's interest in a coal claim; and his son was Ignatius Mullin, one of the Cunningham claimants.[52]

Following Pierce's intervention Glavis began to feel considerable pressure to complete his investigation within the sixty-day deadline laid down the previous April. Despite repeated protests he was told to be prepared with his evidence. At the same time Schwartz implied that Glavis might be removed from the case should he fail to meet the deadline. A Denver lawyer named James Sheridan was dispatched to Seattle to "assist Glavis." In mid-July Glavis precipitated his removal from the case. He called on Ballinger in Seattle and complained that he was being forced prematurely into a hearing. When Schwartz learned that the agent had appealed over his head to the secretary, he peremptorily removed Glavis from the Alaska coal cases and gave them to Sheridan.[53]

It was at this point that Glavis decided to appeal to the Forest Service for assistance. Why he made this decision is not entirely clear. He was in close touch with officials in the Washington office, especially Schwartz, and he was well aware of the general feeling in the department that the claims could not be granted patents. The claimants themselves had insured this verdict in failing to refile under the act of 1908 before the Wickersham decision. The actual point of dispute between Glavis and his superiors was in reality something different than whether the Cunningham claims could be patented. Glavis insisted upon a postponement until a field investigation in Alaska confirmed the evidence already accumulated; department officials ruled that the evidence in hand was sufficient to effect the

---

[52] *Ibid.*, p. 183; 4, p. 973.
[53] *Ibid.*, 2, pp. 20, 42, 73, 516, 519, 522, 525; 3, p. 338.

cancellation of the claims. Both positions were correct. Indeed Glavis admitted that enough evidence existed to cancel the claims; but field investigations were necessary before criminal proceedings could be begun against the claimants, and it was the indictment of the Cunningham group which Glavis seemed to be seeking, not the mere cancellation of their claims. In this, if in no other way, he was radically at odds with his superiors, who took the view that faulty legislation rather than deliberate criminality was the root of fraud in Alaska.[54] Glavis' motives were complex, but from the drastic nature of his response when the cases were removed from his control it seems clear he felt he had much at stake in preventing the mere cancellation of the claims with no effort to prosecute the claimants as criminals. How much he was influenced by the land frauds in Oregon and how much his admiration for Heney led him to see in the Cunningham claimants a chance for a career as a great prosecutor and exposer of fraud are things that will probably never be known. What is clear is his determination to stop the early hearing regardless of consequences.

The interest of the Forest Service in the claims was a late development. By presidential proclamation Theodore Roosevelt had increased the size of the Chugach National Forest in Alaska the day before he left office. Cunningham's luck held and four of his claims were swept into the reserve. Under the law the claims still could have gone to patent, but an agreement between the Departments of Agriculture and of the Interior gave the Forest Service a large degree of influence over land claims in the national forests. Foresters were privileged to make their own investigations and to take part in any hearing which might be held. Perhaps the Land Office was overly concerned about increasing the burdens of its sister agency in the Department of Agriculture; in any event the foresters had never been told of the pending hearings on claims in the Chugach National Forest. On July 16 Glavis remedied this over-

[54] *Ibid.*, 2, pp. 18–19. Dennett remarked on one occasion, "I was astonished . . . at the satisfaction evidenced by Glavis in a coldblooded way. . . . I often have to do something which causes loss, but I never yet have had a feeling of gloat over it." *Ibid.*, p. 125.

sight in a telegram to A. C. Shaw, an assistant law officer in the Forest Service.[55]

The purpose of the Seattle chief was to delay a hearing on the Cunningham case. He must have been surprised at the frenzied activity which followed his telegram. Foresters in the Northwest were instructed to give Glavis any assistance he might require. In Washington City Schwartz learned of the new development when Shaw turned up at the Land Office with a frosty request for access to the Cunningham file. Following a brief but acrimonious debate Shaw marched off with the entire file. On July 21 Secretary of Agriculture James Wilson requested that the Cunningham hearing be postponed until a coal expert of the Forest Service had the opportunity to inspect the claims in Alaska.[56] Schwartz and Pierce had no choice but to acquiesce.

On July 19 Fred Dennett arrived in Seattle on a regular inspection of field divisions to find a forester from Portland poring over the Cunningham file; horrified, the commissioner wrote that Glavis was "endeavoring to 'foul the nest.' " An appeal to the Forest Service could be viewed by a Land Office official only as the rankest kind of treachery. "Glavis," a thunderstruck Dennett exploded, "I would think you would be the last man in the world who would try to take jurisdiction from your bureau, knowing the way I have almost sweat blood in the past year and one-half to retain the authority and powers for you boys."[57] This was the anguished cry of an old trooper discovering that a trusted subordinate had opened the gates to the hereditary enemy. The once moribund Land Office had arisen exhilarated by Ballinger's surgery in 1907, and under new leadership had matched the Forest Service blow for blow in a jurisdictional struggle on the public domain. In Dennett's view Glavis had profited from this war in which youth, vigor, and intelligence were valued assets. Understandably, "calling in the Forestry" looked "a little treacherous" to the commissioner.

[55] *Ibid.*, pp. 242–43; 3, pp. 668, 670.

[56] *Ibid.*, p. 670; 2, pp. 185, 186, 242–43.

[57] *Ibid.*, 7, pp. 4346, 4350; 2, pp. 21, 276.

Dennett was shocked to find the young man speaking the jargon of the foe. "He is . . . talking conservation very strongly," Dennett informed Schwartz. "Glavis talking conservation! All round he is ugly and he is preparing to be as unpleasant as he can."[58]

Bureau patriotism was only one consideration to arise from the intervention of the Forest Service. Schwartz and Dennett were equally bemused by the implication that the Land Office was trying to ram through the Cunningham patents. Since the claimants were "trying to come under the old law," Dennett wrote on July 22, "they have elected to stand without any hope, not receiving any compensation [read "consideration"] if the law should be changed." Schwartz agreed, but the chief of field service feared that an "immediate hearing might be used by the forester for political effect." The larger struggle between Ballinger and the Roosevelt men, which had grown in intensity during the summer of 1909, was too obvious to be avoided. Glavis had handed Pinchot a weapon which could conceivably turn the tide of battle. Schwartz had these larger implications in mind when he asked Dennett to have "Ballinger wire me not fix date of hearing or serve charge until Sheridan completes examination." The request of Schwartz only served to deliver Ballinger more tightly trussed to his foes. On July 22 Dennett wired Ballinger as Schwartz had suggested.[59] Dennett, still in Seattle, dictated his correspondence to F. W. Spaulding, an agent in the Seattle office who saw that Glavis was kept informed of developments. An unfortunate phrase, "subject our talk here," in Dennett's telegram to Ballinger left

[58] *Ibid.*, pp. 122, 272, 273, 519. "Conservation" for a Land Office official meant the program of the Forest Service which had threatened Land Office jurisdiction. Until his break over the Cunningham claims, Glavis seems to have accepted this view. In 1908 when Pinchot moved to consolidate administration of the forests in the Forest Service (see pp. 29–30 above) Dennett had blocked the attempt by securing from the field agents statements that the action would be injurious to administration. Glavis had opposed the move on the ground that "forest service officers have no idea of [the] value of evidence and lack diplomacy in securing same. Few understand land laws." *Ibid.*, p. 149.

[59] *Ibid.*, pp. 21, 48, 119, 244; 7, p. 4347.

Glavis with an impression that the secretary, despite his professed unwillingness to interfere in Cunningham's affairs, had
in the background acted on the cases all along. This view was
reinforced by Ballinger's prompt reply to Dennett, which by
all appearances was an order professing not to be an order.

> Considering my personal reluctance to direct proceedings
> in Alaska coal cases, you should make necessary directions to
> Schwartz.[60]

Yet the intervention of the Forest Service had provided the
situation in which a frightened Dennett had transgressed the
instructions of his chief. Within a week of Dennett's arrival
James Sheridan, who had replaced Glavis, recommended in a
lengthy report that the hearings be postponed until a field investigation had been made. Whether or not this was his real
opinion, Sheridan had been in Seattle too short a time to have
mastered the complex cases, and the possibility that Dennett
had apprised him of the seriousness of the situation is not incredible.[61]

Dennett had not been in Seattle long before discovering that
he had reason to be concerned personally, beyond the questions of bureau solidarity and the growing controversy between Ballinger and Pinchot. "Glavis has written me a letter,"
Dennett told Schwartz anxiously, "giving the history of the
coal cases and running throughout with innuendo against me;
I think he has got me convicted of conspiracy in his mind. He
certainly is a wonder; I would not have his mind for all the
money in the world." The commissioner was shaken. "Now
what do you think of this? Is the boy nutty? . . . It puzzles me
to think what sort of kid he is." The "kid" had already decided
about Dennett "that the man was crooked." Long believing
that the Alaska claimants had an inside man in the Land Office
who kept them informed of the progress of the investigation,
Glavis suspected that Ballinger had on occasion leaked im-

[60] *Ibid.*, 2, p. 21.
[61] *Ibid.*, pp. 43, 44, 74.

proper information, but was absolutely convinced by July 1909 that Dennett was guilty.[62]

Shortly before Dennett arrived in Seattle, at about the same time Glavis called in the Forest Service, he also spoke of his suspicions of the commissioner to Francis Heney, the prosecutor of the Oregon graft cases. The lawyer advised Glavis to be "very frank" with Dennett when he arrived "and see what he has to say." Glavis' method of ensnaring his "culprit" had the pure lines usually found only in detective fiction. On July 27 Glavis handed Dennett the letter which the commissioner spoke of so aggrievedly to Schwartz later in the day. Skimming the letter rapidly while the Seattle chief stood accusingly before him, Dennett saw a flat charge that he had been in collusion with fraudulent coal claimants. The commissioner sputtered incoherently and a painful interview terminated in an atmosphere that crackled with acrimony. Whereupon Glavis, and a witness carefully brought along, drew up a synopsis of the "conversation" which noted the suspicious fact that Dennett had sputtered incoherently when presented with serious charges.[63]

Glavis burned his bridges in the confrontation with Dennett. The break was complete. Yet Glavis only grudgingly ceased to think of Schwartz as a friend, although he supposed Schwartz might be "mad with him" for some of his actions.[64] In a letter written as the month of July drew to a close Glavis revealed something of what was in his mind. He undoubtedly believed a great investigation, perhaps comparable to the Oregon frauds, was about to break in which he would function as both accuser and prosecutor. He made a last effort to retain the friendship of Schwartz; indeed he suggested an alliance in which Schwartz would ultimately be rewarded with the commissionership. The letter revealed that Dennett, not Ballinger, was Glavis' chief target at this point. Ballinger might be in trouble,

[62] *Ibid.*, pp. 6, 10, 34, 76, 427–28; 3, p. 304.

[63] *Ibid.*, p. 300; 2, pp. 50–52, 150.

[64] Dennett to Schwartz, July 20, 1909, *ibid.*, p. 273.

the letter hinted, but Dennett was doomed. Within the month this focus would change. Forest Service officials would assist Glavis in drawing up formal charges against his superiors. Ballinger would emerge as the chief offender. Dennett would be moved from protagonist to chorus in the Glavis drama.[65]

[65] *Ibid.*, pp. 78–79, 215. Glavis' grievances against Dennett may have been longstanding. This appears not to have been the case with Ballinger, who as commissioner had had a hand in the advancement of Glavis. When Ballinger retired from the Land Office, Glavis expressed "regret" that he was leaving "just at the time" when he was "about to see the results" of his "labors." Glavis to R.A.B., January 31, 1908, Ballinger Papers. The animus against Ballinger bloomed about the time of Glavis' own break with the Land Office.

CHAPTER FIVE

The Glavis Charges

George Otis Smith was a safe, conservative man who knew his job and took enormous pride in the Geological Survey, in which he served as director. Smith knew that in certain circles neither he nor his bureau were viewed with equanimity these past months, but the director remained unruffled. Times were troubled indeed, but the survey stood as sound as a citadel, untouched by the struggling forces which swirled about its perimeters.

Smith thought of himself as a Garfield man. The former secretary after all had done much for the survey with his new coal policy. The director was gratified to discover that Ballinger too placed great confidence in the agency, although it was distressing that some of the new secretary's policy decisions were in conflict with the former administration. Smith went to some pains to keep a balanced perspective before his old chief. In May the director wrote Garfield deploring "some unjust criticism in certain newspapers of the present administration, at least as regards this matter of the coal lands"; Ballinger was only "pushing still further along the lines marked out by you." Two weeks later Smith carefully explained that the power sites episode had not been intended as in any way a personal reflection upon Garfield.[1] The director's measured calm was no doubt buttressed by the complacent awareness that the Geological Survey was above suspicion.

Of course no individual was above criticism in the deeply

[1] May 15, 1909, *Investigation of the Department of the Interior and the Bureau of Forestry*, Sen. Doc. 719, 61 Cong., 3 Sess., 6, p. 3318; June 2, 1909, *ibid.*, 5, p. 2046; Garfield's reply, *ibid.*, p. 2047.

personal struggle developing in the federal establishment, and Smith was no fool. He knew that his conservatism always had irked the forester, and in the summer of 1909 Smith was aware of the burden of a new charge whispered abroad by Pinchot. On the whole the director remained unperturbed. This kind of knife-work was a game he well understood. But on July 23 his calm was shattered. Pinchot violated the rules of bureau warfare by bringing the new charge into the open. The forester was in a mood of black anger over the demise of his Indian cooperative plan when his path was crossed by the unfortunate Smith. "Just as I was leaving Washington this p.m.," a perplexed director wrote Garfield, "I chanced to call on Mr. Pinchot, and he said things that I can not yet explain." Among other things he referred to Ballinger as a "yellow dog." Pinchot, continued Smith, "charges me with being loyal to the new Secretary of the Interior at the sacrifice of my loyalty to the former; that people generally are looking upon me as forgetting my obligations to you and acting the turncoat and renegade, and that I'm a marked man."[2]

The aggression against Smith was the opening gun in a struggle which began in earnest as the summer waned. The month of July had witnessed the end of the Indian cooperative agreement, mounting tension over the reclamation certificates, and an intensified newspaper campaign to bring pressure upon Ballinger, who was still traveling through the West inspecting reclamation projects. A number of congresses and conventions annually attended by groups and individuals with special interests in public land management were scheduled in August, and the clans rallied to pack the halls in favor of their champions. The Irrigation Congress, which would feature both Pinchot and Ballinger as speakers, was the object of particular attention, and throughout the month of July the air crackled with prophecy and anticipation.

The long awaited congress opened in Spokane on August 10. Pinchot, the first of the antagonists to arise, basked in a five-minute ovation before he began to speak. The congress was his

[2] Smith to Garfield, July 23, 1909, *ibid.*, 6, pp. 3321–25.

from the beginning. A Seattle newspaper reported to its readers that evening that "war between Pinchot and Ballinger . . . is now open." The effect of the speech nonetheless had been strangely flat. The forester never directly attacked Ballinger, and the president was carefully praised for his "earnest and enthusiastic support" of conservation. With tantalizing indirection Pinchot concentrated his assault upon unnamed opponents of conservation who favored strict construction of the law.[3]

Ballinger arose the following day to scattered applause and delivered a moderate address on reclamation in the West. He left Spokane with Newell that same evening to continue the inspection of reclamation projects, but not before the air had been cleared of all doubt which the mildness of the past two days had encouraged. Shortly after Ballinger left the room George C. Pardee, a former governor of California and a close friend of the forester, stalked to the rostrum. Ostentatiously pushing aside a bulky prepared manuscript, Pardee launched a scathing attack on the secretary of the interior. The weight of his assault bore upon the power site restorations and rewithdrawals of the previous spring. Within eight days of Ballinger's restoration of the Garfield withdrawals, Pardee charged, 15,868 acres—all choice power sites—had been filed upon at the land office in Bozeman, Montana. The governor was repeating a story given him by a friendly newsman which appeared in the Spokane newspapers the same day.[4]

Ballinger was informed several days before the congress that the power sites story would break and for that reason had chosen to leave the hall at the close of his speech. Before retreating from Spokane, however, he took what precautionary measures were possible. Following Pardee's attack the secretary asked George Otis Smith to "go on the department watch service. This meant that I was to refute Pardee's misstatements

[3] *The Seattle Times*, August 10, 1909; *The Seattle Star*, August 10, 1909. *The Spokesman Review* (Spokane), August 11, 1909. *Official Proceedings of the Seventeenth National Irrigation Congress held at Spokane, Washington, August 9–14, 1909*, p. 97.

[4] *Ibid.*, pp. 223–24, 229–41; *Washington Times*, August 10, 1909, dateline Spokane.

and stand out in the open opposed to Mr. Pinchot and his associates." It was not the kind of chore the director relished, but
he loyally made the effort. Smith reported that the ferocious
governor "threatened to skin me alive if I spoke against him,"
but the next day the director resolutely marched to the platform with a *Spokesman Review* folded under his arm. "I notice in this morning's Review," he began, "a ninety-nine percent reduction of this acreage [reported by Pardee and the
newspapers the day before] and the June 11th entry becomes
158.68 acres, and this deserves consideration. . . . The water
power entryman who can make these four forties shoestring
six miles of the Missouri River deserves to become an Indiana
politician." This last referred to the fact that most of the choice
land in the disputed area had long been taken up by settlers.
Smith revealed that a telegram dispatched by him to the land
office in Bozeman failed to turn up any filings by Jeremiah
Collins, the individual alleged to have made the entries for the
power monopoly, and that records of waterpower entries made
by anyone during the period when the Garfield sites were restored were conspicuously absent from the land office files in
Bozeman. He contended that even the reduced figure of 158.68
acres was erroneous, and a strong odor of frame-up hovered in
the air as he left the platform.[5]

The redoubtable Pardee arose to announce that "I am informed as credibly as Mr. Smith has been informed to the contrary that certain of those power sites were taken up." He even
implied darkly that the records at Bozeman had been falsified.
On this inconclusive note the congress dragged to a fitful conclusion. "The congress was organized," Smith reported, "the
issues were shaped, the orator chosen, the newspapers primed
—in short all guns loaded," but the power site charge was de-
fective, and the entire attack fizzled.[6] In contrast to Ballinger
the previous spring, Pinchot had been caught with his withdrawals not showing.

[5] C. S. Ucker to R.A.B., August 9, 1909, Ballinger Papers; Smith to Rizer,
August 16, 1909, *Investigation*, 6, p. 3337; *Official Proceedings of the Seventeenth National Irrigation Congress*, pp. 289–90.

[6] *Ibid.*, p. 297. Smith to Rizer, August 16, 1909, *Investigation*, 6, p. 3337.

The forester had warned Smith in July that if there were any criticism of Garfield at Spokane, Pinchot would lead the fight against Ballinger. There had been no criticism of the former secretary; yet blood was drawn nonetheless. On reflection Smith decided that his spanking by Pinchot was "simply an effort to bring Secretary Garfield in as an issue that could influence me." Clearly by July Pinchot had decided that he and Ballinger could not live together. A friend of both men, Charles Lathrop Pack, pleaded with Pinchot to seek some area of understanding with Ballinger after the Spokane fiasco. Pinchot's reply indicated that compromise, if it was ever conceivable, was out of the question by August 1909.

> Naturally, there can be no question of an agreement between us except on the basis of whole hearted support by him of the Conservation policies. . . . I have been forced to believe that Mr. Ballinger is thoroughly out of sympathy with the point of view which you and I hold as to conservation and the Roosevelt policies. Believing that, of course there can be no question of compromise.

George Otis Smith was in complete accord with the forester. "The whole conservation movement," Smith wrote, "is now linked up with Mr. Pinchot's views on the subject, so that orthodoxy in the cause means agreement with Mr. Pinchot."[7]

In the same letter Smith mentioned something which indicated that the Roosevelt men might not write off the congress as a total loss:

> The Alaska story leaked, much to the disgust of Ballinger's enemies. I would give that charge more consideration if I didn't know that there has been a search high and low to get material and that it was being held back to spring at the right moment. I am afraid that the well-meaning conservationists are using the devil's own weapon to fight the "interests."

The Alaska story of course was the Pandora's box opened by Glavis when he asked the Forest Service to intervene in the Cunningham cases. The Seattle chief's first telegram had aroused the interest of Pinchot; he knew Glavis vaguely, and

---

[7] *Ibid.* Also Pack to G.P., August 14, 1909, and G.P. to Pack, August 19, 1909, Gifford Pinchot Papers.

through George Woodruff the forester had heard the rumor that Ballinger had represented the Cunningham claimants, a fact established once Shaw had seen the Land Office files. Yet Pinchot remained aloof and allowed his subordinates to badger the Land Office until the meaning of the coal cases became clearer. Possibly concentrating on the Irrigation Congress and the power site story as the main line of attack on Ballinger, the forester was unprepared for a telegram which Shaw received from Glavis on August 2 announcing his possession of damaging evidence showing the official misconduct of "parties." When Shaw wired for details Glavis replied that the secretary of the interior and the commissioner of the Land Office were the "parties."[8] Pinchot was forced to leave Washington for Spokane the same day without knowing precisely the import of the Glavis telegrams, but undoubtedly the forester sensed that before long the leverage for which he had searched would be within his reach.

On August 6 Garfield scribbled "the latest Ballinger developments" in his diary, "all bad—if the facts as now developed prove true B. has put himself in a very bad position—his resignation may be necessary. They will be out by next Tuesday when the Irrigation Congress at Spokane meets." If the former secretary's note had a faintly sanctimonious ring, that struck by Pinchot in a letter to his mother sounded only jubilant triumph. "It looks to me as though the time is not far distant when B. and I can't both stay in the Taft Administration. And as B. comes in the alphabet before P., and age before beauty, I think there is no reason why we should advertise 1615 [Rhode Island Avenue] for sale yet awhile. I am much pleased with the situation."[9]

In Spokane Pinchot spoke with Glavis on August 9. He had come bearing a letter of introduction from Francis Heney. Both Pinchot and Pardee listened to a story which made their

[8] Smith to Rizer, August 16, 1909, *Investigation*, 6, p. 3337. McGeary, *Gifford Pinchot: Forester-Politician* (Princeton, N.J., 1960), pp. 128–29. O. W. Price and A. C. Shaw to G.P., January 5, 1910, Gifford Pinchot Papers.

[9] G.P. quoted in McGeary, *Gifford Pinchot*, p. 128.

power site exposure seem like child's mischief. The excited Glavis closed with a threat to publish his tale, but Pinchot restrained him. What Glavis had to say was extremely damaging to Ballinger; a confrontation of Taft with the evidence would be more dramatic and, whatever the outcome, more effective. If Glavis won, Ballinger was finished. If Taft repudiated Glavis there would be time enough to think of publication, which then would be even more damaging. Pinchot ordered Shaw by wire to rendezvous with Glavis in Chicago to assist the Land Office agent in preparing a record to present to the president.[10]

Glavis left Spokane that same day. In his pocket were two letters to the president signed by the forester. The first merely introduced the "bearer." "I have known him for several years," Pinchot fudged, "he has just laid before me . . . statements and documents which, in my judgment, should be in your hands with the least possible delay. The issues are large, and can be handled by no one but yourself." The Cunningham coal case, Pinchot said in the second letter, had recently and only narrowly been prevented from going to patent by the watchfulness of the Forest Service. Pinchot warned that various "parts of Glavis's story are so much known that I believe it will be impossible to prevent its becoming public, in part at least, and before very long. Many persons have knowledge of more or less essential parts of it." The second letter closed with an allusion to the power site "exposure" then about to be publicized at the Irrigation Congress.[11]

Glavis and Shaw spent several days in Chicago bringing form to the mass of records on loan from the Seattle land office. In mid-August they proceeded eastward, Glavis to the vacation White House in Beverly, Massachusetts, while Shaw returned to his more routine duties in Washington. Glavis found Taft preparing speeches for the western trip which he hoped would convince the country that the revision of the Payne-Aldrich tariff had been downward. There is no record of the president's

[10] Price and Shaw to G.P., January 5, 1910, Gifford Pinchot Papers. *Investigation*, 3, p. 370; 4, p. 1217.

[11] Both dated August 10, 1909, *ibid.*, 2, pp. 62–63.

thoughts during this meeting, but he listened attentively to Glavis and asked questions principally about waterpower, since the "exposure" at Spokane had recently enjoyed a vogue in the headlines. Glavis was not informed on the subject but he was anxious to be of service. After leaving Taft the agent wired Shaw in Washington asking him to come to Boston with information on power sites. But the young man never saw Taft again, and the material brought by Shaw went unused. Four days after his visit Glavis was informed by telephone that he could return to Seattle. Still hoping to be useful, Glavis stopped in New York to ask George Wickersham for authorization to proceed to Washington to look for additional evidence against Ballinger, but the startled attorney general demurred. The Seattle chief began his long trip westward.[12]

In all, the story which Glavis laid before the president was a fantastic perversion of the record, marked by disingenuous and at times whimsical selection of evidence. Where a fact disputed his case it was suppressed; where it reinforced, it was given excessive prominence. In some (though by no means all) of the allegations against Ballinger, there was an element of questionable judgment. In the distorted image projected by Glavis there was only collusion or condonation of fraud, purblind folly, and deliberate deceit.[13]

Undoubtedly Glavis bore Dennett the greater hostility, but with an instinct for the dramatic and some assistance from Shaw, the Seattle man turned his heaviest artillery on the secretary of the interior. The single most damaging charge against Ballinger was really an implication that he had used his public office to further private ends. The allegation was significant mainly in the context in which it was set. Ballinger numbered many personal friends among the Cunningham group, Glavis charged, and as commissioner of the Land Office had twice rendered them assistance, once in curtailing Jones's investigation

---

[12] *Ibid.*, 3, pp. 314–16. Shaw and Price to G.P., January 5, 1910, Gifford Pinchot Papers. Pringle, *Life and Times of William Howard Taft* (2 vols.; New York and Toronto, 1939), 1, p. 494.

[13] See complete record of Glavis charges in *Investigation*, 2, pp. 4–62.

and again in clearlisting the claims, though warned by Glavis of their doubtful legality and in spite of incriminating evidence in the Land Office files. After retiring as commissioner, Ballinger had served as the claimants' lawyer. As secretary of the interior he had continued to give them assistance, Glavis insisted, first by sidetracking the Land Office letter to the attorney general requesting an opinion on the act of May 1908; and throughout by keeping in "close touch with the cases" he had secretly guided his subordinates in their efforts to help the claimants fraudulently gain title to the coal.[14]

Most damning was the indisputable fact that Ballinger had acted as attorney for the Cunningham claimants. Glavis made no mention of the 1873 statute which defined the conditions of such representation by former government employees, and probably he was unaware of its existence at this time since, in an article later published by *Collier's Weekly*, he gave it great prominence. The allegation was broached to Taft primarily because Glavis thought it explained the bias which Ballinger had later displayed as secretary of the interior. Yet in giving Pierce the responsibility for the cases Ballinger had taken the only step possible, short of refusing the appointment, to offset his prior association with the claimants. The only evidence presented by Glavis that Ballinger had continued to act in the cases was a telegram from Dennett to Ballinger in July indicating that the commissioner had conferred with the secretary of the interior about Glavis' appeal to the Forest Service.[15] As for the allegation that Ballinger was responsible for the Pierce decision, it was a conclusion an already suspicious mind might reach if uninformed of the background within the department concerning the act of May 1908. The affidavit Ballinger penned for Cunningham in the summer of 1908 might have shown bad judgment, but to stress it was to overlook the fact that the attorney had seen no hope for the claimants under the act of 1904. Then and later in the spring of 1909 he had stressed that the group's only chance to gain title to the coal was to refile

[14] Quote by Glavis, *ibid.*, p. 62.
[15] See pp. 103–104.

under the new act, which he hoped, like Garfield and for that matter Pinchot, could be interpreted liberally to permit coal development in Alaska. An old conflict in the department over the act, dating back to the Garfield administration, was responsible for the Pierce decision.

The most disingenuous presentation in the charges related to Ballinger's career as commissioner of the Land Office. The incriminating evidence which Glavis insisted was in the Land Office file at the time the Cunningham claims were clearlisted simply did not exist. The favorable reports by agent Love dating back to 1905, and the fact that the claimants had been allowed to move to entry, made the Cunningham group unique among all the Alaska claimants. This uniqueness makes even more remarkable the absence of unfavorable mention in the Jones reports, which were not characteristically cautious. Glavis appeared in his own presentation as the sole barrier to the claimants gaining title to the coal. Yet the incredible stupidity of his superiors in even notifying him of the clearlisting goes unexplained. The Juneau office had the plats essential to the issue of patents, and a deliberate attempt to rush the clearlisting could have avoided Glavis entirely, at least until the dirty deed was done. The stupidity was compounded in 1908 when Glavis was transferred to Seattle. The Seattle rather than the Portland division would normally have been responsible for Land Office affairs in Alaska, but the office had been closed for lack of funds when Glavis was first given the investigation. Had there been a concerted effort to thwart Glavis' work, his superiors had only to leave him in Portland when the Seattle Office was reopened.

Despite the absence of selective judgment, Glavis' record cannot be lightly labeled dishonest or insincere. Louis Glavis was a driven man in July and August of 1909. A devious pattern, long vaguely suspected and dimly viewed, had rapidly come into sharper focus as the Washington office unrelentingly pushed him toward what he believed honestly to be a premature hearing of the coal cases. Overwrought by the pressure and the implied criticism, and resentful about his removal, Glavis possibly was incapable of selecting and arranging evidence in any way which did not buttress his case, and it may be doubted that he was otherwise encouraged by Pinchot and Shaw. In any event, the record Glavis compiled could have served as a monument to the prosecutor's mind. Like a court advocate he presented his case in the single-minded pursuit of conviction; it was up to the defense to find the weaknesses in the argument, and if they failed, so much the worse for them.

Very shortly after the telegram of August 2 to Shaw, and several days before the Seattle chief contacted Pinchot in Spokane, rumors of the Glavis charges were drifting through the corridors of government buildings in Washington. To Matthew McEniry, the veteran land office chief at Denver who had once marched with Coxey, Harry Schwartz commented on the circulating gossip:

> Glavis has been patted on the back by Pinchot and Shaw, and led astray by the Lincoln Steffens brand of muckrakers; and these things come to him after a schooling of a year or two at Portland, Oregon (where the finger of suspicion is pointed by each man to his neighbor), with the result that he has worked himself into a mental state that I wouldn't have for a fortune.[16]

That modern instrument of torture the muckrake was indeed brandished a few days later. On August 12 Lawler learned that a friendly newsman had warned Schwartz of a sensational story soon to break charging Ballinger with conspiracy in the Cunningham coal cases. As Lawler warned Ballinger of this development, Schwartz had already wired McEniry to "get into scare heads tonight" to forestall "slanderous newspaper attacks about to be made on" Ballinger and Dennett. The Denver papers carried a story that night informing their public that the secretary of the interior and the commissioner of the Land Office had secured evidence "showing unlawful combinations" of hundreds of coal entries in Alaska. The Land Office was "making every effort to secure speedy action on these cases," the Schwartz account read, but "several of the railroad corpora-

[16] August 5, 1909, *Investigation*, 5, p. 2114.

tions owned by eastern capital are making indirect efforts to delay the hearings, hoping that [the] next Congress will pass further remedial legislation or permit greater consolidation." Having connected Glavis and the Forest Service with "eastern capital" Schwartz sat back to await developments.[17] The next day, August 13, the Spokane *Spokesman Review* published the skeleton of the Glavis story, which the wire services broadcast across the land.

Dennett, too, was aware that unwelcome plans for his future were fleeting through the fevered mind of Glavis. The commissioner retired to Atlantic City at the end of his western tour, early in August. "I came on here to rest for a couple of weeks," he explained to Ballinger, "my nerves were not in good shape. I am improving fast, however, and will soon be back at the desk." But following Glavis' visit to Beverly, the commissioner suffered a relapse. He was "gun shy," Schwartz thought. Lawler feared "that perhaps Glavis has something on Dennett, which is why Dennett hasn't told him to fish or cut bait." It seemed to Lawler that Dennett should "call for a showdown on the letter Glavis has written [to Schwartz]." The commissioner worried intensely about his public image, or rather more accurately, he preferred to be without a public image. "I abhor headlines in the papers," he remarked.[18] It was not an enviable state of mind with which to face the future.

Out West the accelerated attack in the press aroused Ballinger's ire in early August. Wickersham was asked to explain the "misrepresentations" to the president, but the attorney general advised against such a course. Wait, he said, until Taft took notice. A few days later Ballinger was reassured of the president's sympathy through the postmaster general, Frank Hitchcock. Within a week the Department of the Interior learned officially of the Glavis charges. Lawler warned Ballinger not to permit his "feelings to be aroused at this time." Schwartz,

---

[17] *Ibid.*, 2, pp. 266, 424–25; Lawler to R.A.B., August 12, 1909, Ballinger Papers.

[18] *Investigation*, 2, pp. 130, 270; 5, p. 2050. Lawler to R.A.B., August 1909, Ballinger Papers.

Dennett, and Pierce were preparing replies, and "it will be time enough to get indignant when the matter is finally settled: The thing to do now is present it as dispassionately as possible." Lawler cautioned Ballinger to remain absolutely silent. In time, he wrote balefully, "indignation will visit its effects upon those who have acted in a manner deserving of censure." Taft forwarded a copy of the Glavis charges to Ballinger for comment on August 22. An accompanying letter was distantly friendly; but the president warned, "In the Glavis report are certain private and confidential letters between Schwartz and Dennett . . . which indicate an impatience with Glavis and rather a leaning toward the granting of the patents." "My dear Gifford" was informed by Taft that the charges had been placed in the hands of the accused and "I now await their comments on the subject."[19]

Pinchot and Ballinger were traveling over the West during the period when the Glavis charges were breaking into the open. The forester was pleased by his reception in western cities. "Really, I seem to be getting to be a person," he wrote his mother; "strength with the people generally seems to grow by leaps and bounds, so I don't think I am the one to walk the floor."[20]

The now celebrated controversy was expected to erupt again at the Trans-Mississippi Congress in Denver, which opened on August 17. Ballinger and Pinchot had been slated to speak; but Ballinger decided not to attend on the plea of Taft for a cooling off period, an inquisitive press reported. Attention shifted to the National Conservation Congress scheduled to convene in Seattle in the latter part of August. Ballinger had drawn up the articles of incorporation which brought this first congress into existence, and since it was held on his home territory he might have been better represented there than at Spokane. Lawler offered to "see if packing conservation Congress cannot be

[19] Taft to G.P., August 22, 1909, Gifford Pinchot Papers. Wickersham to R.A.B., August 11, 1909; Lawler to R.A.B., August 16, 1909; Lawler to R.A.B., August 1909, Ballinger Papers. *Investigation*, 2, pp. 64–65.

[20] Quoted in McGeary, *Gifford Pinchot*, p. 144.

forestalled," but his efforts were evidently too late. The congress was firmly in the control of the Pinchot forces. A resolution commending the Forest Service and the Reclamation Service was resoundingly carried, after a substitute offered by a Ballinger supporter was roughly squashed. A former private secretary of Gifford Pinchot was elected permanent secretary of the organization. But except for this brief show of force the general theme of the congress was harmony. Pinchot's speech was no bombshell and Ballinger remained absent until the last day, reportedly studying an irrigation project 125 miles away. His speech when he finally arrived in Seattle was unremarkable, and Francis Heney, who was substituting for Pardee as the Pinchot champion in the Seattle action, had difficulty finding an opening for attack when he followed the secretary to the rostrum.[21]

Ballinger had had enough. It had been a hard trip. Originally planning to remain in the West and rendezvous with the president when Taft made his scheduled western tour, on August 30 Ballinger abruptly announced in Seattle that "Department affairs have made it necessary for me to change my plans and go at once to Washington." He arrived in the capital on September 3. His mood was black as he emerged from the train, and the swarm of waiting reporters were disappointed with the hasty interview. Yet a phrase hissed through clenched teeth spoke volumes. "Incidentally," the secretary said tensely, "I intend to kill some snakes."[22]

Richard Ballinger returned to Washington an angry man. But to be effective it was a shade too much the anger of the just. "I stand upon my conscious rectitude," he said as the Glavis charges emerged into the open, "and feel that their efforts to injure me will rebound upon them." In Ballinger's personal code, if a man was intelligent, enterprising, thrifty, honest, and practical, success must inevitably crown his efforts. Failure re-

21 *Addresses and Proceedings of the First National Conservation Congress Held at Seattle, August 26–28, 1909* (Seattle, 1909), pp. 199, 200–202. Lawler to R.A.B., August 16, 1909, Ballinger Papers. *Washington Times,* August 28, 1909. Thomas Shipp was the former private secretary.

22 *Columbus Dispatch,* August 30, 1909. *Chicago Record Herald,* September 4, 1909.

sulted from flaws in individual character, but an upright man had nothing to fear. The attack upon his integrity invested that inner tabernacle, the haven of the idols which no man can see toppled without watching his own destruction. Pinchot claimed to be defending conservation and the Roosevelt policies. Ballinger ended by defending his whole life and everything for which it stood. Appalled by the stakes, Ballinger never fully comprehended the nature of the larger struggle between himself and the Roosevelt men. "It is inconceivable to me," he said many months later, "how anyone, in view of my past record, and professional life, together with my administrative course, could find any possible ground for criticism."[23]

In a sense the resolution of the larger struggle was out of the control of Secretary Ballinger. Just as the first hint of grave charges against Ballinger was exposed to the public, the *Springfield Republican* remarked that Pinchot was demanding Roosevelt methods as well as Roosevelt policies. If the forester was to remain serviceable, the newssheet continued, he would have to become reconciled to Taft methods being appropriate to a Taft administration.[24] Yet this missed the point by a wide margin. Means and ends were too closely identified in the mind of Pinchot to admit of any fine distinction.

The public attack upon the secretary of the interior became more intense after the Glavis charges were presented to Taft. The Forest Service openly supplied the press with information reflecting upon the chief of another department. In reply to a request for information from Lyman Abbott, Overton Price, the acting forester in the absence of Pinchot, outlined the nature of the case against the Department of the Interior as it had been administered under Ballinger. The legal question, Price said, was whether it was best to "act only where there is specific affirmative provision of law or to act in the people's interest where specific affirmative provision is lacking, but where the spirit of existing laws justifies the action proposed." The broader question, Price said, was whether the secretary of the

[23] R.A.B. to Ormsby McHarg, August 25, 1909; R.A.B. to W. H. Cowles, December 9, 1909, Ballinger Papers.

[24] August 14, 1909.

interior had corruptly administered his trust. Even before Glavis left Boston to return to Seattle, Price had given the newspapers in the Washington area a complete copy of the Glavis charges. Much of this activity was known immediately to officers in the Department of the Interior and found its way to Taft. Many of the documents in the Cunningham file, borrowed by Shaw after the first telegram from Glavis in mid-July, were missing when the file was returned to the Land Office. Periodically, they appeared in the press of the capital. The *Washington Post*, friendly to Taft, notified the Land Office when it received the copy of the Glavis charges from Price. The activity of the Forest Service had "every appearance of conspiracy itself," Dennett breathed indignantly.[25]

The conspiratorial atmosphere was heightened by the long delay of the president's findings on the charges. All of the Department of the Interior officials involved had forwarded their replies to the charges to Taft by early September. The record submitted by Schwartz was by far the most complete and finest presentation. The chief of the field service had the least at stake. Glavis "necessarily involved me—or rather certain other government officials, who prepared his statement for him involved me," Schwartz wrote to McEniry, adding that "Glavis, of course, had no such intention." Working late one evening to complete his report, Schwartz was visited by a gentleman he presumed to be an agent of Overton Price. "I was over to the Forest Bureau and had a talk with Mr. Price," the intermediary remarked blandly. Supposedly Price had uttered the encouraging opinion that Schwartz was "all right." "Why don't you see Price?" the nocturnal visitor asked, "I believe he would talk with you." This information also the diligent chief passed on to the president.[26]

[25] *Investigation*, 2, pp. 110–11; and Price to Abbott, September 3, 1909, *ibid.*, 7, p. 3759. Abbott was editor of *The Outlook*. Shaw and Price to G.P., January 5, 1910, Gifford Pinchot Papers. Schwartz to R.A.B., November 22, 1909; Lawler to R.A.B., August 16, 1909; W. E. Clark to R.A.B., September 11, 1909, Ballinger Papers.

[26] Schwartz to McEniry, September 6, 1909, *Investigation*, 5, p. 2116; 2, p. 267.

On September 3 Glavis forwarded to Taft additional evidence relevant to the case against Ballinger: a letter from Cunningham to the Juneau land office dated January 15, 1908, which contained the most damaging single paragraph unearthed in the Cunningham imbroglio. "The commissioner [Ballinger] has furnished us with copies of all the correspondence and telegrams relating to our entries between the various special agents, and also with your office," Cunningham had written. "Up to date everything seems to be approved by each special and department chief. So, now, our only delay will be occasioned through failure to receive plats, according to Judge Ballinger's advice." The letter was written at the time of the clearlisting episode and before the claimants were aware that Glavis would halt the action. Of the claimants only Moore had seen Ballinger during the period in question. Moore was queried by Schwartz after the incriminating letter was exposed by Glavis. The former governor replied "no copies of correspondence furnished me." Yet the letter written by Cunningham was the most difficult accusation imaginable to refute. Its damning words packed more drama than could ever be mustered in an endless string of denials by Moore, who after all could hardly have responded otherwise. "Cunningham may have been attempting to unduly impress . . . [the Juneau] officers" to speed up the forwarding of the plats, Ballinger remarked. Indignantly, Schwartz commented, "Notwithstanding the fact that the varying and different affidavits taken by Mr. Glavis from Cunningham demonstrate that Cunningham is a versatile and willing liar, ready to resort to anything to accomplish the patenting of these claims, Mr. Glavis, without examination as to the probabilities of the matter, accepted as true Cunningham's statement to the registrar and receiver."[27] Unfortunately, the "probabilities of the matter" were weak defenses in the combat arena.

A new champion entered the lists for Ballinger at the end of

[27] *Ibid.*, p. 97; Schwartz to S. J. Colter, October 1909, *ibid.*, 7, p. 3808; Schwartz to Moore, September 10, 1909, and "Memorandum" by D. C. Carr, September 18, 1909, Ballinger Papers. Cunningham did not answer a similar inquiry.

August. Ormsby McHarg had worked with Ballinger in the Northwest during the presidential campaign and had been rewarded with the post of assistant secretary in the Department of Commerce and Labor. McHarg was no admirer of conservation, which he described as "this tendency to place the American people in a condition of tutelage," or of conservationists, "the self-imposed guardians of the Pinchot order, born with millions at their disposal, who have never fought one of the serious battles of life singlehanded." Like Ballinger a self-made lawyer, McHarg learned his creed on a farm in the Northwest where "we used to say that we were so independent during those dry years that we only paid ourselves when we felt like it." Ballinger he loved "as I love my brother," and the Glavis charges and the publicity activity of the Forest Service in August were more than McHarg could stand.[28] The agitation in his sturdy chest burst its bounds during a press conference on August 27. When McHarg ceased speaking he stood in the midst of a rubble which a few moments before had been his public career.

If it did nothing else, McHarg's interview made it difficult to distinguish between friends and enemies as potential menaces to the well-being of Richard Ballinger. McHarg delivered himself of some trenchant remarks on the Forest and Reclamation services. Throughout both agencies, he claimed, visionary theories had replaced common sense in western development. The waterpower trust he described as nonexistent, the Reclamation Service as a financial and engineering failure, and the notion of regulated tree cutting as absurd. Theodore Roosevelt, McHarg was reported as saying, "undertook a task that only the Lord could carry through," adding that "perhaps Roosevelt thought he was the Lord; he acted that way for many years around this place." The following day Overton Price took up McHarg's challenge, and disputed him in every detail.

[28] McHarg to John Marshall, September 20, 1909, W. H. Taft Papers, Presidential series 2. McHarg to Charles Nagel, August 31, 1909, Ballinger Papers.

The slur on the former president, Price said, was deplorable.[29]

On August 30 McHarg resigned undaunted, unashamed, and without apology. The episode was damaging to the administration. Those who suspected that the Roosevelt policies were endangered were confirmed in their views, and the deeply demoralized condition of the executive establishment had been exposed for all the world. The entire episode left Taft more determined than ever to restore the shattered morale of his administration.[30]

Taft's thoughts in the weeks following the Glavis charges were a subject of conjecture. He was reportedly studying the case thoroughly. On September 6 Ballinger delivered a bulky portfolio of documents to the president in Beverly, where they engaged in extended discussions on the golf links safe from prying ears. Both sides were claiming the president's support, but Archie Butt, Taft's military aide, was sure the president would stand by his cabinet officer and "let the reformer go."[31]

"Today Taft's letter sustaining Ballinger appeared," Garfield wrote in mid-September, "something curious behind all this." In a long letter written for publication, Taft completely exonerated Ballinger of all charges alleged in the Glavis report, which the President described as embracing only "shreds of suspicions without any substantial evidence to sustain his attack." In addition, running down the list of policy reversals effected by Ballinger from the power site episode through the prohibition of reclamation certificates, the president asserted his agreement with each change. Privately Taft warned the secretary of the interior that "I have studiously refrained from mentioning Pinchot's name in the matter" and cautioned against involving the forester in any way.

29 *Oakland Inquirer*, August 31, 1909; *Chicago Examiner*, September 1, 1909; *The Washington Post*, August 28, 1909, August 29, 1909.

30 *New York Evening Post*, August 30, 1909; *The Fresno Republican*, August 30, 1909; *The New York Sun*, August 31, 1909.

31 Butt, *Taft and Roosevelt: The Intimate Letters of Archie Butt* (2 vols.; Garden City, N.Y., 1930), 1, pp. 193–94.

> Should it be necessary, as is not unlikely, to submit all this record and evidence to Congress, I shall be glad to have your authority and that of your subordinates to leave out of your answers any references to Pinchot or the part he took in bringing Glavis's report to my attention.[32]

A letter to Pinchot on the same day was conciliatory. "I never reached a conclusion based on a stronger conviction than this one is," the president said, and urged Pinchot not to identify his cause with that of Glavis. "I should consider it one of the greatest losses that my administration could sustain if you were to leave it," Taft said. Indirectly, he broached the question of administration morale and the undercurrent of warfare between the bureaus and departments. "I was especially distressed by McHarg's reported interviews," the president said. "He was an efficient officer, but he talked too much and wildly, and his withdrawal relieved me. I must bring public discussion between departments and bureaus to an end. . . . I want you to help me in this."[33]

Taft set out on a long western trip the day following his letter exonerating Ballinger. The president met Pinchot in Salt Lake City on September 25 and made a further effort to pacify his turbulent subordinate. During an hour-long conversation the forester jotted down detailed notes which described precisely the dilemma of Roosevelt's successor.

> Said he wanted my advice on conservation matters.
> Said he was sure Ballinger would be found most careful not to do anything to hamper the Forest Service but would bring such questions to him. Repeatedly said he was sure it would work out all right.
> He said that he must have unity of action in his administration. That if he did not get it he must take necessary action. I said I fully understood that and yet it might be necessary to fight.
> I said I was not going to resign. He said he was greatly relieved, and said it with emphasis.

[32] Garfield Diary, September 16, 1909, Garfield Papers; Taft to R.A.B., September 13, 1909, *Investigation*, 4, pp. 1187–89; Taft to R.A.B., September 13, 1909, W. H. Taft Papers, Presidential series 3.

[33] Taft to G.P., September 13, 1909, Gifford Pinchot Papers.

I said I might find it necessary to attack Ballinger because I was afraid of what he would do. I used the simile of the wolf guarding the sheep.

Taft said he was going to study the whole conservation problem. He said it was most confused and uncertain, meaning the legal side of it. I begged him to study not only the legal side but the whole problem—what we need as well as what we have. The most emphatic thing he said was—he must have unity of action in his administration.

Thought our press bureau was responsible for the fuss about this fight. I told him we gave out nothing whatever but information on forestry and nothing controversial ever.

. . . Said he wanted to get this waterpower matter "settled one way or the other" by Congress. I said I wanted it settled one way only.

.   .   .   .

I said I did not believe he realized the importance of the stake. He insisted he did (water power matter) but that I exaggerated it. . . .

Throughout Taft looked at the whole question from the legal standpoint. Said I wanted to have him set aside the will of Congress and make law. I said I had never done anything I did not have direct law or the opinion of the Attorney General for, because I realized we should have a Congressional investigation some day.

.   .   .   .

I explained fully that I have no confidence in Ballinger. He said my zeal was so great I tended to think any man who differed as to method was corrupt. I denied it and said I had not accused Ballinger of being corrupt.

I said I would not make trouble if I could avoid it, but might be forced to, and he might be forced to fire me.[34]

Despite the tension of the interview, the following day Taft and Pinchot issued concurring statements to the press presenting a united front of agreement. Taft's statement indicated his eagerness to have Pinchot remain in office. (At first Taft had wanted the forester to make a simple statement that he intended to remain in office, but Pinchot insisted upon something stronger to counteract the impression that he had been rebuked by the exoneration of Ballinger.) Pinchot was author-

[34] "Notes of a talk with President Taft, September 24, 1909, at Knutsford Hotel, Salt Lake City, 11:40 to 12:50 a.m. about," *ibid.*

ized by Taft to publish the laudatory statements in the president's letter of September 13 and to reaffirm strongly Pinchot's own commitment to "conservation within the law." The forester departed with permission to answer at his leisure the president's letter, "stating the facts about the Ballinger matter." Taft thought it a "good plan to have it all in writing now."[35]

As Pinchot took his leave of the president, Lawler was referring to the Glavis charges as the "late unpleasantness." But a harrowing two days had taught Taft otherwise. On the evening of the second day he wired his wife: "I don't know how long I shall be able to get on with him." Writing to Walter L. Fisher at the same time Taft remarked that he had talked with the forester, who "contemplates answering my letter. . . . I do not object to this because I think the matter may just as well be thrashed out between us *dum fervet opus*, and then, if at any time, he wishes to retire, he can have the record of his position to publish, as I shall hope to have mine. I hope it will not come to this however."[36] Taft must have known that Fisher would show this letter to Pinchot.

Glavis of course was dismissed from government service on September 16, an action delayed only by the president's letter exonerating Ballinger. Four days later the president was politely informed by Glavis of his intention to publish the charges. In early October Glavis offered his services to the president in the approaching Cunningham hearings, but Taft replied that "the circumstances under which you were dismissed . . . preclude your employment again for any purpose." Meanwhile, the Forest Service lent its considerable literary talents to the article which Glavis was constructing.[37]

[35] "Account of Interview on train to Saltair, September 25, 1909, Written on September 27, Interview with President Taft," *ibid.*

[36] Lawler to R.A.B., September 25, 1909, Ballinger Papers. Taft to Fisher, September 25, 1909, Gifford Pinchot Papers; quoted in Pringle, *Life and Times of William Howard Taft*, 1, p. 506.

[37] R.A.B. to Dennett, August 26, 1909; Glavis to Taft, October 1, 1909; Taft to Glavis, October 11, 1909, Ballinger Papers; R.A.B. to Glavis, September 16, 1909, *Investigation*, 4, p. 887; Glavis to Taft, September 20, 1909, *ibid.*, p. 888; 8, p. 4576 and *passim*.

Glavis chose *Collier's Weekly* to bring his charges before the public. It was a singularly apt choice. The magazine had reached the peak of its influence in 1909 under the vigorous editorship of Norman Hapgood. It was prepared to begin an attack on the secretary of the interior. In August Hapgood had published an editorial under the provocative title, "Ballinger Should Go," developing the theme "Don't mix up Ballinger and the President." The editor offered three thousand dollars for the story, but Glavis refused remuneration. The article appeared in the November 13 edition. The cover posed the question, "Are the Guggenheims in Charge of the Department of the Interior?" In the crook of a huge question mark the head of Richard Ballinger seemed to blink owlishly at the reader. A sinister black hand hovered menacingly in the background, tensed to tear the riches from the bowels of an unsullied, snow-capped mountain range in faraway Alaska. Between the covers the information was identical to that presented to Taft earlier, though organized under the title, "The Whitewashing of Ballinger," and broken down under such intriguing captions as "The President Whitewashes Ballinger," and "Ballinger Pushes Trial When Government Is Not Ready." Yet Glavis avoided carefully any direct charge of criminality.[38]

The article in *Collier's Weekly* unleashed the pack. In the ensuing months the hapless secretary of the interior was flayed in magazine after magazine. The *Engineering News*, well supplied with information by A. P. Davis, began a steady drumlike tattoo on policy changes in federal reclamation. In an article entitled "Billions of Treasure," by John E. Lathrop and George K. Turner, *McClure's Magazine* greatly augmented the millions of dollars Glavis had said was at stake. *Van Norden's* insisted that Ballinger was in league with Postmaster General Hitchcock to wreck "the whole conservation program." In

[38] "Obituary for Peter Fenelon Collier," *The Outlook*, May 8, 1909, p. 56. *Collier's Weekly*, August 28, 1909, p. 7. The Glavis article, *ibid.*, November 13, 1909, pp. 15–17, 27. The magazine and not Glavis chose the damning subtitles, though of course they suited the organization and tone of the article. See Norman Hapgood, *The Changing Years* (New York, 1930), p. 182.

"The Pinchot-Ballinger Controversy," John L. Mathews argued in *Hampton's Magazine* that Ballinger was the tool of the power monopoly, the railroads, "the Guggenheims and their friends," "the land grabbers, the water grabbers, the coal land grabbers," and the special interests.[39]

Literary "apostles of vomit," Ballinger called them, "scoundrels," and "assassins of character"; but the presses rolled on and eventually covered him with a blanket of abuse. *Collier's Weekly*, in particular, adopted the role of nemesis. "The representatives of Collier's Weekly have been trailing me throughout the United States wherever I have been from my early youth, endeavoring to find some thing with which to besmirch my character," Ballinger complained. Learning that reporters were snooping around New Decatur, Alabama, he defied "them to put their finger on anything in my past history that is worthy of criticism and reflecting on my reputation." Two weeks later *Collier's* article charged that Ballinger had enticed the good people of New Decatur to invest in the Southern Horse Nail Company in the 1880's, and when the company had gone bankrupt through his fraudulent management had hastily left town, only to reappear later in Seattle as a respected pillar. The story was somewhat distorted since Ballinger over the years had repaid several hundred dollars, as a moral rather than a legal obligation, to friends whom he had induced to invest in the bankrupt company. "Ballinger-Shyster" was the result of a brief visit to Seattle during which C. P. Connolly became convinced that "Ballinger is a high-toned crook," chiefly by interviewing everyone in the area who bore the secretary a grudge.[40]

[39] A. P. Davis to Charles Whiting Baker, October 2, 1909, Gifford Pinchot Papers. Baker was editor of *Engineering News. McClure's Magazine*, January 1910, pp. 339–54. *Van Norden's*, October 1909, clipping in Ballinger Papers. *Hampton's Magazine*, November 1909, pp. 659–74, quoted on p. 674.

[40] R.A.B. to Osceola Kyle, February 14, 1910; R.A.B. to C. C. Harris, February 15, 1910; Christopher Harris to R.A.B., February 19, 1910, Ballinger Papers; press release, November 20, 1909, Gifford Pinchot Papers. "Some Lighter Aspects of Ballinger," *Collier's Weekly*, March 5, 1910, pp. 22–23; and *ibid.*, April 2, 1910, pp. 16–17; C. P. Connolly to Norman Hapgood, January 21, 1910, copy in Amos Pinchot Papers.

The surface of the federal establishment seemed to become more placid as the public outcry grew in intensity. Ballinger urged his subordinates to use "extraordinary caution," although he might as well have asked them to saddle a tornado. Schwartz considered leaving government service. Dennett was certain that once the Glavis charges were published a congressional investigation was inevitable, and that it would be "utterly impossible to keep Mr. Pinchot out." In November Taft tried to use his own substantial weight to hold down the lid. An executive order forbade any government official either to volunteer information to Congress or to respond to a request from Congress without specific authorization from the head of his department. A Washington newsman reported that the president had "told Ballinger and all hands to keep their mouths shut. The entire cabinet . . . is bitter against Pinchot." The forester ordered his district officers to keep their hands off the Cunningham claims in all the service's publicity activity. Informing Taft of this action, Pinchot regretted "that certain zealous efforts by the Forest Service to protect the public interest were construed as attacks."[41]

At the close of the meeting in Salt Lake City the president had agreed that the forester should write a letter commenting in detail upon the exoneration of Ballinger. Resignedly Taft admitted that the different positions should be out in the open while memories were still fresh. By November the postponed letter had become an important strategic factor in the continued war upon the secretary of the interior. The overall strategy involved plugging any and all loopholes through which the Forest Service could be attacked, keeping congressmen who were friendly to irrigation and forestry alerted and in general continuing to work through those prominent people interested in conservation who might have influence.[42] Finally, Garfield

[41] R.A.B. to Dennett, October 2, 1909; Dennett to R.A.B., October 11, 1909, Ballinger Papers; "Executive Order no. 1142," November 26, 1909; G.P. to Taft, November 26, 1909, and reply of president, November 27, 1909, Gifford Pinchot Papers; Ashmun Brown to Erastus Brainerd, November 17, 1909, University of Washington Library, Erastus Brainerd Papers.

[42] Garfield to G.P., October 4, 1909; G.P. to Garfield, October 4, 1909, Gifford Pinchot Papers.

collaborated with Pinchot to answer the president's letter of September 13 exonerating Ballinger. In early November each man wrote separately to the president.

Pinchot was respectful. His purpose, he said, was to describe "the facts as I understand them," while recognizing that without Taft's permission to write "this letter would have been a serious official impropriety." The president's own support of the Roosevelt policies, Pinchot said, "I understand and accept," and his criticisms were directed wholly toward "Secretary Ballinger's unfriendly attitude toward conservation." The six pages which followed summarized the conflict over administrative sites on the forest reserves, the waterpower episode, the abrogation of the Indian cooperative agreement, and the attack upon the Reclamation Service. In discussing the Cunningham imbroglio, the forester carefully avoided mention of Ballinger, concentrating instead upon the lack of cooperation rendered the Forest Service by the Land Office and upon the Pierce decision. In all, the letter was a bill of particulars emphasizing the policy changes which had deeply involved the Forest Service.[43]

Garfield's letter also took the form of a bill of particulars. Differences of interpretation he dismissed as irrelevant. "Claims that I acted illegally will be found to rest upon a fundamental difference in policy between Secretary Ballinger's administration and mine." "It is to facts that I call attention, believing that you were misinformed about some of the matters dealt with in your letter" of September 13 exonerating Ballinger. Taft had said that at the time the Garfield sites were considered Ballinger "advised me that it was possible to procure from the Geological Survey an accurate statement of the water-power sites which were available," in order to continue to protect the sites Garfield had withdrawn under the Reclamation Act. The former secretary of the interior had a different recollection. Ballinger "directed the Geological Survey to make the examinations and prepare the list," Garfield explained, "not because the Survey had any more accurate information, but merely be-

[43] G.P. to Taft, November 4, 1909, Ballinger Papers.

cause it controlled a more available appropriation for field examinations."[44]

Taft sent both letters to Ballinger for comment. The secretary replied that he was convinced "since reading these letters that the real animus against me lies in the fact that I have had to treat so many of my predecessor's acts as unsupported by law." Much of the letter which followed reflected those fundamental differences between Ballinger and his predecessor which Garfield had insisted upon. But on two occasions the secretary slipped into evasion and untruth. "The statement that the Reclamation Service had lost the support of the Secretary," he said, "is without foundation." Whereas, as Taft was well aware, Newell's tenure was precarious to say the least. Finally, Ballinger insisted that he had always intended to have the Geological Survey rewithdraw the sites which Garfield had withdrawn through the Reclamation Service. In his final reply to Garfield, Taft adopted this interpretation entirely. To the forester, addressed coolly as "My dear Mr. Pinchot" instead of the usual "Gifford," Taft stated that his confidence in Secretary Ballinger's good faith "had not been shaken in the slightest" and closed the subject on a note of finality.[45]

From the first appearance of the Glavis charges Taft undoubtedly expected a congressional investigation to result. This expectation makes it difficult to understand the lack of frankness displayed by Ballinger and Taft toward the reversals made in the policy of the previous administration. But the Glavis charges and subsequent events changed the nature of the Ballinger-Pinchot controversy. It began as an internal struggle between Roosevelt men over issues which had arisen during the Roosevelt administration. Many policy changes had originated after a struggle within the government, which had left a minority dissatisfied with the changes, but still able to consider themselves Roosevelt men. A new administration was the oc-

[44] Garfield to Taft, November 6, 1909, *ibid.* Taft to R.A.B., September 13, 1909, *Investigation*, 4, pp. 1187–89.

[45] R.A.B. to Taft, November 15, 1909; Taft to Garfield, November 24, 1909; Taft to G.P., November 24, 1909, Ballinger Papers.

casion for change, but the issues debated had originated under Roosevelt. The ensuing controversy had taken the form of a charge that the Roosevelt policies were not being continued, but differences for the most part had been confined within the government. The Glavis charges and the personal attack upon Ballinger had opened the controversy to public inspection. The burden placed upon Taft to defend Ballinger upon specific policy changes forced the president to take a stand upon issues over which he and Roosevelt had always differed. Disagreement under the shelter of a Roosevelt administration was one thing; but with Taft in the White House, it meant coming dangerously close to an open repudiation of the former administration. Such a rupture was doubly distasteful to Taft. Politically it was suicidal. Personally it endangered a cherished friendship.

Taft's dilemma was aggravated by the wilful personality of Gifford Pinchot. The forester used his vendetta with Ballinger mercilessly to force a positive commitment, not alone to Roosevelt ends, which the president had always too comfortably espoused, but also to methods and specific policy. In November 1909 Pinchot still was well satisfied with his strategy. Vindication seemed complete with the appearance of Ballinger's first annual report, which Garfield was convinced would have been different had Pinchot not intervened the previous summer. The forester remarked smugly that the report represented "the goodness of a bad boy recently spanked."[46] A closer examination, however, would have revealed that the secretary had not receded in any fundamental way from his position on public domain waterpower policy.

When Pinchot began (in Taft's words) "defying the lightning and the storm and championing the cause of the oppressed and downtrodden," he spoke for a faction which had been turned out of the seats of power by a former minority. During the spring and summer when the issues were primarily those of changes in policy he looked to men who had been closely

---

[46] G.P. to George Pardee, November 24, 1909; Garfield to G.P., December 4, 1909; G.P. to Garfield, December 4, 1909, Gifford Pinchot Papers.

associated with Roosevelt for support. When attention was focused upon Ballinger's integrity and the president was forced to defend in detail the actions of his cabinet officer, Pinchot was supported increasingly by the insurgent wing of the Republican party, many of whom, like La Follette, Roosevelt while president had looked upon as extremists. The early counsellors of the forester began to fall away from his side. Next to Amos Pinchot and Garfield, probably Henry L. Stimson was Pinchot's closest confidant prior to December 1909. Through the fall of 1909 acting as a check on the impetuosity of his friend, Stimson later told Roosevelt that Pinchot was wrong in "his belief that Ballinger was a crook." Prior to December the Pinchot brothers counted upon the support of Senator Elihu Root, formerly a cabinet officer under Roosevelt. After the turn of the year Stimson, who would seek election to the governorship of New York in 1910, began gradually to withdraw from an active role in Pinchot's affairs. Root, who could not countenance an attack upon the president and the party which could only benefit Democrats, found himself in active opposition to Pinchot. Prominent on the executive committee of the National Conservation Association, founded by Pinchot and Garfield the previous summer to counteract Ballinger, were Henry Stimson, Charles Pack, and Walter Fisher. Stimson and Fisher would later accept cabinet appointments under Taft. Concerned by the increasingly personal turn the controversy had taken, Pack worked tirelessly to effect a reconciliation between Pinchot and Ballinger which would enable both men to continue to function effectively in government service.[47] In March 1909 the controversy centered upon indi-

[47] Pringle, *The Life and Times of William Howard Taft*, 1, p. 506. McGeary, *Gifford Pinchot*, p. 169. A.P. to G.P., November 27, 1909; Pack to G.P., August 14, 1909, Gifford Pinchot Papers. Pack to John F. Bass, January 24, 1910, Ballinger Papers. Philip C. Jessup, *Elihu Root* (2 vols.; New York, 1938), 2, pp. 158–62, discusses the difficult problem the controversy posed for Root, who was a valued adviser and friend of both Roosevelt and Taft. Root saw the affair as a threat to party unity. Richard W. Leopold, *Elihu Root and the Conservative Tradition* (Boston, Mass., 1954), pp. 79–81, although less accurate in some details of the controversy, adopted Jessup's evaluation of Root's role.

viduals whose divisions had originated within the previous administration. By the end of the year the struggle had been transformed, and the lines of division had shifted to delineate party and faction. A controversy over conservation was well on the way to assuming broad political implications which had nothing whatsoever to do with natural resources.

As the year closed Pinchot wrote to Roosevelt in Khartoum, Africa. The letter was symptomatic of the shift which had occurred in the controversy. Sorrowfully the forester informed "Dear Theodore" that the "tendency of the Administration thus far . . . has been directly away from the Roosevelt policies." In an elaborate indictment of Taft, Pinchot claimed a "complete abandonment" of righteousness and virtue by the president, not because of "bad faith" but because of a "most surprising weakness and indecision." Pinchot had discarded an important tactic. No longer would Ballinger be used in an attempt to force the president to come out sharply for the old methods of administration. The president had defended Ballinger's reversal of specific policies, his commitment to the changes being too deeply etched to be erased. Writing only a few days before his final break with Taft, Pinchot was obviously intent upon justifying an action which, without proper knowledge of the background, might be considered rash. The following evening, writing in his diary after a White House reception, he noted, "Taft spoke to me pleasantly. Wished me a happy New Year, and I him."[48]

[48] G.P. to T.R., December 31, 1909, Gifford Pinchot Papers. McGeary, *Gifford Pinchot*, p. 157.

~~~~~~

CHAPTER SIX

The Congressional Investigation

The *Outlook* had imparted comforting news to its readers in August 1909. "Is Mr. Taft's Administration continuing what are known as Roosevelt Policies?" the magazine had asked. "The question may be answered, we think, with a decisive affirmative." Yet the administration had been torn by controversy almost from the beginning. Taft had promised downward revision of the tariff during the presidential campaign, and a group of midwestern congressmen and senators assembled in Washington in the spring expecting his support. Though finally passed, the Payne-Aldrich tariff was scarcely a downward revision, but it belonged peculiarly to Taft, who was committed to its support. The *Outlook* was pleased with the corporation tax, but the group of congressmen rapidly becoming known as "insurgents" pointed accusingly at Taft's alliance with the ultraconservative senator from Rhode Island, Nelson Aldrich, and the tyrannical House speaker, Joseph Cannon of Illinois. A postal-savings bank measure was passed in June. A pet project of Taft, it had been condemned by the American Bankers Association and as vigorously opposed by the insurgents. The party rift was wide by August 1909, when Speaker Cannon stripped the insurgents of their chairmanships on the permanent committees, supposedly in retaliation against thinly veiled criticism of the administration. When Congress reassembled in the winter a band of very disgruntled congressmen in the House was determined to break the stranglehold of Joseph Cannon.[1]

[1] *The Outlook*, August 21, 1909, pp. 919–21. For background see George Mowry, *Theodore Roosevelt and the Progressive Movement* (New York,

Because of the projected attack on Cannon, the Ballinger-Pinchot controversy became the cause of insurgency. The speaker was a near-dictator in the House because he appointed and controlled the powerful Rules Committee, the graveyard of all legislation meeting with his disapproval. In mid-December Representative Gilbert Hitchcock of Nebraska announced to the House that his resolution calling for a congressional inquiry into Ballinger's affairs was before the rules committee. Even if 90 per cent of the House approved, Hitchcock pointed out, the resolution could not emerge without the speaker's consent.[2]

To Hitchcock and the insurgents the resolution was the first move in a parliamentary chess game, but to Taft it meant the long expected ax had fallen. The following day he suggested that Ballinger write a letter to the Senate committee on public lands requesting an investigation which "cannot be made too broad." Instead the secretary wrote to Wesley Jones, senator from the state of Washington, to "court the widest and fullest inquiry by Congress" but insisting that no investigation would be complete which did not "embrace the Forest Service" and "the pernicious activity of its officers."[3] The lid was off again.

Protection of the Forest Service was an important consideration with Pinchot to the end. The threatened attack upon the agency's major weakness, its close association with Glavis, galvanized the forester into action. On the theory that facts were best revealed by the service before they were exposed by an enemy, Pinchot ordered Price and Shaw to make a complete statement of their involvement in the Cunningham imbroglio. Possibly to protect his chief, or possibly as part of a precon-

1960), pp. 36–65; Robert M. La Follette, *La Follette's Autobiography* (Madison, Wis., 1960), pp. 183–203; Pringle, *Life and Times of William Howard Taft* (2 vols.; New York and Toronto, 1939), 1, pp. 480, 519, and *passim*.

[2] *The Outlook*, December 25, 1909, p. 883.

[3] R.A.B. to Jones, December 21, 1909, *Investigation of the Department of the Interior and the Bureau of Forestry*, Sen. Doc. 719, 61 Cong., 3 Sess., 3, p. 177. George Wickersham to R.A.B., December 20, 1909, Ballinger Papers; Butt, *Taft and Roosevelt: The Intimate Letters of Archie Butt* (2 vols.; Garden City, 1930), 1, p. 235.

ceived plan, Price offered his resignation to James Wilson after revealing the whole intricate story. The secretary of agriculture was "astonished at securing this and other information" and requested the forester's recommendation.[4]

In a long letter to Pinchot the two subordinates described their role in promoting the Glavis cause. Price had insured that magazines and newspapers had never lacked material damaging to Ballinger and in general had always been a step ahead of the president in publicizing the Glavis charges. ("We gave out nothing whatever but information on forestry and nothing controversial ever," Pinchot had assured Taft at Salt Lake City.) Shaw had traveled thousands of miles to assist Glavis on several occasions. Most damaging of all was the assistance given in preparing the *Collier's Weekly* article long after the president had officially rendered judgment and had attempted to end the squabbling within his administration. From the "point of view of comity between the departments, our conduct had been irregular" Price and Shaw recognized, but they spurned apology. "We believe that our activities have been pernicious only from the point of view of those who have been hampered in urging fraudulent claims to the public domain. In all that we have said and done, we have been animated by a desire to safeguard the public interest." Although doubtless a worthy desire to be animated by, it hardly obscured the other and more immediate motive of bringing low an official whose policies had been detrimental to the Forest Service. On January 6 Pinchot forwarded their letter to Wilson with the recommendation that "no further action be taken . . . in view of the reprimand already given [and] . . . the purity of their motives."[5]

Besides flushing the Forest Service, Ballinger's letter to Jones had another immediate and portentous effect. With the appearance of Glavis' article, Ballinger had begun to think of bringing suit against *Collier's Weekly* for libel but was deterred by

[4] G.P. to Price and Shaw, December 24, 1909; Wilson to G.P., December 29, 1909, Gifford Pinchot Papers.

[5] Price and Shaw to G.P., January 5, 1910; G.P. to James Wilson, January 6, 1910, *ibid.*

the president's desire to allow the furor to spend its force. (In the spring of the following year when legal suit was feasible Ballinger found himself checked by the impossibility of enticing the publishers to Washington state for trial.) Ballinger's intentions were no secret in the fall, and with the possibility of a congressional investigation looming, the editor of *Collier's Weekly* became concerned. The thought of a "whitewashed" Ballinger emerging from an investigation with a clean bill of health and brandishing a million dollar suit was not a pleasant prospect for Hapgood to contemplate, and gave him a stake in Glavis' vindication. To meet these problems Hapgood sought allies and in the latter part of December gathered at the home of Henry L. Stimson with others of a like mind, Gifford and Amos Pinchot, Robert Collier, and James Garfield. Present also was George Wharton Pepper, the Philadelphia lawyer who had been retained on the advice of Stimson to defend Pinchot in the proposed investigation. Francis Heney had been rumored as a possible counsel for Pinchot. The forester's own first choice, Stimson, had excused himself and persuaded Pepper to take the case. Before adjourning the group agreed to ask Louis D. Brandeis of Boston to serve as counsel for *Collier's Weekly* and Louis Glavis.[6]

While Price and Shaw were laboring over an explanation of their cooperation with Glavis, Stimson and Pepper were helping Pinchot to draft a letter which the two lawyers thought was to go to Secretary Wilson. Senator Jonathan Dolliver, meanwhile, had asked Pinchot what recommendations he "would make to Secretary Wilson as to Price and Shaw." Pinchot was frankly eager to get his case before the public

[6] Frank Baldwin to R.A.B., November 15, 1909; R.A.B. to Baldwin, November 18, 1909; R.A.B. to Alfred Battle, April 9, 1910; Battle to R.A.B., April 9, 1910; J. T. Ronald to R.A.B., December 23, 1909, Ballinger Papers; Hapgood, *Changing Years* (New York, 1930), pp. 183–86, for account of the meeting. McGeary, *Gifford Pinchot: Forester-Politician* (Princeton, N.J., 1960), p. 155, raised the question of Stimson's motives in refusing to serve as counsel, that he was seeking to divorce himself from Pinchot's activity. E. E. Morison, *Turmoil and Tradition: A Study in the Life and Times of Henry L. Stimson* (New York: Atheneum, 1964), pp. 132–33, points out that Stimson persuaded Pepper to serve.

where he thought the controversy with Ballinger would ultimately be decided. On two occasions early in January Pinchot
told James Wilson of Dolliver's request. Through his own in-
advertence, perhaps, the secretary of agriculture remained unaware of the substantive content of the letter Pinchot intended
to send. The Dolliver letter Wilson may have thought identical
to that which he received from Pinchot on January 5 covering
the letters of Price and Shaw. Stimson and Pepper were equally
surprised; Pinchot had changed their letter with a few bold
and imaginative strokes and whisked it off to Dolliver. To
Stimson, Pinchot explained that he "was obliged to modify [the
letter] in certain respects because of information which reached
me after you left." Pepper was not mollified by Pinchot's
apology for the "considerably modified" letter, and considered
resigning from the case. The letter, read by Dolliver from the
Senate floor on January 6, staggered Wilson, who later called
it a review of the "mental processes of the President in passing
upon the Glavis matter." It openly justified the actions of Price
and Shaw, although admitting they had "transgressed propriety." Only the thinnest veil protected the president from criticism. The "action of Price and Shaw was taken with the single
object of protecting the property of the people of the United
States."

> Action through the usual official channels, and finally even
> an appeal to the President, had resulted (because of what I
> believe to have been a mistaken impression of the facts) in
> eliminating from the government service, in the person of
> Glavis, the most vigorous defender of the people's interest.[7]

When the afternoon papers appeared on the day the letter
to Dolliver was read, Taft called an emergency cabinet meeting. The departing officials trooping out at six in the evening
seemed as quiet as clams to excited newsmen. The White House
remained equally silent. Taft was wrestling with a problem
which had come home to roost. "I believe he loves Theodore

---

[7] G.P. to Dolliver, January 5, 1910, *Investigation*, 3, pp. 178–79; 4, pp.
1293, 1297–1305; G.P. to W. K. Kavanaugh, January 20, 1910, Gifford
Pinchot Papers. See also Pepper, *Philadelphia Lawyer, An Autobiography*
(New York, 1944).

Roosevelt," Archie Butt commented, "and a possible break with him or the possible charge of ingratitude on [Taft's] part is what is writhing in him now." However, as Elihu Root remarked, Pinchot had left the president no choice. The following day the forester received a letter.

> The plain intimations in your letter are, first, that I had reached a wrong conclusion as to the good faith of Secretary Ballinger and the officers of the Land Office, although you and your subordinates had only seen the evidence of Glavis the accuser . . . and, second, that under these circumstances, without the exploitation by Messrs. Shaw and Price in the daily, weekly, and monthly press of the charges of Glavis, the administration . . . would have allowed certain fraudulent claims to be patented . . . although the matter had been specifically brought to the attention of the President. . . . Your letter was in effect an improper appeal to Congress and the Public to excuse in advance the guilt of your subordinates before I could act, and against my decision in the Glavis case before the whole evidence on which that decision was based could be considered. . . .
>
> By your own conduct you have destroyed your usefulness as a helpful subordinate of the Government, and it therefore now becomes my duty to direct the Secretary of Agriculture to remove you from your office as the Forester.

That evening Pinchot's mother was entertaining guests. Her son arrived "with President's letter in hand—saying 'Fired.'" "Great Rejoicing," she scratched in her diary, reflecting her son's elation. "Lots of reporters." The air was less festive at 1600 Pennsylvania Avenue. "I would not have removed Pinchot if I could have helped it," Taft sighed.[8]

The dismissal of Gifford Pinchot did not in any sense force a congressional investigation. A resolution prepared by the administration was introduced into the Senate by Wesley Jones of Washington on January 5. Jones was reportedly "scared stiff" at the thought of leaving his favorite stance in the middle of the road, whereas the other senator from Washington, Sam-

---

[8] *The Washington Post*, January 7, 1910; Butt, *Taft and Roosevelt*, 1, pp. 245, 253–56. Quotations in McGeary, *Gifford Pinchot*, p. 161, and Pringle, *Life and Times of William Howard Taft*, 1, p. 509. Taft to G.P., January 7, 1910, *Investigation*, 4, pp. 1289–90.

uel H. Piles, was piqued by what he counted a discourtesy to himself in not being asked instead of Jones. A similar resolution was introduced into the House, and the controversy again became associated with the struggle between Speaker Cannon and the insurgents. On January 7 George Norris of Nebraska offered an amendment to the resolution, providing that the six members of the investigating committee be elected by the House rather than appointed by the speaker. The amendment passed and eventually resulted in the presence of an insurgent on a committee which otherwise would certainly have been staffed on the Republican side with safe party regulars. Its principal effect was to add a third element of faction to the Democratic and regular Republican members already assured positions on the committee. Ironically, the Norris amendment passed because two normally regular Republican members of the House, Butler Ames of Massachusetts and Hamilton Fish of New York, both notorious reactionaries, voted with the insurgents and Democrats because they were personal friends of Gifford Pinchot.[9]

If Ballinger was assured at least a friendly majority on the joint congressional committee, there was no reason to assume in January of 1910 that his case would be lost before the bar of public opinion either. The president delivered his conservation message to Congress in the middle of the month, based upon the recommendations of the secretary of the interior. The content of that message was known on the day Jones introduced his resolution when Francis Newlands of Nevada, whose devotion to conservation was unimpeachable, arose in the Senate to say that he had no objection to an inquiry but would regret to see a long and sensational investigation delay enactment of legislation essential to conservation. Friends of the movement had been seeking practical legislation for a long time, Newlands said, but only recently had an enlightened public begun to push Congress into action. The senator remarked that while he disagreed with some details in Ballinger's recom-

[9] *The Washington Post,* January 6, 1910, January 8, 1910; Ashmun Brown to Erastus Brainerd, January 16, 1910, Brainerd Papers; R.A.B. to S. H. Piles, December 24, 1909, Ballinger Papers.

mendations, they were the most comprehensive yet advanced.[10]

Although many friends of conservation like Newlands were chiefly concerned lest Pinchot in his zeal destroy more than he intended, the forester had his enemies to gloat over his fall. The old split in the executive establishment, which went back to Theodore Roosevelt, was reflected in the observation of an informed reporter on the capital scene. "There is quiet joy in the agricultural department over the fact that Pinchot is to be investigated that . . . extends from the secretary's office down." This same observer felt in mid-January that Ballinger's stock had risen with a wide segment of the public as a result of some not too discriminating tactics employed by Pinchot. Significantly, he added: "Ballinger will never convince the whole country that he is on the 'square.' " The *Outlook*, whose star editor, Theodore Roosevelt, was still abroad sighting near-sightedly down on large African vertebrates, struck the balance of opinion for a large part of the country on the dismissal of Gifford Pinchot. The president could have done no less under the circumstances, the magazine commented.[11]

The composition of the joint congressional committee, which heard testimony between January 26 and May 20 in a total of forty-five sessions, demonstrated the change which had taken place in the controversy after it broke out of the confines of the administration. It was no longer strictly a struggle between "Roosevelt men" and those opposed to certain policies developed under Roosevelt. By far the most prominent Republican member was the senator from New York, Elihu Root, who had served as both secretary of war and as secretary of state under Roosevelt and who occupied a respected place in the tight little circle of Roosevelt advisers. Garfield was certain that Root was "with us in the conservation fight" and with Root on the committee "the truth will come out which ever way it cuts." Yet when questions arose before the committee,

[10] *The Washington Post*, January 15, 1910, January 6, 1910. For other comments upon the Ballinger recommendations, see *The Outlook*, January 29, 1910, pp. 224–25.

[11] Ashmun Brown to Erastus Brainerd, December 30, 1909, January 16, 1910, Brainerd Papers; *The Outlook*, January 15, 1910, pp. 107–8.

the vote was always the seven regular Republicans against the four Democrats and lone insurgent Republican, and Root was invariably numbered among the seven stalwarts. The chairman of the committee, Knute Nelson of Minnesota, was also the chairman of the Senate committee on public lands and a key congressional supporter of conservation. A former populist governor of Minnesota, Nelson had figured prominently in the creation of the Bureau of Corporations, of which Garfield was the first commissioner, and had introduced and supported the Roosevelt coal-leasing bill. During Taft's first year in office, Nelson had been prominent mainly as an insurgent Republican. In the spring of 1909 he took home a tariff schedule to study along with La Follette and Dolliver during the great tariff debate. Largely because of his role in the Ballinger hearings, Nelson was read out of the insurgent movement by La Follette, and Pinchot in his autobiography referred to the Minnesota senator as "Old Guard to the finger tips"; but months after the hearings, in September 1910, Jonathan Dolliver included Knute Nelson among the progressive senators who were enlisted "under the banner of Republican progress."[12] Yet Nelson, like Root, was a close friend of the administration throughout the

[12] Garfield Diary, November 26, 1909, December 28, 1909, Garfield Papers. Pinchot, *Breaking New Ground* (New York, 1947), p. 465; Dolliver, "The Forward Movement in the Republican Party," *The Outlook*, September 24, 1910, p. 172; R. M. La Follette, *La Follette's Autobiography*, p. 193; *The Washington Post*, January 6, 1910. For Nelson and the tariff, see Russel B. Nye, *Midwestern Progressive Politics* (East Lansing, Mich., 1951), p. 249. Background on Nelson can be found in Martin Wendell Odland, *The Life of Knute Nelson* (Minneapolis, Minn., 1926). Other members of the investigating committee included: Senator George Sutherland, Republican from Utah, later a member of the Supreme Court with Taft and Brandeis; Senator Frank P. Flint of California, a lodge brother (Masonic) of Oscar Lawler, a Republican; Democratic Senator William E. Purcell of North Dakota (who replaced Senator Thomas H. Paynter on the committee early in the investigation); Democratic Senator Duncan U. Fletcher of Florida; Republican Representative Samuel W. McCall of Massachusetts; Republican Representative Marlin E. Olmsted of Pennsylvania; Republican Representative Edwin Denby of Michigan, who later as secretary of the navy under Harding had his own conservation problems; Representative Ollie M. James, Democrat from Kentucky; House Democrat James M. Graham of Illinois; and the House insurgent Republican Edmond H. Madison, formerly a judge in Kansas.

investigation. Close association with Roosevelt policies in the past did not always determine loyalty in the congressional inquiry into the dispute between Ballinger and Pinchot.

Ballinger lost ground during the long period when Glavis was on the witness stand. Glavis went through his paces coolly under the guidance of Louis Brandeis. The task of the great Boston counsel was not simple. Representing Glavis and *Collier's Weekly*, to serve them adequately he had to demonstrate in the face of the hostility and open resistance of the majority of the investigating committee that Ballinger was, as a Michigan newspaper bluntly put it, the "Morgan-Guggenheim power trust protégé." Brandeis brought to his task a tough-minded tenacity and a memory for detail approaching the supernatural. His association with Pinchot in the hearings was an anomaly, considering the differences in their approach to that great social problem of the day, the trust. There was little in common between the devotion to the efficiency of bigness espoused by Pinchot and Roosevelt and the emotional aversion to bigness which distinguished the approach of Brandeis.[13]

"Glavis has proved an extraordinary witness," Brandeis remarked at the end of January. "I have never seen his equal. *Der junge Mensch* is only 26." Glavis was remarkable. He was unhurried, always calm in the face of badgering, and had a good memory and a wide array of facts ever on call. He continued to avoid making any specific charge. He provided a

[13] Brown to Brainerd, February 17, 1910, Brainerd Papers; *Saginaw News* (Michigan), June 6, 1910. See Alpheus T. Mason, *Brandeis: A Free Man's Life* (New York, 1946); Theodore Roosevelt, "The Trusts, the People and the Square Deal," *The Outlook*, November 18, 1911, pp. 649–56. It was not so much that Brandeis agreed with Taft or Ballinger on the issue of the trust. It was more that he was not in full accord with Pinchot and the conservationists. With the latter Brandeis agreed that the trust should be considered a condition, not a crime, but he looked on the large economic unit as basically inefficient, which departed from the views of Pinchot. Brandeis was closest to Pinchot in his respect for the expert. Both agreed that the expert made the best reformer precisely because as expert he stood above contending parties and could seek the devices of harmony to heal factionalism. See Samuel Haber, *Efficiency and Uplift: Scientific Management in the Progressive Era, 1890–1920* (Chicago, Ill., 1964), pp. 80–82. Also of interest: Melvin I. Urofsky, "Wilson, Brandeis and the Trust Issue, 1912–1914," *Mid-America*, January 1967, pp. 3–28.

body of selected information and a damaging interpretation and beyond that adamantly refused to be moved. The absence of any specific charge scattered the energies of the opposition and was Brandeis' greatest weapon, as the following exchange indicated:[14]

> *Mr. Denby.* Mr. Brandeis, we are seeking to ascertain specifically what the charges were. Do I understand that they are, first, that upon certain occasions Mr. Ballinger acted improperly, but not entirely corruptly, and upon other occasions he designed and intended to act corruptly, but was prevented from doing so by Mr. Glavis?
>
> *Mr. Brandeis.* I have not used the word "corrupt" in any case.
>
> *Mr. Denby.* I wanted to get it straight in my mind.
>
> *Mr. Brandeis.* I say without due regard to the interests of the people and the Government.
>
> *Mr. Denby.* That is, he acted improperly; that is without propriety; secondly, he intended to act without due regard to the public interests—in other words, corruptly—and was prevented from doing so by Mr. Glavis.
>
> *Mr. Brandeis.* I have not used the word "corruptly." I have desired to bring, and I desire now to bring, without characterization, the facts before the committee. . . .

Glavis demonstrated how to bring facts before the committee "without characterization," thus earning the warm praise of Brandeis already quoted. At one time Glavis used the following words concerning the actions of the secretary of the interior, in a space covering two pages of testimony: "unprofessional," "selfish," "not loyal to his trust," "not faithful to the people," "cowardly," and "unfit man for the office." Something similar would be found in any sampling of Glavis' testimony. Yet the imputations of dishonesty or misconduct remained elusive to the end. After intensive (though not necessarily skillful) cross-examination by Ballinger's counsel, the charges of Glavis could be summarized as follows: There was no charge of criminality against Ballinger, since motive was essential to demonstrate criminality; there was no charge of

[14] Quoted in Mason, *Brandeis: A Free Man's Life*, p. 260. *Investigation*, 3, pp. 26–27.

corruption, because corruption was equivalent to criminality as Glavis defined it; there was misconduct, which meant, apparently, a species of "corruption" for which there was not enough evidence to bring criminal action.[15]

Gifford Pinchot testified at length on the power sites episode, the Indian cooperative agreement, and the Cunningham coal claims. The weight of his testimony he hoped would prove, as he said in his opening statement (distributed to the press just before he took the stand), "that Mr. Ballinger has been unfaithful to his trust as a servant of the people and as the guardian of public property of enormous value."[16] This, with its implication of moral turpitude, went considerably beyond what his own lawyer hoped to prove.

Pepper called Newell and Davis to the stand to develop the following points, each of which was a reasonable approximation of what had occurred the previous spring: (1) Davis and Newell were informed by Ballinger in March 1909 of his intention to restore power sites withdrawn "illegally" by Garfield; (2) Newell protested this course; (3) prior to March 30 Ballinger ordered the Reclamation Service to recommend restoration of the Garfield sites, which Davis did; (4) about April 23 Ballinger told Davis that the president desired the sites withdrawn again and Davis was ordered to so recommend, but

---

[15] *Ibid.*, pp. 434–42, 445–47. The charges against Ballinger brought by Glavis may be fairly summarized as follows: (1) Ballinger told Jones to make a cursory examination in the summer of 1907—suspicious; (2) Ballinger clearlisted the Cunningham claims after being told by Glavis that they were fraudulent (an interesting point since Glavis could not have demonstrated fraud from any evidence then available); (3) Ballinger spoke in favor of the Cale bill; (4) Ballinger represented the coal claimants while out of office—unprofessional conduct; (5) Ballinger turned the decision on the act of May 28, 1908, over to Pierce rather than the attorney general; (6) Glavis concluded: "While there is nothing in any of these things upon which a criminal charge could be predicated, still I think it was far more cowardly for him to take the action he did than if a man actually stole money, for which he could be convicted." Which proved nothing, except that Glavis preferred that his criminals have the courage of their convictions. Quoted in *ibid.*, p. 447.

[16] *Ibid.*, 4, p. 1143.

because of lack of funds in the Reclamation Service, the Geological Survey was given the task instead.[17]

It was Pepper's idea that Ballinger should be revealed as an enemy of conservation and therefore unfit for the office of secretary of the interior. This meshed nicely with Pinchot's estimate of Ballinger as "the most effective opponent the Conservation policies have yet had." If this involved applying a political test to a man's right to hold office, it was justified in Pepper's eyes because Ballinger's lack of frankness in many of his actions was a "shame and a disgrace." To Pepper the nub of the controversy was a "series of successive blows dealt by Mr. Ballinger at interests which were vital to a group of men who had dedicated their lives to a cause." That Pinchot accepted this interpretation was clear in the following exchange with Ballinger's counsel.

> *Mr. Vertrees.* In this movement against Secretary Ballinger?
>
> .   .   .   .
>
> *Mr. Pinchot.* I do not even recognize the movement against Secretary Ballinger.
>
> *Mr. Vertrees.* What I want to get at is, I want to know if you and Mr. Garfield and Mr. Glavis and Mr. Shaw and others have not on hand a movement which means the removal and if possible, the political or official destruction of Secretary Ballinger?
>
> *Mr. Pinchot.* If you ask me whether we have on hand a movement which means the conservation of natural resources and

[17] *Ibid.*, p. 1161. Pepper was afraid Newell would weaken his case, and told Pinchot he would prefer "not to put him upon the stand at all if it were not for the fact that we have in a measure committed ourselves to do so." Newell's role in the power site episode had too many weaknesses, the lawyer felt. "How can he explain satisfactorily the fact that in his interview with Ballinger on or about March 18th he expressed the belief that so large a proportion as 9/10 of the lands withdrawn would have to be restored? He repeated this estimate in his letter to La Follette. If at the time this was his estimate of the proportion of entered lands included in the withdrawn areas that of course is an explanation: but it is an explanation which tends to show either great lack of familiarity with the situation or great carelessness in making the original descriptions for withdrawal." See G. W. Pepper to G.P., March 15, 1910, Gifford Pinchot Papers.

the protection of them, no matter who suffers, I will say to you "Yes."[18]

Yet despite this agreement on fundamentals, Pinchot was at odds with his counsel over method throughout the congressional hearings.

Pinchot was aware of his differences with Pepper. "Your point of view and mine necessarily differ a great deal because our principal objects differ also, yours being . . . to win before the Committee; mine being . . . to win before the country." Pepper never reconciled himself to many of the details necessarily emerging from such a distinction. "I am very anxious," he said, "not to have you tied up with the attempted proof of all of Collier's allegations. I am satisfied that Mr. Brandeis (properly considering only the interests of his client) is going to do all he can to produce evidence generally injurious to Ballinger but based upon facts having no relation to his official life. You must have absolutely nothing to do with any such tactics. Of this I am firmly convinced." Pinchot replied that "the reasoning you give is entirely convincing to my mind and to Garfield's," and at the conclusion of his testimony so far dissociated himself from the case as to leave the country for Europe for a "secret" conference with Roosevelt.[19]

Of course Pinchot did not agree with Pepper's evaluation of the Glavis side of the case. No doubt Pepper was overjoyed to learn from Amos Pinchot that "Gifford, before he left, asked me to advise with you occasionally. . . . I feel as if we somehow did not agree upon the importance of making this particular part of the fight which we are all in against special privilege as keen, clear and easy to understand as possible," Amos continued; "it seemed to me that your conception of the needs of the situation did not sufficiently embrace the necessity of giving the country a clear-cut outline of the methods which are

[18] "Memo for Mr. Pinchot's use in Preparing for his Hearing before the Investigation Committee"; Pepper to G.P., March 15, 1910, *ibid.*; *Investigation*, 4, p. 1320; 9, p. 5002.

[19] G.P. to Pepper, February 5, 1910; Pepper to G.P., March 14, 1910; G.P. to Pepper, March 15, 1910, Gifford Pinchot Papers; Butt, *Taft and Roosevelt*, 1, p. 312.

being used against the people by members of the Administration who are too sympathetic with the special interests." The best way to make the issue keen, clear, and easy to understand, of course, was to support the Glavis contention that Ballinger was crooked and cowardly. Yet Amos was attuned to a larger issue than a personal attack upon Ballinger, who was "merely a sympton [*sic*] of the disease which has attacked the Republican party . . . and I believe that it is of the utmost importance to show up this sympton [*sic*]." Pepper's management of the case continued to irk Amos. At one point he asked Garfield to Washington to act as a "stimulous [*sic*] to Pepper." Shortly after, Amos hired Nathan Smyth as assistant counsel to counteract Pepper's "incompetence."[20]

Pepper was unsatisfactory to other partisans in the Pinchot camp. George Woodruff had heard that Pepper had said that Woodruff's course "had been very weak" and wondered if the statement referred to his seven years as a law officer for the federal government.

> I mention the matter partly because I would value your good opinion highly, but more particularly because I fear the indefinite way in which you spoke of these matters means that you do not agree with the general principles concerning interpretation of the law by the Executive, which were carefully and prayerfully evolved by certain active members of the last administration.
>
> If . . . you disagree, I must say frankly that you are now acting as an attorney on the wrong side of the fence. . . .[21]

In his efforts to win before the country, Pinchot relied heavily on effective publicity, and his experience in the Forest Service had taught him the best methods of getting publicity at a minimum cost. With the help of Amos, in mid-March a summary of the testimony "by the Prosecution in the Pinchot-Ballinger Controversy" was prepared and distributed to newspapers around the country. No markings on the document indi-

[20] A. Pinchot to Pepper, May 3, 1910, A. Pinchot to J. R. Garfield, May 3, 1910, Amos Pinchot Papers; Amos Pinchot, *History of the Progressive Party*, edited, with a biographical introduction by Helene Maxwell Hooker (New York, 1958), p. 15.

[21] Woodruff to Pepper, February 16, 1910, Amos Pinchot Papers.

cated its source. A well-organized selection complete with marginal summaries of page content, it was a handy reference guide for busy editors who lacked the time to plow through the thousands of pages of testimony. By comparison, Ballinger's own efforts to get his case before the public were puny and ineffective. At the end of March he asked Ashmun Brown, a Washington reporter, to attend the hearings and keep newsmen informed on the significance of the testimony, but Brown refused on ethical grounds. Yet even after the testimony of Pinchot and the reclamation officers it was by no means clear that Ballinger was losing, even in the opinion of the public. Up to this midpoint in the hearings, Pepper thought, Glavis' case was strong; but he could only grow stronger, or grow weaker, in what followed.[22] What followed of course was catastrophe for Ballinger, but his humiliation was caused by factors which had nothing to do with the substantiation of the Glavis charges.

On the advice of Taft, Ballinger had no counsel when the hearings began. One or two days of testimony by Glavis revealed the weaknesses in this approach, and after February 3 Ballinger was represented in the hearings. The Land Office officials and Ballinger himself preferred Carl Rasch, a Montana lawyer; but though Rasch had already digested the record in early February and was prepared to begin as counsel, a Tennessee lawyer named John J. Vertrees was suddenly hired as chief counsel and Rasch was relegated to a subordinate position.[23] A personal friend of Taft, the fire-eating Vertrees (indelicately labeled "Pervertrees" by the opposition) did more damage to Ballinger than Glavis could ever have accomplished. Since Ballinger was

[22] A copy of the booklet is in the Ballinger Papers. Its full title is "Advance copy for immediate release—a summary of testimony by the prosecution in the Pinchot-Ballinger Controversy, up to March 18, 1910"; Brown to Brainerd, March 31, 1910, Brainerd Papers; Pepper to G.P., March 14, 1910, Gifford Pinchot Papers.

[23] See the following in the Ballinger Papers: Schwartz to Rasch, February 2, 1910; Schwartz to Rasch, February 2, 1910 [*sic*]; R.A.B. to McHarg, February 3, 1910; Schwartz to R.A.B., February 5, 1910. Before Rasch, Ballinger had asked John Colt Spooner, a New York attorney, to be his counsel. R.A.B. to Spooner, December 23, 1910. Ashmun Brown said "Taft and Secretary of War Dickinson loaded [Vertrees] on Ballinger." Brown to Brainerd, March 31, 1910, Brainerd Papers.

charged with being unfriendly toward conservation, the fact that his lawyer was a genuine anticonservationist was a disaster.

Vertrees charted Ballinger's defense along two courses. The lawyer's first aim was a vindication of the secretary, which necessarily entailed a veiled attack on the previous administration. His second aim was to shift some of the burden of significant policy changes from Ballinger's shoulders to a number of Department of the Interior subordinates. Pierce, Finney, and Lawler took responsibility for many of the administrative decisions which had so irritated Pinchot and Garfield, such as revoking the cooperative agreement between the Forest Service and the Indian service. Neither of these tactics was wise. The first had the effect of hardening the issue. It became progressively more difficult to be simultaneously for both Ballinger and Roosevelt, or for Ballinger to maintain the fiction that he was fighting the willful subordinates, not the chief himself. The second tactic was unwise because it played into the hands of the opposition by fighting the war in their terms. Yet both tactics were of a piece with Ballinger's previous role in the controversy. He had always been off balance. His only hope lay in strongly justifying his actions as resulting from his best judgment under the circumstances. He chose instead to defend himself from the charge that he was an enemy of Roosevelt, even though most of the policy changes implicitly criticized the former administration. The tension created by the paradox inevitably parted the last connections of Ballinger with the Roosevelt administration.

Ballinger's relations with the *Outlook* illustrated the inadequacies of such a defense. Ballinger cared more for the opinion of this journal than for all the rest of the press combined. Not only was it preeminently the watchdog of moral reform in the country and closely associated with the person as well as the policies of Theodore Roosevelt, but Ballinger himself had close ties with the magazine through Elbert Frank ("Frank by nature, and Frank by name!") Baldwin, who was one of the editors and a former classmate at Williams College. With reservations, Ballinger was satisfied with the *Outlook*'s treatment of the controversy through the fall of 1909. But early spring was the turning point; the investigation sealed Ballinger's doom. When it came to conflicting testimony—thousands of pages of complicated testimony that required months of study—the secretary's genial rapport with the magazine broke down. As the hearings developed inevitably into an indictment of the preceding administration, the *Outlook* took off its gloves. Ballinger could not compete with Pinchot for the magazine's sympathy under these circumstances. The break was complete by June, when the editors concluded in their final opinion of the case that Ballinger was not a "trustworthy custodian."[24]

When the hearings were completed, Vertrees said that the "one regret I had in the matter . . . was that I did not have a free hand to say what I really thought about conservation and Mr. Roosevelt for a regard for consequences restrained me." It would have been interesting, at any rate, to see what he called a free hand. Among his few attempts at humor in the hearings, he was fond of saying, "I do not think there is any real difference between conservation and conversation, it is all talk." Before calling his first witness Vertrees provided the committee and the public with a sympathetic summary of his client's case.[25]

> Glavis, suspicious by nature, became perverted by detective service, until apparently he has become incapable of fair judgment. Mr. Pinchot, vain, and flattered as Chief of the Forest Service by his own publicity bureau, had come to regard himself as the most important personality in the Department of Agriculture. "Conservation," like all sound doctrines, when preached by the vain and self-seeking, had become perverted, until it was here a folly and there a reproach. "Reclamation," so called, and "conservation," bellowing, toured hand in hand,

24 See *The Outlook*, September 1909–June 1910, especially 93, pp. 138–39; 94, pp. 643–44; 95, p. 295. In the Ballinger Papers see: Baldwin to R.A.B., August 11, 1909; R.A.B. to Hamilton W. Mabie, October 4, 1909; Baldwin to R.A.B., October 28, 1909; R.A.B. to Baldwin, December 4, 1909; Baldwin to R.A.B., January 20, 1910; R.A.B. to C. L. Pack, January 25, 1910. Vertrees said of this final judgment, "How lacking in generous impulses one of these wormy men of God who writes always is," to Ballinger, June 13, 1910, *ibid.*

25 Vertrees probably took the comparison of conservation to conversation from a January edition of the *Kansas City Journal*, which was in the clipping collection of the Ballinger Papers. *Investigation*, 5, p. 2393; 8, p. 4647.

and those who feel, rather than those who think, appear to see great forests spring up, like Jonah's gourd, in a night, and vast reclamation projects established, not only where such projects can and ought to rightfully flourish, but at every power site which a missionary might describe. Combining these doctrines, their chiefs swept all aside that stood in their way. "Co-operative agreements," "co-operative certificates," "ranger schools," wholesale withdrawals of the people's lands, became the vogue. Here was the reign of men.

March 4, 1909, there came the reign of law . . . [Pinchot] ceased to be the Department of Agriculture. He was exposed, and Mr. Ballinger had committed the unpardonable sin of defeating the ambition of a self-exaggerated man. Mr. Ballinger was now where Mr. Garfield was not, and Mr. Pinchot was confined to the forest reserves. Broad as they are, they are too small for him. Here was the birthplace of that spirit of resentment and revenge which blindly wrote "mistakes" to the President and utilized this Glavis, of the detective service, to attempt to assassinate Mr. Ballinger's good name, and thereby bring reproach upon the President, who had not retained Mr. Garfield and had dismissed Mr. Pinchot.

Vertrees' summary accurately reflected his client's opinion of the Garfield-Pinchot policies and of the origins of the controversy in its broad outlines but was phrased awkwardly for a man defending himself against a charge of attacking the previous administration. Vertrees' own unique flavor of Rooseveltphobia and anticonservationism became closely associated in the public mind with both Ballinger and the president. Being a good Democrat, there was no reason why Vertrees should exhibit fondness for Roosevelt. Yet his party affiliation had partially influenced his choice as counsel, since a Democrat could be expected to arouse fraternal feelings in the minority members of the committee.[26] If such was the theory, it fell short of the mark.

Only slightly less damaging than his attorney was Ballinger's own testimony. The urbane and witty Pepper forced an admission that the secretary of the interior had ordered the Garfield sites restored without having at the time any intention of rewithdrawing them, a fact which to this point both Ballinger

[26] James Hamilton Lewis to R.A.B., February 10, 1910, Ballinger Papers.

and the president had steadfastly denied. As the *Outlook* said, the impression was left that Ballinger "was making decisions from day to day without knowledge of the subject." The nation laughed then at Pepper's parody of Vertrees' opening address. Until "March the 4th, there had been, what Mr. Vertrees picturesquely calls the reign of men, during which there was the policy of broad withdrawals followed by paring down, and that from March 4 to April 23 there was what he has with equal picturesqueness described as the reign of law, during which there was a policy of wholesale restorations, and that after April 23 there was the reign of Lawler, perhaps we will call it that, where there was a policy of rewithdrawals with a carefully chosen form of words to justify it." The overwrought secretary of the interior was no match for the artful Pepper and was unable to fend off the ridicule rolling in with such questions as, "When you cleaned up Seattle and withdrew the dens of vice from entry, suppose your successor had found a defect in the police power and restored them all, would you not have regarded that as a blow to the cause for which you had been laboring?"[27]

No wit cut the edge from the questions of Louis Brandeis. He was savagely aggressive and at times deliberately offensive, a tactic designed to keep the witness in a constant state of irritation and consequently off balance. It was nothing if not effective, and on more than one occasion Ballinger asked the recorder to repeat a question to cleanse it of Brandeis' "intonations." The most significant part of Ballinger's testimony was not immediately apparent to the committee or to the public. In early September Ballinger had journeyed to Beverly accompanied by Oscar Lawler to deliver the replies of himself, Dennett, Schwartz, and Pierce to the Glavis charges, which the president had requested. Casually Brandeis asked what, if anything, Lawler had taken to Beverly. Ballinger's reply, "A grip with some clothes in it," was ludicrously evasive; eventually, under stubborn questioning he admitted that besides a suitcase

---

[27] *Investigation*, 7, pp. 3549–4235. Rather stuffily, Ballinger replied to Pepper, "I certainly would have felt a very sincere regret at any retrograde movement looking to the moral cleanliness of my own city." *Ibid.*, p. 4201; *The Outlook*, May 28, 1910, p. 129.

Lawler had carried a memorandum which was actually a résumé of the Glavis charges, based on an examination of the record.[28] It was the first time the committee had heard of the Lawler memorandum.

On January 6 Taft had forwarded to the Senate the documents and papers upon which he had based his decision in the Glavis case, and among which was a summary prepared by Wickersham for Taft's use dated September 11 (three days before the letter exonerating Ballinger). The astute Brandeis read it over again and again, as many as twenty times was his own guess, and concluded that such a polished piece of work could not have been completed in the five days which elapsed between the time the records in the Glavis case were delivered to Taft by Ballinger and the date on the document. There simply had not been enough time to acquire the familiarity with the record which the Wickersham summary demonstrated, and Wickersham had not been in Washington where the records were lodged before their delivery to Taft. Brandeis concluded that the document had been dated much later, but proof at first eluded him.[29]

In his continued reading of the document, Brandeis discovered internal evidence substantiating his suspicion. Wickersham refuted a charge which had first appeared in the *Collier's Weekly* article of November 13, but never mentioned earlier by Glavis. Still Brandeis was not sure exactly what he had. Edward Finney was testifying at this time, and his face was watched closely by Norman Hapgood while Brandeis casually referred to the date on the Wickersham summary. The consternation which flitted momentarily across the face of the normally imperturbable Finney was all that Brandeis could have desired.[30]

Shortly thereafter, on April 23, Brandeis arose in the hearing

[28] *Ibid.*, p. 140; *Investigation*, 7, pp. 3865, 4092.

[29] "Talk with Louis D. Brandeis, December 30, 1939, in his apartment in Washington, D.C., 5:30 to 6:15 p.m.," Gifford Pinchot Papers.

[30] The charge that Ballinger had violated statute 190 in representing Cunningham in the summer of 1908. *Investigation*, 7, p. 3624. For incident with Finney, see Hapgood, *Changing Years*, p. 187. "Talk with Louis D. Brandeis, December 30, 1909 . . . ," Gifford Pinchot Papers.

with a formal request that the attorney general be asked by the committee to forward all of the documents and papers used in compiling the Wickersham summary, and the names of all individuals involved in its writing. The startled committee voted seven to five to deny this request of Brandeis. A week later the attorney revealed his suspicions to the committee and justified his request as a "question not merely whether Mr. Ballinger was properly exonerated, or whether Mr. Glavis was properly condemned, but whether, after the events which occurred on September 13, steps were taken with the idea of making that appear proper which was not proper when done." Vertrees contended that Brandeis was trying to throw up a smoke screen, that he was making a play for the press, that he was trying to impugn before the public all of the chief advisers of the president and the president himself—but so vociferously that Brandeis was more than ever sure that he was getting somewhere. Edmond Madison, the committee's insurgent Republican, brought the issue into focus. If the administration had heeded this warning at this early stage, the whole case which Brandeis was later to prove would have folded completely. Madison said, "the mere dating back of an instrument which had partially in writing and partially orally been imparted before . . . could make no difference; but the fact that this information . . . is not freely and frankly given might add to the mystery."[31] Nevertheless, Brandeis was again voted down, seven to five.

On the evening of February 16 Brandeis dined with James R. Garfield, who was in Washington to testify at the hearing. Halfway through supper a young man named Frederick M. Kerby called on the former secretary of the interior. Though only twenty-four in 1910, Kerby had already been in the government service five years. He had been Garfield's stenographer in the Bureau of Corporations, and later in the Department of the Interior. Ballinger had kept Kerby as a stenographer and occasional private secretary. During the visit with Garfield, Brandeis learned from Kerby that Lawler had prepared a memorandum for the president's use in September

31 *Investigation*, 7, pp. 3415–17, 3625–29.

1909. Kerby was unwilling to testify before the committee in an appearance which would most certainly cost his position, but within a few weeks his knowledge was magnified in importance by the committee's adamant refusal to give Brandeis what he wanted and by the silence of the White House. In the meantime, Kerby had been offered a job by a news syndicate if he would break the story. He claimed to have been influenced by Ballinger's evasion when questioned about the Lawler memorandum, but the new career opening in the world of journalism was an added incentive; in fact he went on to become a successful newspaper correspondent.[32] He began that career on May 15 when his story appeared in the *Washington Times*. A few days later he appeared before the investigating committee.

Brandeis had performed an end run around the committee by appealing to public opinion with a sensational story. That was the true significance of the tale Kerby repeated to the committee. The question of the dating of the Wickersham summary had been answered six days before Kerby published his story in the *Times*. After Brandeis had been voted down the first time by the committee on April 23, a resolution using almost his exact words was introduced into the House calling on the attorney general to produce the desired documents. Richard Wayne Parker, chairman of the House committee on the judiciary, requested Wickersham to "submit . . . suggestions or information" regarding this resolution. Wickersham answered with a claim of executive privilege; however, he spoke on the question of the postdating of his summary.[33]

[32] Garfield Diary, February 16, 1910, Garfield Papers; *Investigation*, 8, pp. 4395–97, 4416–17. Kerby always insisted that he had not violated the special trust of the private secretary in what followed, since he was a mere stenographer. There are letters in the Ballinger Papers signed by Kerby as "Acting Private Secretary"; see, for instance, Kerby to Franklin McVeagh, September 1909 and McVeagh to Kerby, September 29, 1909. Normally, however, Don Carr was Ballinger's private secretary. Probably the most that could be said was that Kerby was a trusted stenographer.

[33] *Investigation*, 7, p. 4139, for House resolution and correspondence between Wickersham and Parker.

The origins of the resolution . . . [lie] in the fact that the summary and conclusions by the Attorney General . . . [are] the formal record made up . . . from the documents and rough notes . . . which were before the President when he acted upon the charges made against Secretary Ballinger.

This summary was necessarily made up afterwards and properly bore the date of the day when the matter it contained was presented to and considered by the president.

Yet Brandeis' quest for the true date of the Wickersham summary had already turned into something quite different. It now appeared that Oscar Lawler, a lawyer in Ballinger's own office, and not Wickersham, had provided the president with the information used in acquitting Ballinger. According to Kerby, after Lawler had completed his memorandum he consulted Finney, Dennett, Schwartz, and Ballinger and "invited" their "general criticisms." When the criticisms had been incorporated in the final draft, Lawler, Kerby, and two other secretaries had gathered in an office to burn the rough draft copies, which were not to be trusted to the wastebaskets. (One detects the touch of Lawler here, the man who wrote his official correspondence in longhand rather than trust a stenographer.) "The papers blazed up and burned furiously. We stood around the fireplace and watched the smoke curl around the pages and the fire lick up line after line of typewriting. We didn't leave until every bit of paper had been consumed and the drafts were reduced to an unrecognizable mass of black ashes." Kerby implied that the substance of the Lawler memorandum was used by the president in his letter exonerating Ballinger.[34]

The Kerby story smoked out Taft. In a letter to the chair-

[34] *Ibid.*, 8, pp. 4455–58. The response of the public to Kerby's testimony was mixed, to say the least. One widely expressed opinion was summed up by Amos Pinchot: "To condemn your action is not merely an injustice to you personally. It is to advocate that every man in the public service must, in disregard of his oath of office and his conscience, support his superior in wrong doing, and remain silent"; to Frederick Kerby, May 20, 1910, Gifford Pinchot Papers. The other most common reaction was expressed in a clipping from a Toronto journal, in the Ballinger Papers: Kerby said he "regarded himself as the servant, not of Mr. Ballinger, but of the people of the United States." This recalled to the journal the pronouncement of Dr. Johnson, that patriotism was the last refuge of the scoundrel.

man of the investigating committee, the president explained
that he had been on the point of departing on a long western
trip at the time Ballinger arrived in Beverly with his own and
his subordinates' replies to the Glavis charges, and had asked
Lawler to "prepare an opinion as if he were president." The
Lawler brief arrived in Beverly on September 12, but after
examining it the president said he felt its "30 pages did not state
the case in the way in which I wished it stated. It contained
references to the evidence which were useful, but its criticism
of Mr. Pinchot and Mr. Glavis I did not think it proper or wise
to adopt. I used only a few paragraphs from it containing merely general statements."[35] This was the final irony. In September
1909 Taft had written Ballinger, "Should it be necessary . . . to
submit all this record and evidence to Congress, I shall be glad
to have your authority and that of your subordinates to leave
out of your answers any references to Pinchot or the part he
took in bringing Glavis's report to my attention."[36] The Lawler
memorandum with its "criticism of Mr. Pinchot" had remained
in the files of the attorney general when the rest of the documents in the Glavis case were forwarded to Congress, and the
administration had remained silent while the committee had
blocked every attempt by Brandeis to learn the truth behind
the Wickersham summary. When Kerby dramatically disclosed the story of the Lawler memorandum, the resulting impression was that the administration had been hiding something
and had told the truth only after it was exposed by Brandeis.
The anomalous and ambiguous relation between the Roosevelt
and Taft administrations had finally borne fruit. In attempting
to leave Pinchot out when he most emphatically wanted to be
included, Taft had courted and fairly won disaster. Three days

[35] Taft to Nelson, May 15, 1910, *Investigation*, 8, pp. 4393–94. Taft
insisted that his conclusions on Ballinger were "based on my reading of the
record and were fortified by the oral analysis of the evidence and the
conclusions which the Attorney-General gave me." The impression never
died, however, that Taft had reached his conclusions hastily. See, for
instance, Oswald Garrison Villard, *Fighting Years* (New York, 1939),
p. 189.

[36] Taft to R.A.B., September 13, 1909, Taft Papers, Presidential series
3, quoted above, p. 126.

after the Kerby revelations, Gifford Pinchot dashed off a letter to Roosevelt.

> The latest developments in the Ballinger-Pinchot controversy seem to establish my case more completely than ever, but it is a spectacle to make every decent American squirm in his skin when the Attorney General of the United States falsifies an essential public document, and the President transmits the falsification to Congress. That, and the fact, long known to us and now made public, that Taft's letter exonerating Ballinger was prepared in Ballinger's own office, will make it substantially impossible for Taft to be regarded any longer as merely the compliant instrument of stronger men. From now on I think he will have to take his full share of responsibility.[37]

Pinchot to the contrary, what Brandeis called the "awfulness of the President-Wickersham-Lawler frauds" was not especially relevant to proof of the Glavis charges, but neither was the necessity of proving those charges any longer relevant. Ballinger, and with him the administration, were "convicted" before the public by a document which had been postdated and by the failure to admit frankly the existence of another document. The overall effect was to vindicate both Pinchot and Glavis. Clucking over the poor showing made by Taft and his lieutenants, the *Outlook* remarked that it was not "uncommon to date a letter or document back to the time when it was originally prepared," but the most inveterate supporter of the administration would have been forced to agree with Brandeis that "the Lawler memorandum would not have been very damaging except that it was lied about and concealed." Fittingly, Brandeis added the final postscript to the episode. "If only there were a Democratic party," said the future architect of the new freedom, "what havoc would be wrought!"[38]

It was not enough, Pinchot said, for a secretary of the interior to show that he was not actively hostile to conservation. Unless it could be proved that he was actively friendly, it went

[37] G.P. to T.R., May 18, 1910, Gifford Pinchot Papers.

[38] Quotations in Mason, *Brandeis: A Free Man's Life*, pp. 273, 278–79. See also *The Outlook*, May 28, 1910, p. 137, and "Talk with Louis D. Brandeis, December 30, 1939 . . . ," Gifford Pinchot Papers.

without saying that he was unfit for the position.[39] The Department of the Interior was no place for even halfhearted enthusiasm because it held the key to the conservation program in its control of the public lands. With the department occupied by a man bent on reversing the coordinated Roosevelt policies, nothing less than the public good could be at stake; and an attack on the interests of the public could plausibly be launched only by a representative of the special interests. The Cunningham imbroglio provided the opportunity for picturing Ballinger as a stooge of the "Guggies," the "Morganheims," the notorious Morgan-Guggenheim syndicate, which had about as much standing in the hagiography of the muckraking journals as the Cosa Nostra does today. The machinery for taking advantage of this opportunity was found in the same creative technique of publicity—which when used in unworthy causes was sometimes called the technique of "smear"—that had so effectively transformed conservation into a "movement."

"Publicity, like every other great power which is capable of good use, may be grossly misused," Garfield said, but that was "no reason for failing to use it."[40] When it came to defining "good," no better end could be served than the defense of the public interest. Yet in a conflict between two competing views of the public interest—which the Ballinger-Pinchot controversy was, in reality—the line was inevitably drawn between those attacking and those defending established policies. If it had gone no further than this there would have been no Ballinger-Pinchot controversy in the historic sense, with its wake of launched careers and damaged reputations. There remained too much latitude, too little to choose between two sides each insisting on its sincerity and devotion to the public weal. The Ballinger-Pinchot controversy became a national scandal when the sincerity of one side was impugned and its devotion to the public weal was opened to serious question. Ballinger had to be labeled a "high-toned crook" or there would have been no

[39] McGeary, *Gifford Pinchot*, p. 169.
[40] "Review of Roosevelt's Administration," *The Outlook*, February 20, 1909, p. 391.

contest. "If they had brazenly admitted everything," Brandeis said, "and justified it on the ground that Ballinger was at least doing what he thought best, we should not have had a chance." It was the lying that did it, he added.[41] Brandeis was too astute to fail to recognize the true basis for the vindication of Glavis' contention that Ballinger was a dishonest public servant; but he was too much the servant of an adversary system to find the truth it revealed very peculiar.

[41] Hapgood, *Changing Years,* p. 190.

CHAPTER SEVEN

"Go Dispose of Your Illgotten Gain"

Speaking of the press attacks in the summer of 1909 originating in the Forest and Reclamation services, Ballinger took a high plane: "I have felt that the dignity of my office and my record did not warrant a retaliation in kind by me." Subsequently, however, the events of the fall and spring toppled him from this pinnacle of righteousness, and he began vigorously to seek redress. During the congressional hearing the officers of the Reclamation Service, A. P. Davis and F. H. Newell, were particular objects of Ballinger's vengeance. In May and June of 1910 he attempted to dismiss Davis, whose testimony before the committee was especially annoying, but was checked by Taft, who thought it "wiser to wait now," though the action would "have to be taken."[1]

It was no more consonant with political realities to consider dismissing Newell, and effective relations between the office of the secretary of the interior and the Reclamation Service rapidly deteriorated in the spring. The ultimate victim of the strain was the federal reclamation program. Ballinger was sensitive to the charge that his attack upon the leadership as well as the policy of federal reclamation had demoralized the service; yet such was the case. Davis testified that the field engineers had considered resigning in a body in protest against Ballinger's disruptive tactics. During the hearing and after, Ballinger searched eagerly for material damaging to Newell, but the effort came to nothing. Rumors of his resignation continued to circulate, but the director hung on tenaciously and eventually outlasted his

[1] R.A.B. to Ormsby McHarg, August 25, 1909; R.A.B. to Davis, May 11, 1910 (never sent); Taft to R.A.B., May 13, 1910, Ballinger Papers.

superior. One or the other had to go if federal reclamation was to survive. It had become impossible for the two men to work together. In July 1910 a northwestern newspaper editor asked Ballinger for a short memorandum reflecting upon Newell which could be paraphrased in an editorial. Ballinger replied that he could "consistently make no personal comments or criticism," but with the reply went an unsigned memorandum which labeled Newell, among other things, as "weak," "evasive," and "vacillating."[2]

For all the personal character of the contest between Ballinger and Newell, the earlier effort to reconstitute reclamation policy continued apace. With the demise of the reclamation script system other questions claimed attention. In February 1910 as part of the conclusions drawn from his long inspection of irrigation works the previous summer, Ballinger recommended to the chairman of the Senate committee on irrigation and reclamation of arid lands that uncompleted irrigation projects involving land already predominantly in private hands be transferred to the control of the individual states. Since there were few projects where the public lands had not been entered before construction began, this recommendation would probably have destroyed the federal reclamation program had it been acted upon.

Equally far-reaching were Ballinger's efforts to reorganize the Reclamation Service. Authority within the service centered in the office of the director and reached the various divisions directly from there. Policy questions were thoroughly thrashed out before reaching the secretary, a structure that was deliberately designed to protect the agency from political control. To Ballinger this was the arrogance reserved by the expert for the nonspecialist and was based on two erroneous assumptions: that the engineer was by training better equipped than the politician to provide more efficient and objective administra-

[2] R.A.B. to R. E. Sloan, April 7, 1910; E. T. Perkins to R.A.B., June 9, 1910; W. W. Robertson to R.A.B., July 20, 1910 (Robertson was editor of the *Yakima Republic*); R.A.B. to Robertson, July 27, 1910: This memo was probably written by Finney, to whom the Robertson letter had been routed and who was by this time chief law officer of the Reclamation Service; Carr to R.A.B., July 26, 1910, *ibid*.

tion; and that the reclamation of the arid West was primarily an engineering problem in which political considerations should be kept to a bare minimum. In December 1909 Ballinger proposed sweeping changes in the structure of the Reclamation Service. The director's office was to be relegated to the level of a division, one among several in the service, whose immediate superior would be the secretary of the interior. Both Newell and Davis objected strenuously to a measure which, if adopted, would rob the director of immediate control over reclamation.[3] The congressional investigation intervened and the measure was dropped temporarily; but the reorganization of the Reclamation Service remained one of Ballinger's central aims.

Friends of reclamation were exercised in June 1910 when the expenditure of $20,000,000 by the Reclamation Service was authorized by Congress on the recommendation of the secretary of the interior. The admission that the service was overextended financially seemed further to endanger its independence. Yet the additional appropriation was the smallest threat posed by the congressional action; truly hideous to Newell and Davis was the provision that none of the appropriation could be spent until the projects of the Reclamation Service had been inspected by a board composed of officers in the Corps of Army Engineers. The fear was raised immediately that the principal fortification of the Army Engineers, the pork barrel, would be used as a Trojan horse to penetrate the scientific purity of the civilian agency. No comparable action could have duplicated the horror which agitated certain circles, unless perhaps the winds of chance had blown the Forest Service into the tender embrace of the General Land Office.[4]

Taft had been considering the Army Engineers as a tonic for

[3] R.A.B. to Thomas H. Carter, February 9, 1910; memorandum on Newell and Davis, June 29, 1910, *ibid. Engineering News*, March 10, 1910, p. 283. See charts and Newell's testimony in *Investigation of the Department of the Interior and the Bureau of Forestry*, Sen. Doc. 719, 61 Cong., 3 Sess., 5, pp. 2022–23, 2025.

[4] See *Engineering News*, March 10, 1910, pp. 283–84; May 12, 1910, pp. 562–64, 592; June 16, 1910, p. 707; *National Irrigation Journal* (n.d.), 1910, clipping in F. H. Newell Papers; speech before Conservative Club, Rhode Island, January 29, 1910, Ballinger Papers.

reclamation ills from the beginning of his administration. As secretary of war he had been impressed with their efficiency in Panama, where they had rescued the canal from the clutches of civilian engineers, and in April 1909 he had offered the services of the corps to Ballinger. Ballinger had resisted the offer at the time, but in the spring of 1910 the Army Engineers became an instrument for achieving two of his goals: the destruction of Newell and Davis, and the reorganization of the Reclamation Service. In early July the secretary appointed General William L. Marshall, only three weeks retired from the post of chief of the Corps of Army Engineers, to a specially tailored position called consulting engineer to the secretary for the Reclamation Service. Marshall was also ex officio chairman of the Board of Army Investigation appointed by the president to inspect the projects of the Reclamation Service, as provided in the recent act of Congress. Nevertheless, Ballinger was determined, once his ends were achieved, to remain opposed to any permanent disposition of the Reclamation Service in the hands of Army Engineers.[5]

But his ends were never achieved. Frederick Haynes Newell refused to resign, despite the heaviest pressures upon him to do so. Instead, he stubbornly insisted that he be allowed to accompany the army board in their inspection of irrigation projects. Ballinger attempted to block Newell's request, but the director succeeded in winning a favorable decision from the president. It may be doubted that Newell's presence softened the report of the board, but he returned from the junket no weaker than when he left, and his summary dismissal by either Ballinger or Taft was as politically impractical as ever. In its report the board did not hesitate to reflect upon the efficiency of the Reclamation Service. The board substantiated Ballinger's contention that the reclamation fund was overextended. The president sent the report to Congress early in January 1911, but the moment had passed. Ballinger's tenure was known to be short,

[5] R.A.B. to R. H. Thomson, April 19, 1909; R.A.B. to Taft, June 29, 1910; Don Carr to H. M. Teller, July 12, 1910, *ibid.*; *New Orleans Picayune*, June 2, 1910; *Philadelphia North American*, July 3, 1910; *Engineering News*, May 12, 1910, pp. 563–64; *Houston Chronicle*, July 2, 1910.

and little enthusiasm was mustered for the anticlimactic attack on the Reclamation Service, even by Ballinger. When the secretary resigned two months later, Newell and Davis still sat at their desks and the structure of the service remained the same.[6]

The attempted reorganization of the Reclamation Service in 1910 was Ballinger's last significant effort to reverse the major policy decisions of the previous administration. Increasingly during the spring, summer, and fall of 1910 he was more and more concerned with the effects and aftereffects of the congressional investigation. He resisted doggedly all efforts to force his retirement because his usefulness had been impaired to party and country, sensing perhaps the judgment which history would render on such a departure. Yet in the end he was denied the opportunity to make his exit gracefully.

In February 1910 Ormsby McHarg warned Ballinger to "fight like hell." "If you don't do it, your reputation will be shot at and cut at, and it will take a fortune and history to restore it to you." The advice fell on willing ears. Ballinger replied: "I note . . . what you say regarding men in the Department of Justice who have materials which would annihilate Mr. Pinchot. I will be glad to know who the parties are and find the avenues to secure this material." His search for "avenues" led him into the bailiwick of Pinchot's successor, Henry S. Graves, who already chafed under a mountain of restrictions imposed by Secretary Wilson during the congressional investi-

[6] See the following correspondence in the Ballinger Papers: Don Carr to R.A.B., July 12, 1910; R.A.B. to Carr, July 19, 1910; Carr to R.A.B., July 22, 1910; William L. Marshall to R.A.B., July 25, 1910; Carr to R.A.B., July 26, 1910; Frank Pierce to Taft, July 27, 1910; R.A.B. to Carr, July 27, 1910; Pierce to R.A.B., July 27, 1910; Pierce to R.A.B., July 29, 1910; Carr to R.A.B., August 3, 1910; Report of the Board of Army Engineers, Records of the Department of the Interior, Correspondence of the Office of the Secretary, National Archives.

In 1913 substantially the changes suggested by Ballinger in December 1909 were imposed upon the service. In 1914 the offices of director and chief engineer were combined, and in 1915 Newell was replaced by A. P. Davis. Efforts to bring the Reclamation Service under political control continued apace into the 1920's. See Ganoe, "Some Constitutional and Political Aspects of the Ballinger-Pinchot Controversy," *Pacific Historical Review,* 3 (1934), pp. 323–33.

gation. In the spring of 1910 Ballinger unleashed the agents of the General Land Office on the national forests, looking for evidence to use against the opposition in the hearings; but the information obtained was useless. The foresters were not amused by the reverse in fortune, and within a few months of his appointment Graves was threatening to resign, convinced that Wilson had a "definite plan to overturn our organization and discredit me."[7]

The ambiguous figure of Roosevelt was never far from the minds of the antagonists on either side of the controversy, but there was little doubt that the volatile Pinchot had the inside track. The latter's dismissal shocked Roosevelt. He decided to "say nothing at present" because it was "a very ungracious thing for an ex-President to criticise his successor." "But I do wish I could see you," Roosevelt wrote his former subordinate. Pinchot responded to the summons as soon as his testimony was on record, and the two men conferred in Porto Maurizio, Italy, on April 11. Signifying perhaps the effects of Pinchot's story, the former president wrote to Henry Cabot Lodge on the same day, saying that Taft had "completely twisted round the policies I advocated and acted upon."

By virtue of his existence Roosevelt was a political problem for the Taft administration. As early as March 1910 Ballinger was warned that emissaries of Pinchot were fanning out through the West organizing "conservation" clubs which in reality were "Back from Elba" clubs. Yet for Ballinger as well as for Taft, Roosevelt was primarily a deeply personal rather

[7] McHarg to R.A.B., February 3, 1910; R.A.B. to McHarg, February 3, 1910, Ballinger Papers. Graves was former Dean of the Yale School of Forestry and a close friend of Gifford Pinchot. For indication of restrictions imposed by Wilson, see Graves to G.P., January 1910 and August 26, 1910, Gifford Pinchot Papers. A thick folder of reports on national forests made by special agents of the Land Office during the spring is in the Ballinger Papers. In a typical report, an agent who had visited the Kansas National Forest noted that only one small section of the 300,000 acres was fenced in for experimental purposes in growing trees. The balance was treeless and "inclosed with fences by cattlemen, with cross fences built to suit their own conveniences and purposes, and the forest is used exclusively for pasturage purposes under permits from the Forest Service." McEniry to Schwartz, December 28, 1909, Ballinger Papers.

than a political problem. In June Ballinger wrote his "sincere congratulations" on Roosevelt's "safe return" and received a jovially blank reply. Ballinger feared the loss of Roosevelt's good opinion, but the growing strain between Taft and the former president hampered fence-mending.[8]

The congressional investigating committee had adjourned in early May, expecting to gather to render their decision on Ballinger during the second national conservation congress, which was scheduled to meet in St. Paul in September. The approaching congress was an occasion for a frantic regrouping of forces, and again the administration was outmaneuvered. Pinchot and Garfield arrived in St. Paul in June to confer with the group of Twin Cities businessmen who were handling the local arrangements for the congress. In the friendly afterglow of a luncheon, Pinchot magnanimously "suggested that the local committee submit the program for entertainment and he . . . would submit a program of speakers and subjects." The gratitude evoked by this sacrifice wilted when the list of speakers finally arrived in St. Paul. Among those proposed were Pinchot himself, Roosevelt, and Brandeis, whereas the absence of President Taft and Ballinger was conspicuous. The local committee revolted and for awhile threatened to scuttle the congress. Eventually they agreed to compromise; Brandeis was stricken from the list of speakers and Taft (but not Ballinger) was added. Despite the uproar, except for the federal territories of New Mexico and Arizona and one or two western states which sent delegations friendly to the administration, the congress belonged to Pinchot.[9]

---

[8] T.R. to G.P., March 1, 1910, Gifford Pinchot Papers; McGeary, *Gifford Pinchot: Forester-Politician* (Princeton, N.J., 1960), p. 177; A. P. Sawyer to R.A.B., March 7, 1910; R.A.B. to T.R., June 18, 1910; T.R. to R.A.B., June 23, 1910, Ballinger Papers.

[9] W. R. Logan to C. D. Norton, July 13, 1910; W. J. Mills to R.A.B., July 7, 1910, Ballinger Papers; *Minneapolis Journal*, July 15, 1910; *Proceedings of the Second National Conservation Congress at Saint Paul, September 5–8, 1910* (Washington, D.C., 1911), *passim*. Pinchot asked Brandeis to withdraw: "I believe I was mistaken, and that it would be wiser for you not to come . . . counting up the time you would necessarily take from other things, I believe the total effect would be better if you

Maneuvering to control the conservation congress interested Ballinger much less than the approaching committee report. He was warned by friends that a report before the congressional elections would be disastrous, whereas after the elections a minority report would be unlikely. Hope and despair combined in Ballinger's yearning for a "unanimous" opinion and resulted in paralyzing inaction; yet there was little anyone could have done to control the situation. The end might have been the same in any case, but when the investigating committee agreed in May to convene in St. Paul before the fall elections, the administration was deprived of the only possible chance to prevent a divided report.

When the committee gathered in St. Paul on September 8, four of its members, including Elihu Root, were absent. Root, who had been abroad, landed in New York two days earlier and a frantic effort was made to rush him to the scene, but he arrived too late for what transpired. Among the eight members present, the minority party was temporarily in the majority. Two Republicans left quickly to insure the absence of a quorum, but Chairman Nelson remained behind to observe. Undismayed by the lack of a quorum, the rump proceeded to adopt two resolutions. The first, presented by Edmond Madison, declared that the charges against the secretary of the interior brought by Louis Glavis were sustained. The second resolution adopted two committee reports. The report presented by the four Democrats found that "Ballinger has not been true to the trust reposed in him." Likewise, in a report filed independently insurgent Edmond Madison declared that the secretary of the interior was "not a faithful trustee," not a "friend ... of conservation," and that he should be dismissed. In a futile effort to gather the reins of his stampeded authority, Knute Nelson announced that a meeting of the full committee would be held in Chicago the following Tuesday, but the rump had

---

declined. I hate to write this way, but I know you want me to tell you just what I think." July 17, 1910, Gifford Pinchot Papers. Taft advisers thought the president should stay away because of the initial insult. See C. D. Norton to K. Nelson, July 16, 1910, and Nelson to Norton, July 29, 1910, Taft Papers, Presidential series 2.

temporarily thrown parliamentary procedure to the winds. They adjourned to meet again in Washington on December 3.

Richard Ballinger was "deeply chagrined at the action of the minority." He was "astonished that the majority of the committee should have allowed themselves to be duped by this gang of dishonest politicians, and I hope they will undertake to retrieve the ground they have lost." Yet there was no retrieving what was already surrendered. Six Republicans gathered glumly in Chicago on September 13. This time it was the majority which lacked the quorum, and the favorable report drawn by Nelson could not be adopted, since they were protesting the action of the minority. Croaking their protest they quickly disbanded, uncomfortable and outmaneuvered.

Only with Congress again in session was Nelson able to gather enough of his truant committee under one roof to constitute a quorum. After clubbing down a motion to adopt the Democratic report as that of the committee, offered on the grounds that it had been accepted in September, a majority of seven adopted the chairman's report. The majority report exonerated Richard Ballinger of the Glavis charges and justified policy changes as having been made in good faith. As for the Cunningham coal claims, whose hearings had been incorporated as part of the official record of the committee, the majority recommended that Alaska coal be leased. In the end only the one report was actually adopted by the committee when a full quorum was present, but though an interesting parliamentary point, as a victory it lacked luster.[10]

The Cunningham claims continued to hang on as the albatross of the Taft administration. Hearings on the claims had

[10] C. Rasch to R.A.B., July 1910; M. D. McEniry to R.A.B., September 8, 1910; R.A.B. to W. M. Crane, September 10, 1910; R.A.B. to Alice Hull Lieb, December 12, 1910; R.A.B. to C. Rasch, July 1, 1910, Ballinger Papers. *New York Sun*, September 9, 1910; *New York Evening Globe*, September 8, 1910; *The Outlook*, September 17, 1910, pp. 91–92; September 24, 1910, pp. 138–39; December 7, 1910, pp. 839–40. *Louisville Courier-Journal*, December 8, 1910. The majority and minority reports comprise volume 1 of *Investigation*. K. Nelson to C. D. Norton, September 6, 1910, Taft Papers, Presidential series 2. Amos Pinchot to Pepper, May 3, 1910, Amos Pinchot Papers.

been held finally in the fall of 1909 and lodged in the Land
Office for consideration. In March 1909 Ballinger had been able
to shift responsibility for the claims to his assistant Pierce, but
after the congressional investigation no one remained in the
Department of the Interior, in the opinion of the secretary, who
could render a just decision. In June 1910 Ballinger and Taft
had a bill introduced in the House providing for "appeals from
the final decisions of the Department of the Interior to the
Court of Appeals of the District of Columbia in land cases."
The committee on public lands was still sitting on the bill
when Congress adjourned for the summer and fall.

On November 7 Amos and Gifford Pinchot wrote to Taft
expressing concern for the safety of the claims, and requesting
that they be allowed to submit a brief in the event that the
department recommended that Cunningham and his associates
be granted patents. The brothers released the letter to the press
on November 13. To counter this new attack Ballinger released
an advance of his annual report for 1910, recommending again
that the District of Columbia Court of Appeals be given final
decision in land cases. The Cunningham claims were destined to
be settled by Ballinger's successor. Nevertheless, in January
1910 the brief, a rehash of the minority reports, was forwarded
to Taft.

Clarence Cunningham had become unwittingly a terrible
burden to Richard Ballinger, who was never able to escape the
consequences of the summer of 1908 when he had served as
legal counsel for the coal claimants. Presumably he had acted
with some regard for the ethical implications of the situation
after becoming secretary of the interior, when he shunted responsibility for the claims to Pierce; yet even this action was
interpreted as designing. "Pierce knows where his chief stood,
before appointed Secretary, and Pierce will be an anomaly if he
bites off his own official head," said one newspaper. The *Outlook* believed Ballinger should have refused the appointment
because he had represented the claimants. The proposal to give
the Court of Appeals the final decision on land claims, it said,
would favor "big business interests" which had the means to

pay for litigation. Other newspapers interpreted the proposal as meaning the law officers of the department had decided that the claimants were entitled to their land but political expediency ruled otherwise. Senator Robert M. La Follette saw it as a not too subtle attempt to win the claimants another trial. The public outcry had its effect and the Taft-Ballinger measure died aborning.

Some months after Ballinger's retirement, Commissioner Dennett canceled the Cunningham claims "practically on the order" of the new secretary of the interior, one newspaper thought. A growl of protest was heard from the direction of Seattle, and the president questioned "the propriety" of some of the remarks credited to his former cabinet officer. Ballinger's reply revealed the dimensions of the crisis which the claims had caused in the department. Ballinger had asked Dennett to step aside and allow an assistant commissioner to handle the final disposition of the claims. Dennett had refused on the grounds that it would reflect unfavorably on his objectivity. When the claims were canceled, Ballinger felt "keenly the impropriety of the Commissioner," and called the decision "political" and not "judicial."[11]

With a little less compunction for objective standards of justice Ballinger might have displayed more courage. The plan to give the Court of Appeals the final decision in the Cunningham claims was an attempt to avoid responsibility. Yet clearly no action of his would have met with satisfaction in the tents of the enemy camp, where knives were kept whetted as long as he remained in office.

"Ballinger should go" was the flat statement by *Collier's Weekly* in August 1909. The demand gained an ever wider currency in the nation's press, particularly after the congres-

[11] R.A.B. to Taft, October 22, 1910; R.A.B. to Wayne McVeagh, January 17, 1911; Taft to R.A.B., July 31, 1911; R.A.B. to Taft, August 7, 1911, Ballinger Papers. *New York Tribune*, November 13, 1910, November 14, 1910. *Springfield Republican*, November 14, 1909. *Minneapolis News*, August 25, 1909. *New York Call*, February 11, 1911. *The Washington Times*, June 26, 1911. Brief prepared by Amos Pinchot and Nathan A. Smyth. Copies are in the Ballinger Papers, and in the Amos Pinchot Papers. *The Outlook*, November 26, 1910, p. 653.

sional hearing. On this subject the president was torn by conflicting motives. On the one hand Ballinger had to be recognized as a political liability after May 1910; but the president
believed Ballinger to be the victim of a conspiracy. Later Taft
concluded that the actual target of this conspiracy had been
himself and that Ballinger was only the instrument for this
larger purpose. In any event, Taft dreaded the thought of adding to his subordinate's humiliation, and in the end was guided
by his sympathies. As for Ballinger, he thought he stood "se-
curely" on his "conscious rectitude," but it was proving to be
a precarious perch.

The conflicting motives of the president with respect to
Ballinger's tenure became apparent in curious fashion. Taft was
a judicious man. His habit of weighing and qualifying his judg-
ments before hesitantly determining upon action had more than
once been a handicap in his struggle with impulsive men. One
observer was sure that "Teddy would have fired Ballinger at
the start off and very kindly ruined him, knowing that he must
give the people a sacrifice."[12] Whatever Roosevelt's action
might have been, Taft was seemingly unable to act decisively
in the face of such political realities. But he recognized them—
and occasionally he seemed on the point of acting.

In the summer of 1910 citizens of the state of Washington
were stirred by a hotly contested Senate race. During the primary, four regular Republicans and insurgent Miles Poindexter
were battling for the same seat, though the regulars were sap-
ping their energies by fighting one another. Having been a
vigorous critic of Ballinger in the House, Poindexter was the
favorite of Pinchot, who arranged for an interview at Oyster
Bay in July to secure the benediction of the Leader. Taft
thought it "very important that nothing" be said about the interviews with Roosevelt and reprimanded Ballinger for certain
ungracious remarks elicited by Poindexter's visit. But Ballinger

[12] Taft to R.A.B., March 7, 1911, Ballinger Papers; speech before the
Denver Chamber of Commerce, quoted in *Daily News* (Denver), September 22, 1910; Butt, *Taft and Roosevelt: The Intimate Letters of Archie Butt*
(2 vols., Garden City, 1930), 1, p. 347 and *passim;* Brown to Brainerd,
February 17, 1910, Brainerd Papers.

continued to warn that "Poindexter cannot be defeated" except by quick action, and Taft eventually came to agree. By the end of August he was asking his secretary of the interior to help "save the country from the disaster of Poindexter."

Ballinger reported that after the president's plea for assistance "I made an effort to secure the elimination of one of the Seattle candidates and was successful. I have had some fear that the stronger man was eliminated." This fear was not the only ludicrous aspect of Ballinger's labors in the Washington vineyard. Even before writing to Ballinger the president had taken steps to render his subordinate's efforts ineffective.

On August 3 newspapers around the country had carried a story that Ballinger had been asked to resign for the good of the party by W. Murray Crane. The story gained added credence because it seemed to emanate from Beverly and because Senator Crane ("Old Pussyfoot," Taft called him) was known to serve the president in political matters requiring delicacy. Ballinger was annoyed and publicly consigned "these scurvy politicians" to "the devil."

The origin of the story had indeed been Beverly. The president's private secretary, Charles Norton, had concocted a plot with Crane, to which Taft had given his tacit support for a short time. Crane was to suggest diplomatically to Ballinger that he resign and enter the Senate race in Washington in order to prevent the election of Poindexter. Crane had dutifully set out to accomplish this end, but Norton had prematurely given the story to the press. In the meantime the president had had second thoughts. "In my opinion the president will neither ask for nor accept your resignation," the mercurial Crane reassured Ballinger.

This comedy of errors took its toll. Once again Taft was left looking like a "stranded whale." Norton lost the confidence of the press which resented being used, and consequently lost much of his value to the president. Poindexter might have emerged successfully from the primaries in any event, but Ballinger's efforts to swing the election to an administration candidate were not strengthened by the Crane-Norton scheme or the president's hesitant support of that scheme. As for Ballinger, he seemed more than ever determined to hold fast.[13]

Yet a scant five months later Ballinger was through. His health had begun to decline and progressively worsened during the fall. His resistance was already sapped when the rumor began to circulate that a Democratic-insurgent coalition would begin impeachment proceedings in the spring. Possibly the thought of a renewed public outcry was more than he was prepared to endure. Ballinger first sought to resign on January 19, 1911, but the president asked him to remain at least through the congressional session and "until after all unjust attacks are ended."

On March 6 Ballinger asked "to be relieved" on grounds of "health and financial interests," and the president consented. Taft had two opportunities to vent publicly his feelings in the Ballinger-Pinchot controversy. The first occasion was the letter dismissing Gifford Pinchot; the second was the letter accepting the resignation of Richard Ballinger. The latter had been the object of one of the "most unscrupulous conspiracies for the defamation of character that history can show," but Taft believed that he "was certainly the ultimate object of the attack." Ballinger's enemies had made use of a "malicious and unprincipled plan" to use the press to "torture every circumstance" to "misrepresent you and your actions." The "conspirators" had resorted "to the meanest of methods," yet plumed "themselves like the Pharisees of old, as the only pure members of society, actuated by the spirit of self-sacrifice for their fellow men."

The prose was spare and muscular. Yet the affair was flabbily handled by Taft right to the end. He consulted no one before accepting Ballinger's resignation, and his cabinet filed out of a routine cabinet session to meet waiting reporters, unaware that

13 Taft to R.A.B., July 7, 1910; R.A.B. to W. M. Crane, September 10, 1910; Taft to R.A.B., August 24, 1910; Don Carr to R.A.B., August 16, 1910; Crane to R.A.B., September 19, 1910; R.A.B. to Hill, August 26, 1910, Ballinger Papers. Brown to Brainerd, September 9, 1910; September 16, 1910; August 15, 1910; August 14, 1910; February 20, 1911, Brainerd Papers. *Boston Herald, New York Evening Sun, Brooklyn Daily Eagle*, all August 3, 1910; *Portland Oregonian*, August 17, 1910. Butt, *Taft and Roosevelt*, 2, pp. 456–57, 461, 463.

Taft had earlier given his letter to the press for publication. To a man they stoutly denied the malicious rumors of the resignation of their colleague.

If Ballinger's detractors were chagrined by the president's lively analysis of the controversy, the feeling was short-lived. Gifford Pinchot assured newsmen that the resignation had been "inevitable and will be received with general satisfaction." Likewise, Louis D. Brandeis thought the news welcome to the vast majority of the people of the United States. *Collier's* was magnanimous. They hoped that the best of his life was "yet to come" now that he had "ceased to be a misplaced official" and had become "a single human being" with a "wife and children" in need of "help and mercy" like all men. But "Your former Classmate and compaion [*sic*]" of Red Oak, Iowa, said much the same thing more succinctly: "Go dispose of your Illgotten Gain and seek Peace by Joining the Penitents."[14]

[14] On Ballinger's health, see Archie Butt, *Taft and Roosevelt,* 2, pp. 434, 591–92, and Colt to R.A.B., March 7, 1911, Ballinger Papers. On impeachment see *New York Call,* March 9, 1911. Amos Pinchot said the threat of impeachment led Ballinger to resign, in "The Syndicate's Losing Fight to Grab the Cunningham Claims," MS in the Amos Pinchot Papers. R.A.B. to Taft, and reply of Taft, January 23, 1911; Taft to R.A.B., March 7, 1911, Ballinger Papers. *Collier's,* March 18, 1911, clipping *ibid.* Butt, *Taft and Roosevelt,* 2, pp. 603, 604. "Statement of Mr. Gifford Pinchot on Ballinger's resignation," March 7, 1911, Gifford Pinchot Papers; *St. Louis Republic,* March 8, 1911.

The controversy flared anew a few months after the resignation. In June a young Radcliffe graduate named Myrtle Abbott published a sensational story charging both Taft and Ballinger with conspiring to turn Alaskan resources over to the Morgan-Guggenheim syndicate. Norman Hapgood of *Collier's* had commissioned the story but refused to publish it, and it appeared in the papers of the Newspaper Enterprise Association and the United Press. Miss Abbott wrote her story from files made available to her by Secretary Fisher, whose intention was to quash an earlier story making similar accusations. The Abbott article contained a postscript of a letter to Ballinger which indicated conspiracy and also that Charles Taft, the brother of the president, was the go-between for the president and the syndicate. A congressional investigation was authorized and the committee hired Brandeis as counsel. The investigation was never held because the "Dick to Dick" letter, as the papers named the letter with the infamous postscript, was evidently the forgery of a too anxious reporter. In any case Brandeis recommended against it after studying the record. In the end the flare-up principally served as a platform for Brandeis to bring his recommendations on Alaska before the public; but it also kept

For Ballinger the past was not so readily disposed of; nor was peace easily found. He had affirmed traditional values—the same values that carried him from an obscure Iowa farm to the highest councils in the nation—but in the end they failed him. "Conscious rectitude" was not enough. He returned to Seattle, but somehow he was unable to pick up the pieces of his life. Public criticism weighed him down. He found himself shunning the old business haunts, the law practice failed to offer quite the same rewards, and gradually he went to seed. By 1915 the textbooks began to appear. One text in particular he felt libeled him by repeating the Glavis charges as proven facts; but although this text was destined to serve thousands of high-school children, Ballinger found he was without recourse. The bad opinion of all those future generations seemed more than he could bear. Years later in a possibly apocryphal story which was at least aesthetically true, the columnist Drew Pearson recounted the details of Ballinger's death. In the fall of 1921 "a newspaper was placed in his hand reporting the election of Gifford Pinchot as Governor of Pennsylvania. Ballinger read the headlines and fell dead."[15]

---

the Ballinger affair alive in the overcharged political air of 1911–12. Mason, *Brandeis: A Free Man's Life* (New York, 1946), pp. 282-89. "Preliminary Examination of Persons Having Knowledge of Controller Bay Matters, Washington, D.C., July 26, 27, 28, 1911," Taft Papers. Taft to R.A.B., July 31, 1911; R.A.B. to Taft, August 7, 1911, Ballinger Papers. *Boston Evening Transcript,* December 4, 1911.

[15] R.A.B. to George Wickersham, April 14, 1915, Ballinger Papers; *The Washington Post,* February 10, 1940. Pearson sided with Ickes in 1940.

CHAPTER EIGHT

Perspectives on the Controversy

The great prominence of Theodore Roosevelt in the first decade of the century has obscured the extent to which progressives were at odds over the role of the state in modern America. All too frequently in the history of the period this divergence does not become apparent until the sudden dramatic clash of the new freedom and the new nationalism in 1912, and then it often appears to be a sharply partisan clash. In this view Democratic progressivism emerged victorious over Republican progressivism almost by accident because conservative Republicans led by Taft successfully retained control of the Republican party. The progressive wing bolted with Roosevelt, and the divided Republicans went down to defeat before the united Democrats. In this general theory the Ballinger-Pinchot controversy was seen as one of a sequence of events, along with the Payne-Aldrich tariff and the rise of insurgency, which demonstrated the betrayal of the Roosevelt policies by the reactionary Taft administration. The theme of betrayal was part of the partisan propaganda of the time, but as a key to understanding the significance of the controversy it is now useful only to neo-Bull Moosers whose chief aim is to refight the battles of 1912. Betrayal was an essential element in this partisan interpretation of the Taft administration because it was in so many ways an extension of the preceding regime. Nothing less than treason could explain the events of 1912.

An alternative and more fruitful approach has to begin with the acceptance of the essential progressivism of the Taft administration. It is possible of course to argue that both administrations were basically conservative; but to preclude the theory of the great betrayal requires only the admission that the one was at least as progressive as the other—that is to say, they both contained about the same range of progressive and conservative elements, and had a high degree of continuity with one another. It then follows that the trouble which arose between Taft and Roosevelt was rooted in the way in which power was exercised. Taft and Ballinger were the same men in 1909 and 1910 as they had been in 1907 and 1908. Their differences, both temperamental and philosophical, with the Roosevelt mood, had always existed. They did not become fundamentally important until the fortunes of politics forced Taft and Ballinger to exercise power. The Ballinger-Pinchot controversy revealed significantly different attitudes among progressives on the role of the state in modern society.

An astute delineation of these differences was drawn in 1909 by Herbert Croly in the *Promise of American Life*. "Reform," he said, was all sorts of things. Reformers were all for "the People and against the Octopus, but beyond this precise and comprehensive statement of the issue, [they had] endlessly different views about the nature of the disease and the severity of the necessary remedy." He added that they would "never be united on the basis of allegiance to the traditional American political creed, because that creed itself [was] overflowing with inconsistencies and ambiguities," which afforded a footing "for almost every extreme of radicalism and conservatism." Their strongest allegiance was to the Jeffersonian creed of equal rights for all, special privilege for none. But they discovered with dismay that their opponents believed the same thing. Nor had they recognized that the Jeffersonian creed, with its distrust of institutional restraints, inevitably led to inequality. Croly chided reformers for espousing a "species of higher conservatism," for being reactionaries rooted in a preindustrial past.[1]

The moral assumptions of Roosevelt, and men like him, were also rooted in an older America—probably his great appeal to reform-minded Americans was partly attributable to his dy-

---

[1] Croly, *Promise of American Life* (New York [Dutton reprint], 1963), pp. 143, 147.

namic adherence to conventional moral principles. Nevertheless, education, social position, and temperament combined in him to produce a broader view of his nation's historical development and role in world affairs than was common to most of his countrymen. Indeed, it might be argued that "progressive" is a confusing term to apply to Roosevelt. He could more appropriately be called a tory, using the word in its nineteenth century sense. That is, he advocated a militarily strong state, extension of the nation's influence abroad, and adjustment to the facts of industrialism at home.[2]

It was the rare progressive who favored all three positions with quite the same vehemence as Roosevelt. Most were more parochial in the sense that they viewed national problems from a standpoint which might in one instance be narrowly sectional, and in another, involve the identification of specific evils which could be eliminated by institutional reform. Most of the different shades of progressivism, as well as some not so progressive, were to be found in the Roosevelt administrations. Roosevelt shared with the rest a conventional moral tone, a determination to apply the canons of middle-class morality to public affairs, an unwillingness to question the "system," an insistence that the problems of society were problems of good and evil rather than the irresistible clash of overriding social forces which swept men along regardless of the morality or immorality of their individual actions.

Yet Croly admired Roosevelt almost alone among progressives. As president, Roosevelt had attempted to forge the federal government into an instrument for attaining truly national ends. Although his continual mouthing of the "Square Deal" seemed to be no more than a reiteration of the Jeffersonian

2 While running the risk of presumption by invoking an analogy to the complex British political scene, I only seek to draw attention to a general tendency in which nineteenth century liberals found themselves deeply implicated in industrialism, while social and factory legislation was sometimes championed by aristocratic landowners who had little to lose and much to gain by espousing the cause of the urban proletariat. Both "Whig" and "Tory" parties in Britain as in America embraced upper, middle, and lower classes, so that there is no intention to make a hard and fast line between parties in the use of the analogy.

creed, in practice Roosevelt had revived "the Hamiltonian ideal of constructive national legislation."[3] His domestic program—the regulation of giant economic enterprise, the welding of economic power to national ends, the controlling of conditions under which natural resources, the basic wealth of the nation, could be used—was in marked contrast to the stated aims of most reformers who wanted to restore the pristine purity of an earlier America, break up the trusts, and revitalize individualism. Croly deplored the extent to which the same tendencies appeared in Roosevelt's public statements. But more than any other leader, Roosevelt had striven to create the kind of state Croly thought necessary: a great regulatory state which could mobilize the energies of the entire nation, but resting on a democratic base.

Nevertheless, Roosevelt's success had been limited; the goal remained more an ideal than an actuality. Conservation was thus seen as part of a larger system. It was important not only because of its essential place in the total scheme but also because it was the most successful part of it. Ballinger's changes threatened a working program, and precisely because the program was in full operation he was bound to run into opposition from the bureau chiefs who had the most at stake in the perpetuation of established policies. Furthermore, any position on conservation was certain to involve conflict. The questions of how, and by whom, resource decisions were to be made touched on the vital interests of too many people to be resolved placidly. Yet the controversy had ideological implications which raised it to a level of significance that a squabble between bureaucrats or even a fratricidal war of competing interest groups would never have reached.

Croly pointed to an ideological division among "reformers" which was a potential source of internecine conflict. On the one hand, he said, the adherents of the Jeffersonian creed still looked for greater equality to be attained through a minimum of institutional restraint. On the other hand, many had combined the Hamiltonian bent for strong central power with the

[3] Croly, *Promise of American Life,* p. 168.

Jeffersonian emphasis on equality, and emerged with the belief that greater equality could only be attained by the active regulation of the government. The potential conflict became a reality when the contradictory ideas of Ballinger and Pinchot clashed. For in their respective positions the two men dramatized sharply the dichotomy between the Jeffersonian and Croly's "neo-Jeffersonian."

Ballinger had been called on to reform the Land Office in much the same fashion as he had earlier cleaned up Seattle, by eliminating the corruption and inefficiency. It might be said then that the very limitations which Croly attributed to the Jeffersonian contrived to make Ballinger adequate to the task at hand. Although he was something less than a success from Pinchot's standpoint, Ballinger in the Land Office did act like a man accustomed to shutting down dens of iniquity and tossing out rascals. These "limitations," in Croly's terms, became truly menacing only when Ballinger shifted to a position of power under another administration. For Ballinger and everything he stood for had been a threat to the conservation program from the very beginning. He was a threat as a bureau chief because he defended the traditional lines of jurisdiction of his agency and because he left it sufficiently reformed to defend itself in the future. He was a threat because he vigorously questioned the elitist assumptions of bureaucracy and expertise which were the underpinnings of the new regulatory state. In the Land Office he was an incipient threat to every effort to forge the executive into an effective instrument for the central control of resource use. When he became secretary of the interior the threat to coordinated planning became a reality.

The working out of these developments can be seen by following the underlying dialogue between the two adversaries. Ballinger often referred to Pinchot as a "preservationist," meaning one who wished to lock away remaining resources where they would remain safe for future generations. At first glance it seemed an oddly erroneous label, perhaps deliberately contrived to mislead. In any case, Pinchot was just as quick to use the same word in reference to Ballinger, and maintained with some justification that the Roosevelt policies were more likely to encourage utilization than were the modifications of Ballinger. Yet in political issues of this kind, subjectivity and personal interpretation play a large role. Ballinger stood on a vantage point from which his views appeared neither mistaken nor misleading.

Ballinger's attitudes to conservation were formed in Seattle. The city was the economic center of a region which sought to encourage the immigration of capital, a region which was badly in need of technical and entrepreneurial assistance from older established sections of the country whose control was, nevertheless, feared. Absentee ownership was an issue that aroused deep passions where men thought the economic growth of their region was restricted and opportunities for investment limited by decisions arrived at thousands of miles away. Conservation policies roiled the waters of an already muddied pond.

Although the rhetoric of conservation had a distinctly Jeffersonian cast, the opponents of the program in the West were by no means the "interests," the giant corporations. A number of large concerns directly affected by conservation were strong supporters of the program. Smaller, less established firms bitterly fought against it side by side with small grazers and farmers, while their more prosperous neighbors were often complacent. Conservation was "preservation" to the enemies of the movement. It seemed that others had been allowed to plunder and fatten on the wealth of the land and finally had been protected in their riches by a benevolent government; yet equally ambitious men who wished to follow in their footsteps were prevented from doing so. Ballinger could speak from this frame of reference and with perfect sincerity maintain that the Pinchot policies locked up the resources of the West and retarded development.

> The grazing lands were to be leased to the influential and more powerful stockmen; the forests held or disposed of in conjunction with the timber barons; the mineral lands mined on lease or royalty to those who would contribute their support to this politico-bureaucratical combination, and the water

powers and rights of way distributed on a permit basis so as to hold the permitee as a vassal to the service.[4]

Ballinger could honestly support a policy which in many respects resembled such aspects of the Garfield-Pinchot program as the principle of classification. But against the "discriminatory" character of conservation he was adamant.

"Reformers begin by piously reiterating certain phrases about equal rights for all and special privileges for none," Croly remarked. Having in this way "proved their fundamental political orthodoxy, they proceed to interpret the phrases according to their personal, class, local, and partisan preconceptions and interests."[5] Ballinger closely followed this pattern. He thought of conservation in concrete, practical terms of his own background and saw it benefiting some people but not others. Emotionally he was allied to the man-on-the-make who saw the forest reserves as game preserves and grazing monopolies which supported the status quo. Pinchot, Garfield, and Roosevelt took a less parochial and seemingly more national view, which in reality was the view of men holding the reins of the central controlling apparatus; the needs of the center attempting to co-ordinate the pluralism promoted a somewhat different view than the needs of the individual unit attempting to survive with other competing units. The distinction was symbolic, for the one side emphasized cooperation where the other saw never-ending struggle. In the view of the conservationists regulation was impartial, affecting as it did both large and small; the forest reserves were, as Amos Pinchot said, "the conservation and regulation of the great forests belonging to the people."[6] Yet such were the conditions of political reality in a plural society that "impartial" often meant only that a significant portion of those affected endorsed the policy; the Ballinger controversy revealed that the opposition was also significant.

[4] From an address by Ballinger delivered at the Public Lands Convention, Denver, September 1911, MS in Amos Pinchot Papers.

[5] Croly, *Promise of American Life*, p. 150.

[6] Amos Pinchot to Brandeis, June 5, 1910, Amos Pinchot Papers.

The elitist assumptions of the conservationists were anathema to Ballinger. The expert had acquired new stature under Theodore Roosevelt. Natural resources were the province of specialists partly because of a tradition of excellence in this area of federal science harkening back to John Wesley Powell. But there also existed a presumption that questions involving the allocation and use of natural resources could not be suitably answered in the conventional political arena by conflict and compromise. Science and the efficiency of sound business management should replace the anarchy of conflicting interest groups with cooperation and control, much the way that consolidation of economic enterprise had emerged from the bloody field of laissez faire. This was to be accomplished by the specialist, who stood above social and economic class. Although this might have resulted in an "establishment" along British lines, a separate class of government servants, the American environment was hostile to such a conclusion. Both as bureau chief and as leader of a coordinated program Pinchot necessarily assumed the role of broker to a plural constituency. Yet the elitist assumptions remained, their implications open to evaluation for what they might embody.

Ballinger rejected the notion that the expert was inherently better suited to resolve critical social issues because he was "nonpolitical." In fact, he tended to read more than a little political motivation into the actions of the conservation bureaucracy, for instance, in its ability to mobilize public opinion by welding often disparate groups into impressive coalitions. The Roosevelt conservation movement sought to introduce order into the use of natural resources by means of continuous administration and supervision imposed from above by a disinterested permanent bureaucracy. But Pinchot's power rested on the methods of the modern promoter who understood how to take advantage of the greater concentration of population and the advanced techniques of mass communication, rather than on the calculated restraint of the scientist in his laboratory. In common with other "right thinking" men Ballinger deplored the inefficiency and corruption of spoilsmanship, and advocated a civil service based on the merit system. But he had an entirely different notion of the role of the bureau chief, the specialist, than the view held by the Roosevelt men. The "specialist," he said, had no direct obligation to the people. He had no party affiliation in any conventional sense. He sought "power through publicity . . . for influence that [would] give extended authority to the bureau." This was hostile to the "representative system," which fostered local interests through compromise and negotiation with competing interests.[7] The program of the regulatory bureau was founded on its alliance not so much with the affected interests as with the dominant elements of those interests.

In his only public effort to arrive at a broad understanding of his experience in the Taft administration, Ballinger concluded that the villain had been bureaucracy.[8] Yet he also recognized that the size and complexity of modern government made the growth of bureaucracy inevitable. Indeed, he specifically excluded the bureaus of "investigation and research" from his censure. But regulatory bureaus, wielding virtually autonomous power founded on the support of specific interest groups and modern methods of promotion, were repugnant to him. That they could control the economic development of whole regions by determining how land was to be used and by making priority decisions between competing users was bad enough to a man temperamentally suspicious of all institutional restraints; but that these decisions seemed to be made in conjunction with the same absentee owners who were suspected of deliberately retarding western economic development was enough to convince this lawyer from Seattle of the threat of a "politico-bureaucratical combination" that dwarfed in size the dens of vice he had faced earlier.

In assuming his stance as the enemy of "bureaucracy," Ballinger sometimes sounded as if he thought he was standing against government by decree. This was particularly true when differences appeared in the interpretation of law. Ballinger

[7] Ballinger address to Public Lands Convention, Denver, September 1911, *ibid.*

[8] *Ibid.*

questioned the supervisory power of the executive, and took a strict constructionist, formalistic view of the law. The dialogue that ensued can be reconstructed from the public statements of Pinchot and Ballinger. " 'The letter killeth, but the spirit giveth life,' " Pinchot quoted.

> To follow blindly the letter of the law, or the form of an institution, without intelligent regard both for its spirit and for the public welfare, is very nearly as dangerous as to disregard the law altogether.[9]

Ballinger replied:

> When the public officer transcends the powers with which the constitution and the laws clothe him, he becomes a menace to popular rights and to all the safeguards surrounding them.[10]

Pinchot demanded "use of the law for the public good, and the construction of it for the public welfare."[11] Ballinger replied:

> Men love power and they will generally exercise it when they can get it and abuse it in popular governments under declarations of lofty patriotism to disguise the assumption. Even when carefully restrained within strict limitations "Power is of an encroaching nature."[12]

Doubtless both Taft and Ballinger were temperamentally inclined to take a narrower view of the law than Pinchot and Roosevelt. But caution is required in interpreting the differences of Ballinger and Pinchot over the law as even a secondary cause of the controversy. Their positions are partly explainable by their respective roles in the conflict. Pinchot was defending a program the full legal implications of which had yet to be worked out, while Ballinger was attacking that program and was naturally led to strike at its shaky legal foundations. How

[9] *Official Proceedings of the Seventeenth National Irrigation Congress Held at Spokane, Washington, August 9–14, 1909* (Spokane, 1909), p. 9.

[10] Address of Ballinger before Good Government Club January 22, 1910, at Williams College, Ballinger Papers.

[11] *Official Proceedings of the Seventeenth National Irrigation Congress,* p. 99.

[12] Address of Ballinger before the Good Government Club January 22, 1910, Williams College, Ballinger Papers.

basic his feelings were is conjectural. In American political history more than one strict constructionist has found himself defending a more flexible view in changed circumstances. Nevertheless, once the qualifications have been made, what remained was the rhetoric in which each antagonist couched his arguments. A "liberalism" which distrusted power and looked for progress primarily in the absence of institutional restraints confronted a "liberalism" which loved power and looked for progress primarily in the planning and regulation that only an active central government could provide. That dangers lurked in either position the subsequent history of the twentieth century has amply demonstrated. Perhaps the controversy was a minor benchmark in this continuing demonstration: that ideas become dangerous in direct ratio to the blind devotion in which men regard them.

Yet whatever its philosophical and ethical implications, conservation was first a technical program engaging the efforts of the federal science establishment. Beyond that it was an attempt to fill the need for a central apparatus to oversee resource policy in a plural system in which bureaus competed independently for their own programs and so turned into a nightmare any effort to advance an overriding scheme. And somewhere in the background lurked the vision of an integrated program to promote the material well-being of the nation on every level. Ballinger operated from the position of the agency chief attempting to preserve the autonomy of his bureau; but although Pinchot too had played that role, he had become more concerned with the needs of the center to overcome the pluralism even before Ballinger became secretary of the interior. It was a concern which led to important changes in the character of the conservation movement before the Roosevelt years ended.

Discouraged by congressional failure to approve an emerging program, which until then had been chiefly the concern of federal administrators and specific interest groups, Pinchot and other administration leaders began searching in 1908 for ways to give the conservation movement a broader base of support. In a sense, the controversy was a continuation of these efforts.

But the search for broader support had a narrowing effect, too, especially as Pinchot and his following became increasingly involved with insurgent attempts to discredit Taft. Conservation acquired partisan overtones which became quite marked as the Ballinger controversy played a large propaganda role in the campaign of 1912, and the movement emerged as an important feature of the new nationalism.[13] Indeed, never had conservation been given as wide expression as in the proposals of Roosevelt to create a master state with extraordinary powers to direct the economic life of the nation.[14] He offered a heady brew.

Too heady for the taste of many. The broader the conservation movement became in the political arena the more the interest groups, the constituent parts of the movement, feared that their own limited aims would be swamped in the widening movement. In a letter to Pinchot in July 1910 E. T. Allen of the Oregon Conservation Association tried to convey some of these fears. In Oregon and Washington, he said, "conservation" had become synonymous in the minds of many people with "Pinchotism." It no longer meant the protection of local resources; but with the controversy with Ballinger it now evoked questions concerning the ownership and use of waterpower, coal, and grazing. People would work for better state fire laws or state waterpower laws who did not sympathize with Pinchot on questions of ownership and use. "Should we risk their support in our coming strenuous campaign before the state legislature by saddling these local measures with [these] apprehensions?" Allen thought not. "I honestly believe the most useful thing we can do is to devote our immediate open effort to saving our local resources from waste by appealing to local patriotism and selfishness alike. . . ." He could only end with the hope that such an approach would result in a more

[13] "Theodore Roosevelt and William Howard Taft, What Each Has Done for the People of the United States," tract put out by Roosevelt League of New York State, copy in Ballinger Papers; Richardson, *Politics of Conservation: Crusades and Controversies, 1897–1913* (Berkeley and Los Angeles, Calif., 1962), *passim*.

[14] Roosevelt, *The New Nationalism* (Englewood Cliffs, N.J. [Spectrum ed.], 1961), pp. 21–39, 50–85.

enlightened electorate sometime in the future which would "support the broader principles" of Pinchot.[15]

Allen was a devoted follower of the former forester; indeed, he was the first person Glavis approached after his decision to seek the assistance of the Forest Service. There were others whose devotion was more obviously founded on expediency. Their desertion of the "broader principles" could be followed through the national organizations, which were the clearing houses of the various interest groups. Even before his resignation Pinchot was forced to admit that he could not retain control of the American Forestry Association, which resisted his attempts to broaden its scope. He founded the National Conservation Association partly in recognition of this failure. But its scope remained limited because it dwelt primarily on the issues of waterpower and mineral leasing which interested Pinchot. Where once it was intended to broaden the movement, by 1912 it had lost all contact with state activities, as Allen had warned. The National Conservation Congress experienced a similar decline. During the 1912 campaign it was virtually impossible to prevent the word "conservation" from becoming associated with one side in the political battle. In subsequent years, because of Pinchot's dominant influence, the movement came eventually to be regarded as an attempt to influence federal legislation, with little or no contact with activities in the states.[16]

The fragmenting of the grand coalition contrived by Pinchot during the Roosevelt years continued apace in the decade after the Ballinger episode. One after another the interest groups which had supported coordinated waterway development fell away, while the opposition of the Corps of Army Engineers never slackened. Pinchot himself fell out with the civilian engineers of the government over the question of how multiple purpose development should be financed. After 1910 a change in the composition and rules of the House committee on rivers

[15] E. T. Allen to G.P., July 20, 1910, Gifford Pinchot Papers.

[16] Hays, *Conservation and the Gospel of Efficiency: The Progressive Conservation Movement, 1890–1920* (Cambridge, Mass., 1959), pp. 175–88.

and harbors, the chief congressional obstacle to waterway development, made it possible for the waterway associations to obtain approval for their own measures through established channels, and they ceased to support the broad planning of the Newlands bill. In 1917 the waterways commission died ignobly, and Pinchot realized he would have to settle for federal regulation of hydroelectric power as a substitute. When the act was passed in 1920 he claimed victory, but the Roosevelt program had been compromised. Regulation of hydroelectric power was no substitute for the broad planning of the envisioned waterways commission.[17]

The shift from the general to the particular was equally evident in the federal government. In 1916 after ten years of agitation by many groups—nature lovers in the Sierra Club, sportsmen's organizations such as the Boone and Crockett Club, economic interests such as travel agencies, railroads, and highway associations—Congress finally created the National Park Service. When the new bureau came into existence Pinchot was already identified as an enemy by its supporters as a result of his position in the Hetch Hetchy affair. The creation of the park service signified the shift in the conservation movement which was to be characteristic of the nineteen twenties. Great bureaus cultivated their own constituencies and promoted their own programs, sometimes with brilliance, but without the vital coordination of the Roosevelt years.[18]

But if the dream of national planning seemed a chimera, it did not die. In a sense, it lived because it was built into the federal science establishment. Among scientists and technicians in a given era certain kinds of activity will enjoy greater prestige than others; while in the larger community certain kinds of problems will elicit greater response than others. In the framework of a given number of technical bureaus in the government servicing a broad spectrum of interests in the wider community, the confluence of activity of great appeal to the

[17] *Ibid.*, pp. 184–86, 199–240.

[18] Donald C. Swain, *Federal Conservation Policy, 1921–1933* (Berkeley and Los Angeles, Calif., 1963) is excellent on conservation during the decade of the twenties.

scientists with a related set of problems of concern to the general community can result for a time in fruitful creative coordination of federal programs.[19] Conditions were right in the Roosevelt era.

For a generation, after the time of John Wesley Powell, federal scientists had studied land, water, and resource problems as an interrelated whole and, in the tradition of Powell, were accustomed to thinking of them in terms of social as well as technical parameters. At the same time, in the first decade of the century large numbers of Americans were increasingly concerned with the varied problems that had accompanied rapid industrialization. Pinchot had the wit to seize upon the confluence of the two conditions, weld them into a single system, and for a time give them both focus. At first he used this power to further his own program in the Forest Service. But Pinchot was a great scientific administrator precisely because his ambitions transcended the technical mission of his bureau. The great outburst of activity in resource planning and policy testified to his own growth. As scholars have been quick to point out, the conservation movement was the product of many men's thinking, and Pinchot was by no means the most creative among them. But he was a great promoter, and the times called for a great promoter. The characteristic pluralism of the American political community itself gave rise to the need for periodic unity in the midst of plurality in order to give the structure direction. For a time the need for a focus where priority decisions on natural resources could be made by federal scientists in the name of the general community was met by the Forest Service of Gifford Pinchot.

Ballinger did not bring these times to an end, he merely signified the end. After 1909 bureau chiefs concerned with conservation ceased to be endowed with extraordinary powers. Those powers had depended on the peculiar relationship of Pinchot and Roosevelt in conjunction with the support of a wider political community. Focus for that support was removed when another administration chose another approach to

[19] See the provocative article by A. H. Dupree, "Central Scientific Organization in the United States," *Minerva*, Summer 1963, pp. 453–69.

the solution of the community's problems. The controversy with Ballinger was really Pinchot's bid to perpetuate the system of the previous administration. He failed and the movement subsequently fragmented into its individual components. But again, the Ballinger affair only sealed a process already begun. The broader the movement grew at the end of the Roosevelt years, the more unwieldy it became; its natural divisions were increasingly apparent as policy became more concrete. The great crusade of 1908 in its recognition of the need for broader support attested to this deterioration. The Ballinger affair merely accelerated the decline of coordinated policy by turning it into a partisan question in the political arena. "The special interests are in politics," Pinchot had said. In the event, the general interests of conservation gave way before its special interests. It may not have been the way to run a business, but it turned out to be the only way to run the country.

Bibliographical Note

1. Personal Papers

The papers of Richard Achilles Ballinger in the University of
Washington Library were an important source in this study.
The collection is small, but highly concentrated in the years
1907–11. The Erastus Brainerd Papers, also in this depository,
yielded material rich in human interest.

A number of collections in the Library of Congress were
searched. The Gifford Pinchot Papers, although awesome in
size and difficult to use, were worth the time and effort their
sifting required. The Amos Pinchot collection was smaller, as
were the collections of James Rudolph Garfield and Frederick
Haynes Newell, but each in its own way was a valuable source
of information. The papers of William Howard Taft were in
the process of being microfilmed when I wanted to use them,
but I would like to thank the staff of the manuscripts division
of the Library of Congress for their efforts in prying large
segments of the collection out of the photography division for
my use. The Walter L. Fisher Papers were less useful for my
purposes but easy to use because of the printed index.

2. Public Documents

As is obvious from the footnote citations, a central source
for this work is Senate Document 719, Sixty-first Congress,
Third Session, *Investigation of the Department of the Interior
and of the Bureau of Forestry*. Its thirteen volumes are a gold
mine for historians of conservation. The first volume contains
the majority and minority reports and the separate report of
E. H. Madison; the second, the Glavis charges and the material
submitted by the Department of the Interior to Taft, bearing

on the Glavis charges. Volumes 3 through 8 contain 4,902 pages of testimony and related evidence. Volume 9 comprises the arguments and briefs of Louis Brandeis, George Wharton Pepper, John J. Vertrees, representing Glavis, Pinchot, and Ballinger, respectively. Volumes 10 through 12 are the hearings on the Cunningham coal claims, incorporated by the Nelson committee in their final report. Volume 13 contains the mining laws of Australia and New Zealand.

3. Public Archival Material

In the National Archives, Record Group 48, Records of the Department of the Interior, Correspondence of the Office of the Secretary, and Record Group 95, Records of the United States Forest Service, were searched. Two points should be made about these sources with regard to my own system of footnoting. In the first place, most of the official correspondence even vaguely relevant to the controversy was introduced into the record of the congressional investigating committee. Wherever possible I followed the general rule of citing the more accessible source, and hence many citations from the hearing of the congressional investigating committee to be found in this work could just as well have been to any of several sources including the National Archives. In the second place, Ballinger and Pinchot kept much of their correspondence—this was especially true of Pinchot who walked off with practically a duplicate set of the Forest Service archives relevant to the controversy. Again, wherever possible I cited the hearing of the congressional investigation. However, many of the citations from these personal collections are to be found in the archival record groups mentioned above. Where this is true, the reason for citing the personal collections rather than the National Archives was quite simply that they were searched first. I offer this explanation in order to make the reader aware of the National Archives as a source rich in the history of conservation policy—a fact that those aware of the work of Samuel Hays will find familiar.

4. Published Material

The books, periodicals, and newspapers used in preparing this work are listed in the footnotes. Those interested in the controversy may compare my work with earlier studies. In the order of their appearance, they are: Rose M. Stahl, "The Ballinger-Pinchot Controversy," in Harold U. Faulkner and Sidney B. Fay (eds.), *Smith College Studies in History*, 11 (1926), 65–136; relevant chapters in Henry F. Pringle, *The Life and Times of William Howard Taft* (2 vols.; New York and Toronto: Harcourt, Brace & Co., 1939); Harold L. Ickes' article, "Not Guilty! Richard A. Ballinger," in the *Saturday Evening Post*, May 25, 1940, p. 9, and the longer *Not Guilty: An Official Inquiry into the Charges Made by Glavis and Pinchot against Richard A. Ballinger, Secretary of the Interior, 1909–1911* (Washington, D.C.: United States Government Printing Office, 1940), by the same author; Alpheus T. Mason, *Bureaucracy Convicts Itself: The Ballinger Pinchot Controversy of 1910* (New York: Viking Press, 1941); and his *Brandeis: A Free Man's Life* (New York: Viking Press, 1946); George E. Mowry, *Theodore Roosevelt and the Progressive Movement* (Madison: University of Wisconsin Press, 1946); Gifford Pinchot, *Breaking New Ground* (New York: Harcourt, Brace & Co., 1947); Samuel P. Hays, *Conservation and the Gospel of Efficiency: The Progressive Conservation Movement, 1890–1920* (Cambridge, Mass.: Harvard University Press, 1959); and *Gifford Pinchot: Forester Politician* (Princeton, N.J.: Princeton University Press, 1960), by M. Nelson McGeary; Elmo R. Richardson, *The Politics of Conservation: Crusades and Controversies, 1897–1913*, University of California Publications in History, vol. 70 (Berkeley and Los Angeles: University of California Press, 1962).

Index

Abbott, Lyman, 121
Abbott, Myrtle, 179
Agriculture, Department of, 48, 101, 154–55; center of science in the government, 2–3; cooperation with Department of the Interior, 28–29; *see also* Forest Service; Wilson, James
Alaska, territory of, 27, 39, 79–81, 83–85, 92–94, 96–97, 100–102, 104, 111, 116–17, 173, 179
Alaska coal; *see* Ballinger, Richard A.; Cunningham coal claims
Alaska railroads, 82–83
Alaska syndicate; *see* Morgan-Guggenheim syndicate
Aldrich, Nelson, 137
Allen, E. T., 192–93
American Forestry Association, 4, 193
American Mining Congress, 5, 96
American National Livestock Association, 4
American Smelting and Refining Company, 82
Ames, Butler, 143
Appeals, Court of, District of Columbia; *see* Court of Appeals, District of Columbia
Arizona, state of, 171
Army Engineers, Corps of; *see* Corps of Engineers, U.S. Army
Atlantic City, 118
Attorney General, and reclamation script, 70–72; *see also* Wickersham, George

Bache, Alexander Dallas, 2
Baldwin, Elbert Frank, 43, 54, 153
Ballinger, Richard A., 9–10, 30, 59, 74–76, 84, 102–12, 124, 126, 131–36, 140, 143–44, 147–49, 152, 155, 158, 160–61, 163–70, 174–75, 182, 192, 195–96; accused of misconduct, 114–19, 123; and Alaska coal, 84–87, 92–96; appointment as commissioner of the Land Office, 21–23; appointment as secretary of the interior, 41–43; attacked in periodical press, 129–30; and coal land policy, 77–78; commissioner of the Land Office, 23–28; early career, 19–21; exonerated by Taft, 125–26; and Forest Service program, 43–47; and hydroelectric power sites, 47, 50–58; ideas on conservation, background of, 31–38; majority and minority reports of congressional investigation, 171–73; and Oregon land frauds, 89–91; and presidential campaign of 1908, 41; as progressive, 39–40; reaction to Glavis charges, 120–21; receives copy of the Glavis charges, 119; and reclamation policy, 60–61, 66–72, 165–69; relations with *Outlook*, 153–54; retirement as secretary of the interior, 175–80; seeks Newell's resignation, 72–73; testimony in congressional investigation, 155–57; views on conservation contrasted to Pinchot's, 185–91

201